MORE PRAISE FOR HOW TO LAND A TOP-PAYING FEDERAL JOB

"This book will become an instant classic. It is chock full of make-or-break advice—available nowhere else—about every phase of the job-search process and about getting ahead in government."
    —**Kelly Paisley**, former Deputy Director of the Vice-President's National Partnership for Reinventing Government

"This book pulls together needed and hard-to-find information on ways to get a job in federal government. It is a very helpful resource."
    —**Sandy Hessler**, Director of Career Advancement, Harvard Kennedy School

"[T]he layman's field guide to a federal job search…based on hundreds of interviews with federal hiring managers and job hunters."
    —*Roll Call*, the newspaper of Capitol Hill

"Have you ever gone to a bookstore and sorted through all the books about getting a federal job? Well I have and I want to let you know they are all horrible. Basically, they are all scam books re-purposing content that is available for free on sites like USAJOBS.gov. Further, most of the authors have never worked as a fed and are just trying to get a quick book.

Which brings us to *How to Land a Top-Paying Federal Job*. It is totally different. In this book, Lily brings together the highlights of her years of *Federal Times* columns and adds her experience as a federal employee and federal hiring manager. The best part are the examples culled from years of working as a fed, hiring feds, and helping people get hired as feds. It provides all the insider tips of the process and informal guidance you need.

In summary, this book rocks. This is not a book you read at the bookstore over 10 minutes. This is a book you buy. Read. Read-again. And reference. If anyone asks you how to get a federal job, just tell them to buy this book. If they ask you again, tell them to read it twice as there are tons of little gems dispersed throughout the book. And if you are already in the federal system, this is an essential career guide as it tells you how to navigate the waters, find your next job, get promoted, and negotiate your salary (yes you can do this as a fed)."
    —**Steve Ressler**, Founder and President of http://www.GovLop.org, the leading social networking site for public sector employees

"An excellent resource for undergraduate and graduate students who are interested in securing an internship in the public sector. . . . A great resource for new-career professionals and mid-career professionals who seek a federal career and are interested in 'insider' tips to navigate the federal hiring process . . . describes the myriad of diversity programs for women, minorities, and disabled job seekers . . . provides for easy reading and a straightforward approach . . . will almost certainly ensure that job-seekers submit an A+ application . . . . Anyone looking for a federal job, or any job for that matter, would definitely benefit by reading this book."
    —*Journal of Public Management & Social Policy*

"The strength of Lily Whiteman's manual lies in her ability to present information in an easy-to-digest format. . . . In addition, Whiteman does an admirable job of providing extensive "how-to" examples for her readers. From sample ways to transform 'boring' résumé accomplishments into attention-grabbing statements to her many self-assessment worksheets, the author focuses on really showing, not just telling job-seekers how to be successful."
    —The Eastern Association of Colleges and Employers

"This book is a must-read. Anyone who aspires to a federal position or promotion within the federal service will find Whiteman's advice invaluable as they prevail over obstacles of entry and advancement throughout their federal careers. Whiteman gives her readers access to a wide range of information on the federal service application process, interview techniques, and how to successfully sell your résumé to hiring managers. Her 'hot tips' are excellent resources that are appropriately positioned throughout the book to help the reader gain additional insights. This is a superb reference book and action plan for all prospective and current federal employees."

    —**Farrell J. Chiles**, former Chairman of the Board, National Organization of Blacks in Government

"This book is essential reading for anyone who wants to decipher the federal government's hiring system. Don't apply for a federal job without it."

    —**Paul C. Light**, Paulette Goddard Professor of Public Service, Robert Wagner School of Public Service, New York University

"Great information. . . provides a 'behind-the-scenes' perspective from hiring managers…liberally interjects humor."

    —National Career Development Association (NCDA)

    Excerpts from an article about a previous edition of this book that originally appeared in NCDA'S web magazine, Career Convergence at www.ncda.org. Copyright National Career Development Association, March 2006. Reprinted with permission.

"Most books on how to find a federal job are about as interesting as the tax code. But [this book] offers a mountain of helpful advice in a visually appealing, easy-to-read format."

    —*Government Leader*

"Bottom Line: This book provides clarity, insider advice, and hot tips into the federal government and its hiring process in an entertaining and informative way….An easy read using everyday language, Whiteman explains the often difficult and hard to navigate human resource system within the government, making it easy for both the neophyte and the well-seasoned government expert to move through the book with limited bumps and hurdles."

    —OhMyGov! (OhMyGov.com)

"Overall, a broad and optimistic view of federal jobs and the employment process that should both prepare readers for the job hunt as well as inspire them."

    —*Career Opportunities News*

"From lesser-known ways of finding openings to negotiating salary and getting quickly promoted, this is an outstanding guide recommended for any library strong in job opportunities and career guidance."

    —Midwest Book Review

"Whiteman's enlightening, entertaining book will teach you everything you need to know about how to put the right spin on your credentials on paper and in person."

    —**Ray Kurzweil**, recipient of the National Medal of Technology; best-selling author of *The Singularity Is Near: When Humans Transcend Biology*

HOW TO LAND A TOP-PAYING FEDERAL JOB

HOW TO LAND A TOP-PAYING FEDERAL JOB

Your Complete Guide to Opportunities, Internships, Résumés and Cover Letters, Networking, Interviews, Salaries, Promotions, and More!

SECOND EDITION

LILY MADELEINE WHITEMAN

AMACOM
AMERICAN MANAGEMENT ASSOCIATION
New York • Atlanta • Brussels • Chicago • Mexico City • San Francisco
Shanghai • Tokyo • Toronto • Washington, D. C.

Bulk discounts available. For details visit:
www.amacombooks.org/go/specialsales
Or contact special sales:
Phone: 800-250-5308
E-mail: specialsls@amanet.org
View all the AMACOM titles at:
www.amacombooks.org

This publication is designed to provide accurate and authoritative information in regard to the subject matter covered. It is sold with the understanding that the publisher is not engaged in rendering legal, accounting, or other professional service. If legal advice or other expert assistance is required, the services of a competent professional person should be sought.

This book represents the views of Lily Whiteman and not the views of the U.S. National Science Foundation.

Library of Congress Cataloging-in-Publication Data

Whiteman, Lily.
   How to land a top-paying federal job : your complete guide to opportunities, internships, résumés and cover letters, networking, interviews, salaries, promotions, and more! / Lily Madeleine Whiteman. —2nd ed.
      p. cm.
   Includes bibliographical references and index.
   ISBN-13: 978-0-8144-2022-5
   ISBN-10: 0-8144-2022-2
   1. Civil service positions—United States—Handbooks, manuals, etc. 2. Career changes—United States—Handbooks, manuals, etc. 3. Internship programs—United States—Handbooks, manuals, etc. 4. Job hunting—United States—Handbooks, manuals, etc. 5. Job hunting—United States—Computer network resources—Handbooks, manuals, etc. 6. Vocational guidance—United States—Handbooks, manuals, etc. I. Title.
   JK692.W45 2012
   351.73023—dc23   2011049586

About AMA

American Management Association (www.amanet.org) is a world leader in talent development, advancing the skills of individuals to drive business success. Our mission is to support the goals of individuals and organizations through a complete range of products and services, including classroom and virtual seminars, webcasts, webinars, podcasts, conferences, corporate and government solutions, business books and research. AMA's approach to improving performance combines experiential learning—learning through doing—with opportunities for ongoing professional growth at every step of one's career journey.

Printing number
10 9 8 7 6 5 4 3 2 1

*This book is dedicated to the **Whiteman** and **Gregg** wings of my family,
a band of survivors who have again and again intrepidly soldiered
on through adversities—and in memory of my young nephew, **Lucian Gregg**,
an adventurous climber who literally and figuratively reached great heights in his short life.*

CONTENTS

A copy of the files on the CD accompanying this book can also be accessed at
www.amacombooks.org/go/FedJob2E.

WHAT'S ON THE CD...

➤ KSA and ECQ Prep
  Includes: Outlines, Cheat Sheets, Tips, and Essay Examples

➤ Internships and Special Recruitment Programs
  For Young Professionals, Women, Minorities, and People with Disabilities

➤ Fellowships for Experienced Professionals
  For Nonfeds and Current Feds

➤ Going Global

➤ *Washington Post* Articles, by Lily Madeleine Whiteman
  Articles on Federal Internships, Interview Skills, International Opportunities,
  and Networking in Professional Organizations

➤ Résumé Prep

➤ Interview Prep

➤ Application and Interview Warm-Up Tip Sheets

➤ Get Ahead Cheat Sheets

FOREWORD

Lily Whiteman's neat, well-organized book demonstrated that my many years on the subcommittee with direct oversight over federal employees haven't taught me all I want to know. This nugget of a book will tell you what you don't know, what you need to know, and what you may not have thought to ask about federal employment and promotion. Whiteman, herself a federal writer who has served as a federal hiring manager, is skillful in culling the essentials and meticulous in providing accurate information. She draws on other federal experts on the inside as well to provide information not easily available elsewhere. At the same time, this readable paperback has much to offer a wider audience seeking up-to-date approaches to employers in today's competitive job and promotion market.

The book's breadth (interns to managers as well as Congress and agencies) is matched by attention to detail. Yet, Whiteman does not take you in the weeds. Discussion that could get complicated, such as job qualifications and the ranking of applicants, is uncannily concise. In plain-speaking language, she concentrates on the basics for a fruitful federal job and promotion search while also offering helpful tips and insights.

Whiteman's book is being issued as federal employment is becoming more attractive and more available. The collapse of prestigious companies has made the private sector less glamorous. Federal jobs seem a lot more inviting today as the country experiences the most serious economic crisis since the 1930s.

However, this good news about federal employment also assures a large pool of applicants. More Americans seeking jobs and promotions are likely to be attracted by government stability and benefits. Baby boomers, who have been quick to retire, may respond to the poor economy and its impact on retirement savings by staying in place longer. As federal job and promotion opportunities become more competitive, the information in these pages will grow even more valuable.

The varied and increasingly important missions of the federal sector virtually assure that the federal sector will grow. Federal employment offers a version of virtually all the major job categories in the private sector. No single employer has this range of opportunities for jobs and promotions and locations in the U.S. and overseas. *How to Land a Top-Paying Federal Job* is an invaluable tool for the federal job and promotion search, but the guidance in these pages will serve the reader wherever good jobs are available.

— **Congresswoman Eleanor Holmes Norton**
   (Washington, D.C.)

PREFACE

Common Myths About Federal Jobs

1. **Government salaries are low.** *No!* Studies and anecdotal reports show that federal salaries compare very favorably to private-sector salaries. And federal "benies" and job security are unparalleled. Plus, some feds receive up to $60,000 in student loan repayments. This book provides the most complete, accurate guidance available anywhere on federal salaries.

2. **Federal salaries are nonnegotiable.** *No!* Federal salaries are usually negotiable. This is the *only* book that explains how to negotiate federal salaries.

3. **The applicant with the best connections usually gets the job.** *No!* The applicant who impresses hiring managers the most usually gets the job. This is the *only* book that provides application advice straight from federal hiring managers—the gatekeepers to federal jobs.

4. **Federal internships are voluntary and do not pay.** *No!* Tens of thousands of undergrads, grad students, law students, and recent grads currently enjoy well-paying federal jobs and internships. This book provides the *most* comprehensive list available anywhere of such opportunities.

5. **The federal workforce is not diverse.** *No!* Minorities are generally better represented in the federal workforce than elsewhere, and federal agencies are aggressively recruiting women, minorities, people with disabilities, and veterans. This book provides the *most* comprehensive advice available anywhere on special federal hiring programs for job hunters in these categories.

6. **The federal government is a monolithic mass.** *No!* Federal agencies are as different from one another as are private organizations. This book provides the *most* comprehensive advice anywhere on how to get the inside scoop on your target agencies.

"I had the dream about meaningful employment again last night."

7. **The federal hiring system is a big, mysterious black hole.** *No!* The federal government

now uses straightforward, streamlined hiring practices.. This book is the *only* book that clearly and concisely explains how the federal system *really* works and how to *really* work the system.

8. **It takes forever to get hired by the feds.** *No!* Applicants for federal jobs are frequently interviewed soon after applying. And many agencies have reduced the entire hiring process to 45 days, which is comparable to the private sector.

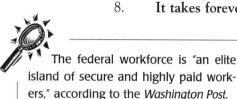

The federal workforce is "an elite island of secure and highly paid workers," according to the *Washington Post.*

9. **You have to pass a civil service test to become a fed!** *No!* The civil service test is history. Today, only a few types of federal jobs require tests.

10. **Most feds are lazy and dim-witted.** *No!* Forget oddballs like Neuman on *Seinfeld* and Cliff Claven on *Cheers.* Most feds are smart, tech-savvy go-getters.

11. **Most federal jobs are in Washington, D.C.** *No!* Almost 85 percent of federal jobs are located outside of D.C., in nationwide and overseas locations.

12. **Government work is dull and unimaginative.** *No!* Feds use creativity and judgment to carry out policies that significantly impact millions of people and precious resources.

13. **Only insiders can land federal overseas jobs—never outsiders.** *No!* Varied types of professionals from recent grads to midcareer professionals to stay-at-home parents returning to work are currently being recruited into exciting overseas jobs. This is the *only* book that provides advice straight from federal hiring managers on how to land these jobs.

14. **If your political party is not currently in power, you would have to abandon your principles to work for the federal government.** *No!* Federal agencies must fulfill their legally mandated missions no matter which party is in power and so most federal jobs are generally insulated from politics; federal staffers continue their work day in and day out, even after the political pendulum swings.

15. **Federal work schedules are rigid.** *No!* Most white-collar feds can, within reason, set their own daily arrival and departure times and work longer days in exchange for taking three-day weekends every other week. In addition, a significant and growing percentage of white-collar feds work at home part of the week.

16. **If you have previously been rejected for a federal job, it's useless to apply for another.** *No!* Federal agencies hire more than 200,000 new employees and promote hundreds of thousands of others every year. Your standing in any particular job selection has absolutely no bearing on your standing in others.

17. **The federal government is being downsized.** *No!* The size of the federal workforce has remained fairly steady in recent years, and the federal government hires about 200,000 people of all professions and all career stages every year.

18. **All feds ascend the career ladder at the same pace—no matter what.** *No!* Feds can accelerate their career ascents by using the potentially pivotal career advancement strategies that are provided in this book (and nowhere else).

HOW TO LAND A TOP-PAYING FEDERAL JOB

PART

I

GEARING UP TO APPLY

And you're off . . . in hot pursuit of a new and better job. Part I explains why this is a great time to go federal, provides leads to hot openings, and presents simple, easy-to-follow instructions on landing domestic and overseas jobs—either by walking through the federal government's front door or by using little-known strategies to slip through its back doors. Part I also reveals how federal hiring managers really think—absolutely essential information for acing your applications and interviews.

In addition, the CD that accompanies this book features the most comprehensive directories available anywhere of: (1) well-paying federal internships, student jobs, and special recruitment programs for young professionals; and (2) fellowships for experienced professionals—including nonfeds and current feds.

Armed with this book's previously unavailable, behind-the-scenes guidance, you will easily and expertly navigate the federal system, whether you are seeking your first federal job or a promotion.

1

A Great Time
to Go Federal

U.S. News & World Report *describes a government job as a terrific deal
and includes "governement manager" on its list of best careers.*

With about 2 million civilian employees, the federal government is the nation's largest employer. Every year, about 200,000 new hires join the federal workforce and hundreds of thousands of current feds are promoted.

Why spend your career toiling in obscurity when you could be on your way to becoming a power broker? Feds contribute to the high-stakes, hot-button policy issues that cover the front pages of the nation's newspapers every day.

U.S. News & World Report describes a government job as a terrific deal and includes "government manager" on its list of best careers.

Do you want to land an interesting job that pays a top salary, provides unbeatable, rock-solid job security, and will advance the public good in important ways? If so, you're probably primed to work for the federal government.

What does the federal government do? The federal government literally runs this country. To do so, it protects the strength and vitality of the U.S. economy; creates foreign policy; manages precious natural, cultural, and high-tech resources; forecasts tornadoes and hurricanes; oversees the nation's planes, trains, and highways; secures our food and water supplies; protects the health and safety of workers; keeps unsafe products off the market; and funds most of the nation's scientific and medical research, to name just a few examples.

To run the country, feds do everything that private-sector employees do—and more. So like the private sector, the federal government hires almost every type of white-collar professional, including engineers, teachers, IT experts, scientists, business managers, lawyers, PR specialists, policy wonks, medical professionals, accountants, program managers, and almost every type of blue-collar professional, including auto and aviation specialists, equipment operators, mechanics, electricians, property managers—and many more.

Plus, the federal government has jobs that you won't find anywhere else. Feds work as spies, volcano watchers, park rangers, terrorist hunters, disease detectives, curators of precious historical documents, and diplomats. The possibilities are endless.

Feds work in every imaginable setting, from offices, laboratories, museums, libraries, hospitals, parks, forests, and marine sanctuaries located throughout the United States to embassies located in far-flung countries. And they access and control resources—including huge budgets—that are unavailable to private-sector employees.

Another important advantage: the federal government provides one of the precious few workplaces where you can work exciting jobs, earn competitive salaries, and still have a life. Most feds stick to a 40-hour work week. The federal government also offers these first-rate perks:

> **Job Security:** The federal government continuously hires for all types of jobs and internships—even when other organizations are laying off. And while nongovernmental employees may be "pink-slipped" when the economy falters, feds are rarely laid off. Also, it is generally much harder to fire federal employees than employees in other sectors.

> **Top Salaries and Advancement:** Studies and anecdotal evidence show that federal salaries are very competitive with private-sector salaries and that feds in many fields earn more than their private-sector counterparts. Plus, feds receive regularly scheduled promotions, merit-based promotions, and annual cost-of-living salary increases. For more information about federal salaries, see Chapter 16.

➤ **Generous Vacations:** Full-time federal employees enjoy 10 paid holidays and 9, 13, 20, or 26 days of vacation each year, depending on their seniority. They can take up to 12 weeks of unpaid leave to attend to a birth, adoption, or seriously ill family member.

➤ **Top-Notch Health Insurance:** Feds choose from the nation's best health insurance, dental insurance, vision insurance, long-term care, and life insurance programs.

➤ **Facilities to Help You Stay Close to the Kids:** Many agencies have on-site childcare facilities.

➤ **Coverage for Health Care and Dependent Care Costs:** Feds can pay up to $4,000 annually for childcare, up to $5,000 annually for health care, and up to another $5,000 for adult dependent care, from tax-free accounts that are set aside from their paychecks. Depending on expenses and tax brackets, these benefits may yield individual tax savings totaling thousands of dollars annually.

> **Forget Stereotypes of Sour-faced Feds!** Recent surveys show that the overwhelming majority of feds consider their work important and like their work; public service is a rewarding choice.

➤ **Excellent, Secure Retirement Packages:** As corporate scandals and cutbacks erode private-sector pensions, feds remain covered by secure pensions that feature a defined benefit based on length of service (with cost-of-living increases), and a 401(k)-like investment program with matching. Moreover, unlike most retired private-sector employees, retired feds get another coveted benefit: lifetime health insurance coverage.

➤ **Flexible Schedules:** Flexible work schedules and telecommuting options are freeing feds from the straitjacket of 9-to-5 schedules. In addition, many feds can opt to work 9 hours per day in exchange for taking off every other Friday. Surveys show that the overwhelming majority of feds feel that their supervisors support a work-life balance.

➤ **Repayment of Academic Loans:** Some feds receive up to $60,000 in student loan repayments. In addition, the College Cost Reduction and Access Act forgives the outstanding student loans of public service employees—including feds—after they have made 10 years of payments.

➤ **Opportunities to Be a Do-Gooder:** The ultimate aim of most federal jobs is—in one way or another—to better the world. In the words of a Peace Corps staffer, "I am doing what I love to do, and it's all for a very good cause." Moreover, even entry-level employees can wield tremendous responsibility in the government. "I have only been out of college for a year-and-a-half, and I

"True, the private sector has its benefits, but, then again, so does the public trough."

am influencing huge budgets on environmental programs," observes a program analyst at the Environmental Protection Agency.

Ride the Hiring Wave

The federal government, which currently employs almost 2 million people, is currently perched on the edge of an unprecedented retirement wave, according to the Office of Personnel Management. More than 25 percent of federal employees have already reached the minimum retirement age of at least 55 years old, and every year, hundreds of thousands of feds are retiring. By 2016, 37 percent of feds are expected to retire.

The retirement wave is currently rolling over the federal government's executive corps (the senior executive service) with particular ferocity; about 50 percent of federal senior executives are currently eligible to retire; about 90 percent of them will become eligible to retire over the next 10 years; and, in some agencies, this figure has already reached 50 percent.

To backfill for retirees and other employees lost through normal attrition, the federal government is vigorously recruiting all types of professionals at all levels of their careers. Indeed, large percentages of new federal hires are now experienced professionals. Moreover, every retirement at top grades is expected to trigger multiple staffing actions as lower level employees ascend to fill the resulting power vacuum. This means that the retirement tsunami will make it easier than ever to move up in the federal government.

New Blood

When you think of government employees, do you visualize dowdy, schoolmarmish women and frumpy, pocket protector–clad men toiling in musty offices? If so, your perceptions are due for an update.

Indeed, statistics from the Office of Personnel Management, which is the federal government's main personnel office, show that the federal workforce—which is already generally more educated than the private-sector workforce—is steadily becoming more skilled and more educated. In addition, largely because of the ongoing retirement wave and because of renewed zest for government service inspired by various factors, including the fight against terrorism and political and economic factors, "a potential for a quasi-youth movement in the government job sector" promises to infuse the federal government with new, revitalizing blood and fresh ideas, according to the Web site Monster.com. In other words, the feds are registering lower and lower on the stodgy meter.

CHAPTER
2

The Search Is On

Finding Openings

"The best way to predict your future is to create it."
— ANONYMOUS

Your job search is on and you have issued an "all points bulletin" (APB) for appealing openings. You can continue your quest online anytime, anywhere—at home dressed in your sweatpants while nursing your cappuccino, or between meetings at work while nursing your resentment of your current boss. This chapter explains how to find federal openings and provides leads to hot opportunities.

> **Hot Tip**
>
> Each federal organization and congressional office has its own Web site that: (1) explains the who, what, where, when, and why of what it does; and (2) features a career section. To find opportunities in any particular agency, check the agency's own career Web site, as well as the career Web site of the department in which it is housed. A hyperlinked A-to-Z directory of federal organizations is posted at http://www. usa.gov.

Where Do You Want to Work?

Contrary to popular belief, the federal government is not a single, monolithic mass. Indeed, federal organizations differ from one another as much as do private organizations.

Some of these differences hinge on each organization's mission—from the National Science Foundation's collegial academic-like ambience to the National Clandestine Service's cloak-and-dagger secrecy to the Security and Exchange Commission's "We're the good guys" ethic. Other differences hinge on factors such as the agency's pay scales, willingness to reward producers with bonuses and promotions, workforce diversity, age demographics, degree of office formality, hierarchy, and level of staff teamwork.

More tips on how to research federal organizations are provided at the end of this chapter, and tips on Capitol Hill jobs are provided in Chapter 5.

What Credentials Do You Need?

Almost every type of white-collar and blue-collar job that exists in the private sector also exists in the federal sector. So, no matter what your field of expertise, there is a good chance that the federal government employs professionals just like you.

Many types of professionals are hired by virtually every agency. These types of professionals include lawyers, project managers, and specialists in human resources, information technology, accounting, communications, contract management, logistics, property management, budget management, and administrative support. But the hiring of some types of specialized professionals is limited to certain agencies that address their specialties.

Some federal jobs require specific certifications or college degrees and some require graduate degrees. But many desirable federal jobs do not require college degrees, and many others, including some management and executive jobs, accept work experience or specialized knowledge in a particular field as a substitute for a degree. The Office of Personnel Management, which is the federal government's human resources agency, explains: "The nature of your specialized experience is what really counts."

Examples of appropriate job titles for administrative staffers who do not necessarily have college degrees include administrative officers, procurement specialists, contract managers, grants managers, audio-visual specialists, property managers, printers, equal opportunity specialists, human resources specialists, information technology specialists, recreation instructors, public affairs assistants, and Web site developers.

Examples of the types of blue-collar jobs (usually called *wage-grade jobs*) that exist in the federal govenrment include mechanics, building engineers, gardeners, farmers, electricians, fleet managers, drivers—and the list goes on.

The requirements for each job opening are spelled out in its announcement. For more information about federal salaries and what salary range you should aim for, see Chapter 16.

The Federal Jobs Web Site

USAJOBS (http://usajobs.gov) is the official jobs Web site of the federal government. Clicking on USAJOBS is like hitting the mother lode of federal job openings; the site announces more than 15,000 jobs per day and is continuously updated throughout the day, every business day.

> **Hot Tip**
> Several commercial Web sites charge members to search lists of federal job openings and to be e-mailed customized lists of openings. USAJOBS provides the same service for free. Why pay for what you can get for free?

Included among USAJOBS's listings are jobs located all over the world and jobs that are at every level of almost every conceivable occupation. USAJOBS also announces some state, local, and private-sector job openings and features links to the employment Web sites of many federal and state organizations.

Vacancy Announcements

Federal job openings are advertised in vacancy announcements—the government's version of "Help Wanted" signs. You can search USAJOBS's collection of vacancy announcements by various criteria, including keywords, salary, geographic location, job title, and hiring agency. See Chapter 6 for more info on vacancy announcements.

If you are unsure of which federal job titles best match your skills and interests, conduct keyword searches on USAJOBS's job listings using common job titles in your field and words representing your areas of expertise. Also, consult the Federal Classification and Job Grading Systems, which can be obtained by typing that term into the search window at http://www.opm.gov.

> Wonder which government organizations are in your city? Check the blue government pages in your local phone book.

The Window of Opportunity

The window of opportunity for applying for federal job openings varies. Some jobs are advertised for several weeks or longer. But others are advertised for the minimum amount of time required by law: five business days for jobs that are open to all applicants and three business days for jobs that are open only to current federal employees. Surf through USAJOBS every few days so that you don't miss out on any hot openings.

Which Jobs Are Not Posted on USAJOBS?

Most federal agencies are required to advertise most of their job openings that are open to the public (i.e., are not just open to their own employees). They usually meet such advertising requirements by posting their announcements on USAJOBS. Nevertheless, some types of federal jobs are not necessarily posted on USAJOBS. These jobs include:

➤ Jobs that the hiring agency opts to advertise in other venues instead of USAJOBS, such as their own Web sites, newspaper classifieds, indeed.com, Facebook and other social media outlets, and online jobs boards

➤ Most of the internships, recruitment programs, and fellowships that are covered in Chapter 3

➤ Jobs in the legislative branch (Congress) and judicial branch (the courts)

➤ Jobs that are open only to the hiring agency's own employees

➤ Jobs that are filled exclusively by attendees of career fairs

➤ Most contract and temporary jobs

➤ Most jobs in the Foreign Service

➤ Jobs that are in the excepted service rather than the competitive service

What is the difference between competitive service jobs and excepted service jobs? *Competitive service* jobs—which account for the majority of federal jobs—must be advertised and filled through open competitions. By contrast, *excepted service* jobs can be filled through relatively flexible procedures that are designed by the hiring agency; these procedures do not always involve advertising openings and holding open competitions for them.

Excepted service jobs include: (1) all federal jobs for certain types of professionals, including attorneys, chaplains, doctors, dentists and nurses, and certain other professions; and (2) all jobs that are in excepted services agencies, which include the the FBI; CIA; State Department; agencies in the intelligence community; many agencies that address trade, finance, and unilateral issues; and various other agencies. For a list of excepted service agencies, look up *excepted service* in Wikipedia.

To find excepted service openings, regularly check the Web site(s) of the appropriate agencies. (Though not required, some excepted service jobs are advertised on USAJOBS.) Also, inquire with the human resources departments of excepted service agencies about openings that suit your background and interests, and seek opportunities for networking with employees of excepted service agencies by, for example, joining appropriate professional organizations that are listed on the CD accompanying this book.

Other Sources of Agency Openings

You may also find vacancy announcements for jobs in federal agencies via:

➤ **Federal Web Sites:** In addition to regularly checking USAJOBS, also regularly check the Web sites of your target agencies. Why? Because some agency openings appear on agency Web sites before appearing on USAJOBS while some never appear on USAJOBS. If you don't know which agencies match your interests, surf the hyper-linked A-to-Z list of all federal agencies at http://www.usa.gov. When you do so, you may be surprised to discover a large number of agencies that you have never even heard of before—but that appeal to you.

➤ **Clearancejobs.com:** A database of government and contract jobs requiring security clearances. (See Chapter 7 for more information about jobs requiring security clearances.)

➤ **The National Academy of Sciences (NAS) Web Site:** NAS is a quasi-government organization that employs scientists, policy experts, and administrative personnel. See http://www.nas.edu. (NAS openings are not posted on USAJOBS.)

➤ **Social Networking Web Sites:** Many agencies advertise jobs and career fairs, and provide opportunities for job-seekers to obtain answers to career-related questions from agency experts via Facebook, Twitter, and other social networking media. Another potential source of openings and other career information is http://www.gov-loop.com —a social networking site for future and current government employees at all career stages. *Hint:* I know of job seekers who have used the site to start or participate in online discussions with feds about various timely issues and thereby have generated pivotal job leads or connections.

➤ **Intelligence Jobs:** Career information on 17 intelligence agencies is posted at http://www.intelligence.gov.

➤ **Job fairs:** See this chapter's discussion of job fairs.

➤ **Newspapers:** Check the Sunday classifieds and papers that cover Capitol Hill, including *Roll Call* (http://www.RollCall.com) and *The Hill* (http://www.HillNews.com) and *Politico* (http://www.politico.com).

➤ **The Human Resources Offices of Federal Agencies:** These offices can tell you about unadvertised openings that will be filled through special streamlined procedures for special categories of applicants, including veterans and people with disabilities.

➤ **The Senior Environmental Employment Program (SEEP):** SEEP hires retired and unemployed Americans who are at least 55 years old for clerical, administrative, communications, and technical jobs that support Environmental Protection Agency programs throughout the United States. See http://www.EPA.gov/ohr.

Openings in Congress

Find openings on congressional staffs at the following:

➤ **The Senate Employment Office:** Go to http://www.senate.gov; click *Visitors*.

➤ **The House of Representatives Employment Office:** Go to http://www.house.gov; click *Employment Opportunities*. In addition, after every election, the Committee on House Administration hosts a résumé drop area through which résumés are distributed to new House members.

➤ **Publications that Cover Capitol Hill:** These include *Roll Call*, *The Hill*, *Politico*, and *Congressional Quarterly*. Also, subscribe to "Opportunities in Public Affairs" at http://www.opajobs.com.

Chapter 5 discusses jobs on congressional staffs, and Chapter 16 discusses the salaries of those jobs.

Hot Tip

Volunteer, Seasonal, and Short-Term Jobs. By working volunteer or temp jobs while you job-hunt, you may earn helpful references, gain new skills, generate pivotal networking contacts, and avoid creating holes in your work history.

Organizations that run volunteer programs offering substantive assignments include: (1) the Civil Air Patrol of the Coast Guard Auxiliary; (2) reserves and hatcheries that are managed by the U.S. Fish and Wildlife Service (http://www.fws/gov/volunteers); (3) marine sanctuaries and other facilities that are managed by the National Oceanic and Atmospheric Administration (http://www.sanctuaries.noaa.gov/involved/volunteer_future.html and http://www.volunteer.noaa.gov/index.html); and (4) federal museums and other cultural institutions.

In addition, seasonal and short-term jobs are offered by various agencies, such as: (1) the U.S. Forest Service (http://www.fs.fed.us/fsjobs/openings.html); (2) FEMA (http://www.fema.gov/ plan/ehp/employment.shtm); (3) the IRS (http://jobs.irs.gov/seasonal); (4) the U.S. Census Bureau; and (5) the National Park Service (http://www.nps.gov.personnel/seasonal.html).

Also, see (1) the websites of particular national parks, forests, and monuments that interest you; (2) the discussion of National Park Service internships that is included in the internship directory in this book's CD and http://www.serve.gov; and (3) volunteer programs discussed at http://www.volunteer.gov/gov; and (4) http://www.volunteer.gov/gov, which is America's Natural and Cultural Resources Volunteer Portal.

Another option: Many federal agencies run summer and year-round non-paying internship programs for high school students, undergrads, grad students, and recent grads.

Take Note!

Ten Ways to Land a Federal Job

1. Answer an announcement posted on USAJOBS or an agency or Congressional website.

2. Get hired at a federal job fair.

3. Get recruited into one of the internships, student jobs, or special recruitment programs for studnets, recent grads, and experienced professionals covered in Chapter 3 and on this book's CD.

4. Land one of the fellowships covered in Chapter 3 and on this book's CD.

5. Segue into a permanent job from a temp job or a contract job.

6. Progress from a volunteer job into a permanent job.

7. Use your networking and other professional activities to impress a federal manager enough to compel him to create a position for you or recruit you into an existing position.

8. Get accepted into the senior executive service (SES) by landing a place in the Federal Candidate Development Program (Fed CDP).

9. Join the Foreign Service.

10. Receive a political appointment.

Job Fairs

The federal government frequently participates in nationwide job fairs. At a single event, you may meet hiring managers from many agencies recruiting for jobs at all levels. Some agencies use these events to fill high-priority jobs or internships through fast-track procedures or even make on-the-spot offers. Therefore, you may find openings at career fairs that are not advertised anywhere else.

Take Note!

Attention Women, Minorities, and Disabled Job Seekers!

If you are a woman, a member of a minority, or a job seeker with a disability, you may be eligible to participate in programs that promote diversity in the federal workforce:

- College students, grad students, and recent grads should consider the internships and recruitment programs for women, minorities, and people with disabilities, as covered in Chapter 3 and on this book's CD.

- Experienced professionals should consider applying for the senior executive service, which is discussed in Chapters 6 and 18.

- Special programs for veterans are discussed in Appendix 1 and special programs for people with disabilities are discussed in Appendix 2. Also, the SEEP program for retired professionals is covered in this chapter.

- Federal programs that go by various names, including the Special Emphasis Program, the Selective Placement Programs Employment Program, and the Employment Initiative, are designed to promote the hiring of veterans, Native Americans, Asian Americans and Pacific Islanders, African Americans, Hispanics, people with disabilities, women, and in some cases, military spouses. Each agency has a program manager who helps applicants improve their applications, match jobhunters with appropriate openings, and keep jobhunters apprised of appropriate openings. Access a list of these program managers by typing *selective placement coordinator directory* into the search window at http://www.opm.gov, and feel free to call them to use their services.

Agencies that are aggressively recruiting minorities and women for various types of positions include the FBI, the Federal Deposit Insurance Corporation, Foreign Service agencies, and some intelligence agencies. So check their Web sites for their openings and job fair schedules. Wonder which agencies are the best promoters of workforce diversity? Check out the rankings of federal agencies in workforce diversity at http://www.bestplacestowork.org.

Two more tips: (1) Many federal agencies regularly recruit professionals at conferences and other venues sponsored by minority organizations, such as the National Association for the Advancement of Colored People, the Society of Black Engineers, and the American Indian Science and Engineering Society. (2) Many federal agencies recruit at minority colleges and universities. So if you attend such a school, ask your career office for leads to federal jobs.

Federal employers frequently recruit at their own job fairs and job fairs that are co-sponsored by other federal and private sector employers.

Find job fairs that are attended by federal recruiters by regularly:

➤ Surfing through the career sections of the Web sites of your target agencies and target offices.

➤ Reviewing the Sunday classifieds of the *Washington Post* and/or your local newspaper for ads for job fairs. (Some job fairs exclusively invite jobhunters with security clearances.)

Take Note! _____

Ten Tips for Faring Well at Job Fairs

1. Before the fair, check which agencies will attend. Then, troll through the Web sites of your target agencies so that you will be able to pepper each meet-and-greet conversation with evidence of your knowledge of the agency's goals and high-profile activities.

2. Practice introducing yourself with a 30-second, punchy opener that highlights your key qualifications and how they would benefit your target agency.

3. Present yourself as a decisive, goal-oriented job seeker who knows what type of job you want. Recruiters are universally turned off by job seekers who expect career guidance from them.

4. Prepare yourself for an on-the-spot job interview by reviewing Chapter 15.

5. Pack the following items in a professional briefcase: your ID, pens, pad, résumés, college transcripts, reference lists, business cards, your success portfolio as discussed in Chapter 15, documents verifying your eligibility for veterans' preference, if appropriate, and your most recent Notification of Personnel Action, if you are a current fed.

6. Dress as nicely as you would for a job interview. No eating or gum chewing, or sucking out of a water bottle in the interviewer's face.

7. Attend the fair alone, without bringing parents or friends with you. By doing so you will help prove that you're a sure-footed professional who doesn't lean on others or bring personal baggage to the office.

8. Collect the business cards of contacts so that you will have their names, titles, and contact info.

9. If a recruiter does not have openings that are suitable for you, ask her for other leads.

10. Immediately send thank-you letters to helpful contacts and follow up on promising leads.

On the CD. . . _____

More Info on International Jobs

For more information about overseas jobs, see the "Going Global in Government" chapter on this book's CD. Also, see the directory of federal internships, as well as my *Washington Post* articles on international careers and federal internships.

➤ Conducting Google searches using (1) the name of each of your target agencies along with keywords, such as *job fairs* and *career fairs*; (2) and the name of your target city along with keywords, such as *job fairs* and *career fairs*.

➤ Checking D.C. Congresswoman Eleanor Holmes Norton's Web site (http://www.norton.house.gov) for information about her annual job fairs in Washington, D.C., which always feature dozens of federal agencies.

➤ Seeking information about job fairs sponsored by the Partnership for Public Service at http://www.ourpublicservice.org/.

In addition, if you are a member of a minority group, attend conferences and other events that are sponsored by minority organizations, such as the National Association for the Advancement of Colored People, the Society of Black Engineers, and the American Indian Science and Engineering Society. Federal employers frequently recruit at such events. And if you are a student, ask your school's career office about upcoming job fairs at your school and at other local venues. (Note that federal employers regularly recruit at minority colleges and universities.)

Hint: Some agencies in the intelligence and defense communities, the State Department, the FBI, the EPA, and agencies that address banking and corporate finance are veritable job fair junkies. So, regularly check the career sections of their Web sites.

"*To be completely frank, we have now discovered all your country's secrets, except how to make a million dollars in one's spare time at home with no personal investment.*"

Leads for Particular Types of Professionals

Provided below are job-hunting tips for professionals in some selected specialties.

Going Global in Government

Are you a globe-trotting adventurer longing for adventure in far-flung countries? If so, consider joining the tens of thousands of civilian feds who currently work overseas.

What types of professionals does the federal government send overseas? Virtually *all* types of professionals. In fact, almost all types of professionals are needed overseas. So no matter what you currently do or want to do for a living, you could probably do it overseas.

What types of projects do feds work on overseas? They provide humanitarian and disaster relief; reduce world hunger; promote conflict resolution; train scientific researchers; conserve natural resources; fight diseases; identify and confront threats to the United States such as terrorism and other illegal activities; and hammer out international agreements on health, environmental problems, defense, trade, and immigration—to name just a few of their activities.

In addition, overseas feds provide all manner of administrative support and maintain the federal overseas infrastructure by working on construction projects, running the administrative and accounting aspects of offices, procuring goods and services, protecting the security of diplomats and other Americans overseas, advancing IT projects, and contributing to other types of projects.

In surveys of feds, the State Department consistently ranks as one of the best places to work. Also, the State Department ranked among the 10 best employers in a recent *Business Week* survey of undergrads and college recruiters.

Hot Tip

Insider Info on Going Global. Stay informed on international affairs and prepare for interviews for international jobs by reading *Frontlines,* which is published by USAID (find it by Googling *Frontlines* and *USAID*), *State Magazine,* which is published by the State Department (find it via the search window at http://www.state.gov), and *The Foreign Service Journal,* which is published by the American Foreign Service Association at http://www.afsa.org.

Leads for Legal Eagles

The federal government is the United States' largest employer of attorneys. What's more, attorneys are among the highest paid feds.

Federal lawyers work throughout Capitol Hill and in virtually every federal agency—not just the Justice Department—and they are qualified for various types of jobs: They shape policy, write federal regulations that impact huge populations and important resources, liaison with Congress, advise political appointees, write congressional testimony, enforce regulatory and administrative programs, work on ethics issues, and serve as trial lawyers and judges, to name just a few possibilities.

Many agencies hire legal interns and newly minted lawyers through their summer internship and Legal Honors Programs, which may or may not be advertised on USAJOBS. Find information on agency Legal Honors Programs by checking the careers Web sites of your target agencies and by Googling the names of agencies that interest you along with keywords such as *Legal Honors Program.*

Also, the Congressional Research Service sponsors a Law Recruit Program. And many other agencies recruit through an Office of Attorney Recruitment or an Attorney Recruitment Coordinator under their Office of General Counsel or human resources office. Find such offices by calling your target agency's main number or by checking its organizational charts posted on its Web site.

In addition, many types of legal jobs for lawyers of all levels are advertised on USAJOBS. You may find them by using keywords such as *attorney, counsel, legal, law,* and *solicitor.* But beware. Many legal jobs are only advertised on agency Web sites. And review the internships covered in Chapter 3 and on this book's CD. Also, if you want to clerk for a judge or explore other opportunities in the federal judiciary, go to the jobs section of the Web site of the U.S. Courts at http://www.uscourts.gov.

You may find unadvertised federal openings by networking with professional organizations, such as the Federal Bar Association (http://www.Fedbar.org) and the Public Service Law Network. In addition, do a Google search for the *NALP Legal Opportunities Guide,* which provides an excellent overview of federal attorney jobs and guidance on how to land them.

Leads for PhDs

With many excellent universities, a dynamic intellectual life, and employment possibilities for both halves of academic couples, Washington, D.C., offers an attractive alternative to academia.

Although PhDs are hired by virtually all federal agencies and labs, several organizations are particularly popular among PhDs because they offer "think tanky" environments and manage studies, reports, and programs on multidisciplinary topics involving foreign affairs, education, information technology, social issues, economics, public health, and the sciences. These organizations include the Library of Congress, the Government Accountability Office, the Congressional Budget Office, the Office of Management and Budget, the National Academy of Sciences, and the National Science Foundation.

The Departments of Agriculture, Energy, and State; the CIA; the FBI; NASA; the Office of Naval Research; the EPA; the DOD; the Department of Health and Human Services; the National Endowment for the Arts; the National Endowment for the Humanities; and agencies in the intelligence community are also popular destinations for PhDs. In addition, many Capitol Hill offices, particularly congressional committees, hire professionals with advanced degrees. (See Chapter 5 for more information on jobs on Capitol Hill.)

Also, many federal fellowships recruit PhDs. For more information about them, see Chapter 3 and the directory of fellowships featured on this book's CD.

Another lead: Many federal agencies, particularly science-based ones, have post-doc programs. The EPA, the National Institutes of Health, and various other federal agencies have earned high rankings in surveys of the best places to work for post-docs, according to surveys that have been conducted by *The Scientist*.

Leads for Enviros and Public Health Advocates

Do you want to save the Earth or protect people from diseases and other public health threats? Federal environmental and public health advocates advise political appointees, write congressional testimony, manage trail-blazing research and education programs, investigate industrial disasters, write and enforce national laws, manage precious natural resources, reduce the impacts of natural and unnatural disasters, and promote sustainable development.

Opportunities for enviros and public health advocates are offered by many agencies, including the Agriculture Department; the Army Corps of Engineers; the Chemical Safety Hazard and Investigation Board; the Congressional Research Service; the Consumer Product Safety Commission; the Council on Environmental Quality; all agencies in the Department of Health and Human Services (particularly the Centers for Disease Control and the U.S. Public Health Service); the Office of Science and Technology Policy, the Departments of Defense, Energy, Justice, and Labor; the EPA; the Federal Energy Regulatory Commission; FEMA; the Government Accountability Office; NASA; the National Atmospheric and Oceanic Administration; the Peace Corps; the Smithsonian; the State Department; the Transportation Department; USAID; the U.S. Public Health Service Commissioned Corps; the Veterans Administration; the U.S. Geological Survey; and the World Bank. Also consider the organizations listed under *Leads for PhDs*, and explore congressional committees addressing natural resource and public health issues.

Leads for Medical Professionals

Almost 25,000 medical officers are employed by the federal government; the average annual salary of this in-demand group of professionals exceeds that of every other occupational group in the federal government.

Which federal agencies employ physicians, mental health professionals, nurses, physical therapists, and other types of medical practitioners? The VA is currently aggressively recruiting physicians and nurses. Other employers of medical practitioners include the Departments of Defense and State, USAID, FAA, the intelligence community, the U.S. Public Health Service Commissioned Corps, the VA, the FBI, and agencies in the Department of Health and Human Services, particularly the Centers for Disease Control.

Leads for Generalists

You may be a generalist if you have: (1) a liberal arts degree; (2) excellent research and communication skills; and (3) diverse interests rather than a passion for one esoteric issue that only about five people in the world really understand.

Find generalist jobs by searching USAJOBs on these keywords: *public affairs, communications, outreach, writer, editor, congressional affairs, legislative affairs, external affairs, coordinator, media,* and *Web*. In addition, look for job titles like *program analyst, policy analyst, program manager, program analyst,* and *special assistant* because many jobs associated with such titles involve policy and communications issues—some with requirements for specific technical knowledge and some without such requirements. And explore opportunities in the organizations discussed previously under "Leads for PhDs."

Leads for Teachers

Many federal agencies run training programs, professional development programs, and/or public education/outreach programs that hire teachers, trainers, instructors, guidance counselors, and education aids. These agencies include the EPA, agencies within the Department of Interior, NASA, NOAA, the Office of Naval Research, the Department of Energy, and the National Institutes of Health, to name just a few.

Other employers of teachers include federal training institutes, including the State Department's Foreign Service Institute, the Federal Law Enforcement Training Center, FEMA's National Training and Education Division, TSA's Training and Development Office, the Defense Acquisition University, the Federal Acquisition Institute, the Department of Interior University, and many DOD training facilities. Others federal employees of teachers and instructors include the training centers for current feds that are covered in Chapter 18.

If you are a globe-trotting teacher, look for openings in the the Department of Defense Education Activity, which hires teachers and administrators to teach children in military bases in the United States and all over the world. For more information, see http://www.dodea.edu/home, as well as the Web sites of regional sites.

In addition, the Peace Corps and USAID hire teachers to manage and deliver international education programs. And the State Department's Bureau of Education and Cultural Affairs manages various education programs. Also, the Defense Language Institute Foreign Language Center delivers foreign language training to some members of the military, some DoD civilians, and other feds. The center currently employs about 1,700 instructors and is continuing to staff up. Jobs are currently available on the West and East Coasts. Look for them by conducting keyword searches on "language" in USAJOBS or by visiting http://www.dliflc.edu.

Teachers and instructors are also employed by the child care facilities of many federal agencies.

Also, federal employers sponsor various fellowships for teachers, which are listed in the directory of internships and fellowships included in the CD accompanying this book. One more thing: A great resource for current or wannabe federal teachers/trainers is the Training Officers Consortium at http://www.trainingofficers.org.

Leads for Experts in Finance

Federal hiring trends are often impacted by current events. For example, recent corporate finance scandals are compelling agencies that regulate corporate financing to staff up.

Agencies that address finance include the Consumer Financial Protection Bureau, the Securities and Exchange Commission, the Bureau of the Public Debt, the Federal Financial

---

Take Note! _____

Wanted: Intelligence, Security, and Language Experts

In the wake of 9/11, the departments of Defense and Homeland Security have been offering recruitment bonuses to some new hires. In addition, several agencies are aggressively recruiting intelligence and language experts.

- The National Security Agency (NSA), which offers signing bonuses worth up to $7,500, is seeking experts in languages, intelligence analysis, signals analysis, math, computer science, the physical sciences, and acquisition. Go to http://www.NSA.gov; then click *Careers*.

- The National Geospatial-Intelligence Agency, which studies imagery from spy satellites and other systems, the Defense Intelligence Agency, and the FBI, which offers recruitment bonuses to some types of professionals, will also hire large numbers of intelligence specialists and other professionals in the coming years.

- The Central Intelligence Agency's Corporate Language Hiring Bonus Program offers some language specialists recruitment bonuses worth up to $35,000. Go to http://www.cia.gov; then click on *CIA Careers* and then *Language Positions*.

- The Secret Service offers recruitment bonuses worth 25 percent of annual salary to language experts.

For more leads on opportunities for language experts, go to http://www.makingthedifference.org and click *Foreign Language Programs* in the Federal Government.

Examination Council, the Federal Reserve Board, the Federal Trade Commission, the National Credit Union Administration, the National Technical Information Service, the Office of the Comptroller of the Currency, the Office of Thrift Supervision, the Consumer Financial Protection Bureau, the FDIC, the Commodities Futures Trading Commission, the Office of Financial Research, the Federal Finance Housing Agency, the Board of Governors of the Federal Reserve, the Bureau of Economic and Business Affairs (State Department), the Office of Economic Adjustment, the Bureau of Economic Analysis, the Economic Development Administration, the Economic Research Service, the Economics and Statistics Administration, the Overseas Private Investment Corps, and the new Office of Financial Stability.

Leads in the Intelligence, Security, and Defense Communities

Without doubt, the news event that has most profoundly affected federal hiring in recent years is 9/11. Since the attacks, agencies in the intelligence, security, and international communities—including the departments of Homeland Security, Defense, and the FBI—have been aggressively recruiting.

Find more information about career opportunities in the CIA and 17 other intelligence agencies at http://www.intelligence.gov. Remember to check the career site of each organization and of each subagency. Also, remember that military agencies don't just employ members of the military; they also employ many civilians.

Keep in mind that many agencies besides those in the intelligence community address security and intelligence. As examples, consider the Defense Security Cooperation Agency, the Department of Commerce's Bureau of Industry and Security, and the National

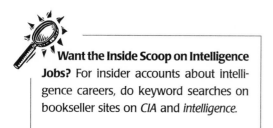

Want the Inside Scoop on Intelligence Jobs? For insider accounts about intelligence careers, do keyword searches on bookseller sites on *CIA* and *intelligence*.

Nuclear Security Administration. To find more agencies in the intelligence community, go to the hyperlinked list of federal agencies at http://www.usa.gov, and look for agencies that start with the word *defense* and agencies that address international issues.

Another tip: Agencies in the intelligence and security communities hire various types of professionals, not just security and intelligence experts. Believe it or not, the CIA even employs makeup artists and fashion experts to help groom its spies for undercover operations. *Who knew?* Also, the Drug Enforcement Administration frequently snaps up finance experts and accountants to track the money trails of drug cartels and terrorist organizations. And scientists are employed by various federal agencies, including the Agriculture Department, to help fight bioterrorism and other security threats.

When searching on USAJOBS and agency Web sites for openings, use keywords such as *intelligence, terrorism, threat,* and *national security*. (See box, "Wanted: Intelligence, Security and Language Experts.") Also, participate in networking opportunities provided by the Association of Former Intelligence Officers, which sponsors various programs and speakers on intelligence, and the National Military Intelligence Association.

Follow the News: Find Hiring Blitzes

If you want to become a fed, become a news junkie. Why? Because current events, the priorities of the president and Congress, and industry-specific developments influence the job market in general and help determine which agencies receive budget boosts that trigger hiring blitzes. For example, recent corporate finance scandals compelled many agencies that regulate corporate finance to staff up, and triggered the recent formation of the Consumer Finance Protection Bureau.

As you follow the news, follow the money. Look for organizations that receive budget increases and/or are assigned new legislation and programs to implement; new organizations, task forces, and commissions; and organizations that are reorganizing. Why? Because they are probably hiring.

I know, for example, a federal project manager who read about a reorganization at the U.S. Postal Service. Through minimal research, he identified an agency office director who was likely to need his skills, and then he submitted to the office director his résumé with a cover letter explaining how his skills would meet the office director's needs. Soon after, the project manager followed up with a phone call to the office director. The result: Within a few weeks the project manager had a new job (a promotion) in the reorganized office.

High-Demand Professionals

The following types of professionals are in particularly high demand by the government.

> **IT professionals.** Particularly those skilled in cyber security are being aggressively recruited throughout the government. (The salaries of IT experts are significantly higher in the federal government than in the private sector.)

➤ **Intelligence analysts.** These people are wanted by intelligence and defense agencies. According to the *Washington Post*, "being an analyst is almost an academic profession—part taught, part absorbed, part intuition—that requires weighing volumes of information and boiling them down into reports for policymakers in the executive branch and in Congress."

➤ **Professionals with language skills.** High-demand professionals include those who know Middle Eastern languages, Asian languages, and Russian, and other professionals who are knowledgeable on intelligence issues, such as weapons of mass destruction, are in high demand.

➤ **Contract specialists.** These people manage and negotiate the purchase of goods and services and oversee projects. Contracting specialists are being snapped up throughout the government—which is the world's biggest buyer, spending more than $400 billion per year. Note that agencies in the Department of Defense have been aggressively recruiting contracting staffers.

But you don't necessarily need a contracting or acquisitons background to land a contracting job. For example, professionals with diverse backgrounds—ranging from biology to computer science to telecommunications—are frequently recruited for contract jobs and then trained in contracting by hiring agencies. See http://www.fai.gov and http://www.dau.mil.

➤ **Auditors, budget specialists, and business managers.** These people are also in high demand throughout the government. Accountants are also wanted, particularly by the IRS.

➤ **Patent examiners.** The U.S. Patent and Trademark Office (USPTO) needs experts to help manage the technology revolution. (A bachelor's degree in engineering or science is required.) Note that the USPTO is aggressively recruiting mid-career professionals with generous recruitment bonuses, and that a large percentage of patent examiners work at home.

➤ **Engineers.** The Defense Department, NASA, the Nuclear Regulatory Commission, and the Departments of Defense, Transportation, and Energy have high demand for engineers. Many of these agencies offer recruitment bonuses to some new hires.

➤ **Tax examiners.** Thousands of tax examiners will be hired by the IRS over the next few years.

Political Appointments

Granted, you probably won't be named secretary of state if you don't already have serious inside pull and instant name recognition. But take heart: Many of the approximately 7,000 political jobs in the federal government are filled by ordinary, hard-working professionals whose names have never graced *Time* magazine.

What They Are

Political appointees include ambassadors, cabinet members, agency heads, members of regulatory commissions, judges, lawyers, and policy specialists. Many of the assistants and members of the immediate staffs of high-ranking officials are also political appointees.

All political jobs in the federal government are filled via nominations from the White House. (Some political jobs require Senate confirmation.) Professionals who have strong affiliations with the president, an administration staffer, or the president's political party have the best chances of landing political jobs. But many accomplished professionals who have no inside track also land political jobs simply by applying for them.

Political appointees usually spend most of their time designing and advocating administrative policies and working closely with key officials. READ: power, influence, and prestige. But the flip side to political positions is that they offer little job security and most appointees lose their jobs when the administration changes. And the stresses experienced by political appointees are reflected in memoir titles such as *Leaving Town Alive* by former National Endowment for the Arts Chairman John Frohnmayer and *Locked in the Cabinet* by former Labor Secretary Robert Reich.

Applying for a Politcal Appointment

If you apply for a political appointment, treat your quest like a campaign. The more endorsements you get from powerful advocates, the better. Exploit any White House connections—even distant ones—that you have. Perhaps, for example, your congressman works closely with an administration official. Recommendations from associations, nonprofits, unions, academics, and business leaders will also help.

The best time to apply for political positions is right after a presidential election. Nevertheless, many political positions turn over between elections.

Resources

A list of political positions is available in *The Plum Book*, which is published after each presidential election. To find it, Google *The Plum Book*. Also, *A Survivor's Guide for Presidential Nominees* is posted at http://www.brookings.edu/papers/2000/ 1115governance. aspx. Applications for political appointments are posted at http://www.whitehouse.gov/ appointments.

Follow the Money: Contract Jobs

Many federal contractors work on federal projects without being full-fledged federal employees. That is, these contractors do federal work, are supervised by federal managers, and are based in the offices of federal agencies. But such agency-based federal contractors are not employed or directly paid by the federal government. Instead, they are employed and paid by consulting firms that hold a contract with the federal government.

Because agency-based federal contractors work cheek-by-jowl with federal employees, agency-based contracting assignments provide ideal opportunities for networking, gaining government experience, and earning a salary while you job-search. Indeed, many agency-based federal contractors are eventually hired into full-time federal positions.

Take Note! _____

Career Transition Success Story

By Barry Phelps, Supervisory Writer/Editor

A few weeks after I left my position as communications director for a small nonprofit organization, I decided to resume my career with the federal government. An Internet employment Web site ad soon caught my eye. The ad, which had been placed by a temporary-placement firm, was for a temporary writer/editor at a federal Homeland Security agency.

I followed up and things moved quickly. I interviewed with the firm on a Friday and was working at the federal agency by the following Monday. When my initial three-month stint ended, the agency offered me a full-time federal position as a senior writer-editor with its Office of Human Resources. The salary negotiations went well and I am now making more in compensation than at the nonprofit and at several other federal jobs I have previously held. Since starting my federal job, I've been transferred to the Office of Communications and Public Affairs as a supervisory writer-editor.

The type of seamless segue that I experienced from a temporary contract position to a permanent federal position is not unusual because the federal government has special, streamlined procedures for filling positions that address critical needs.

Types of Federal Contractors

There are three major types of federal contractors:

1.   Contractors who work for consulting firms that have contracted with a federal agency to provide specific services. You can find job openings with federal contractors by checking job Web sites such as http://www.monster.com and, and the Sunday classified sections of newspapers, particularly the *Washington Post*, which occasionally includes a special section devoted to government contracting jobs. In addition, US Media Services (http://www.usmediaservices.com) places contractors in federal agencies.

2.   Professionals who work for employment agencies that are contracted to help a federal agency fulfill its short-term staffing needs for various types of professionals, including lawyers, accountants, contract managers, writers, IT professionals, and administrative assistants. Note that temp jobs aren't just for receptionists anymore! Employment agencies (which may go by such names as temporary staffing or human resource agencies) advertise their contract openings on job Web sites and the classifieds sections of newspapers. Also, ask employment agencies listed in your local phone book if they help federal agencies staff up.

3.   Personal service contractors are professionals who directly contract with an agency for a job for a specified time period. Many (but not all) personal service contracts are for overseas assignments. (See "Going Global in Government" on this book's CD.)

Finding Federal Temp Jobs

Here are some tips for finding temp agencies that contract with the federal government:

> Temp firms that help federal agencies staff up include PoliTemps (http://www.polite mps.com); Adecco (http://www.adecco.com); PRofessional Solutions, LLC (http://www.prstaffing.com); AmeriTemps (http://www.ameritemps.com); Snelling Personnel Services (http://www.snelling.com); Hire Standard Staffing (http://www.hirestandard.com); Answer Staffing Services (http://www.answerstaffig services.com); and Legal Personnel, Inc. (http://www.legalpersonnelinc.com).

> GCS (http://www.gcsinfo.com) specializes in helping government contactors staff up.

Hint: Treat your applications for temp jobs as seriously as your other applications. Most temp agencies look for the same qualities in applicants that other types of employers look for.

Finding Temp Jobs If You Have a Security Clearance

Professionals who have security clearances are in high demand by federal agencies and federal contractors, and generally command significantly higher salaries than their noncleared counterparts. KellyFedSecure (http://www.kellyfedsecure.com) and http://www.ClearanceJobs. com place cleared professionals in security-related jobs throughout the United States. Also, Tek Systems (http://www.teksystems.com) places professionals with and without security clearances in federal agencies and government contractors throughout the United States. If you currently or previously held a security clearance, cite this credential prominently on your résumé and other application documents.

Find Out Who Is in the Money

It is a good bet that a consulting firm that has just won a new federal contract will soon be staffing up. Therefore, such firms—flush with federal funds—provide strategic targets for searches for contracting jobs.

As recipients of huge federal contracts, top federal contractors provide particularly good grist for job searches. WashingtonTechnology.com publishes lists of the top 100 federal contractors. Find the latest list by Googling the term *top 100 government contractors*.

Find More Leads: Research

By researching the federal community, you may identify managers and experts that you may want to contact for informational interviews, learn about promising networking events, and get tips on how to impress hiring managers. You may also identify agencies that:

> Promote an organizational culture that jives with your style.

> Are in the hiring mode because their budgets are increasing, are creating new programs, are reorganizing existing ones, or are leading special recruitment drives that feature recruitment bonuses or fast-track hiring procedures.

> Offer particularly enticing salaries. (For more information about federal pay scales, see Chapter 16.)

What's more, the knowledge you gain about agency-specific priorities through your research will help you gear your application to your target agency. Here are some free online resources that provide truckloads of information about federal agencies:

➤ *Federal Times*, which is a weekly publication available for free at http://www.FederalTimes.com.

➤ *My Career Matters* column, which appears twice a month in *Federal Times*. (Go to http://www.FederalTimes.com; then click *Careers*.) In addition, my *Washington Post* articles and WashingtonPost.com online chats on federal jobs are linked to the *In The News* section of my Web site at http://wwww.IGotTheJob.net.

➤ Surveys of employee satisfaction in the federal workforce and information about the culture of federal agencies are posted on http://www.BestPlacestoWork.org.

➤ *FedSmith.com*: an information portal for feds (http://www.FedSmith.com).

➤ Every other year (usually in October or November), *Washingtonian* magazine ranks the best places to work in Washington, D.C., including the best federal agencies.

➤ *GovernmentExecutive.com*. Also peruse monthly issues of *Government Executive* magazine. *Federal Computer Week* (http://www.FCW.com) and *Government Computer News* (http://www.GNC.com) cover trends in federal IT hiring and management.

Resources for Young Professionals

If you are a newbie to the working world, or even have a decade or two of work experience under your belt, various resources for young federal professionals may be particularly helpful to you.

➤ The Partnership for Public Service's site at http://www.makingthedifference.org is overflowing with practical information about landing federal jobs, including a directory of opportunities for young professionals.

➤ Young Government Leaders, a very active group of under-40 feds, sponsors professional development and social activities. See http://www.YoungGovernment Leaders.org.

➤ Various professional organizations that are devoted to young professionals are listed in the directory of professional organizations included in the CD accompanying this book.

Rolodex-Stuffing Activities

You certainly don't *need* to have friends in the federal government to land a federal job, but it never hurts to have friends in high places. They can advance your job search by:

➤ Hiring you into a current opening or creating a job for you. Yes, a hiring manager can tailor a job opening to the credentials of a particularly desirable applicant, and thereby ensure that the applicant will be a shoo-in for the position.

➤ Pulling strings for you with other hiring managers.

➤ Informing you of job openings as they develop.

➤ Referring you to other promising contacts.

Make a Rolodex Connection

Remember the idea about the six degrees of separation? It implies that every person on Earth is connected to every other person through six contacts or fewer. Well, you're probably connected to a promising lead through only one or two degrees of separation. I know this because I have met many feds who were steered toward their current jobs from people in their orbits.

For example, I know a federal writer who learned about her current position through a conversation with a stranger in an elevator; a marketing manager who was invited to apply for her current position after one of her clients, a government contractor, put in a good word for her at her current job; and a public affairs specialist who landed her position after a family friend had greased the skids for her.

What worked for these feds could work for you, too. Increase your chances of hitting employment paydirt by working your Rolodex. Tell everyone you know about your job search and ask everyone you know to tell everyone they know . . . and so on. In other words, use a more aggressive approach for publicizing your availability.

Create a Networking Card

Make it easy for your contacts to sing your praises by arming them with your networking cards—that is, business cards that provide a concise list of your credentials and your contact info. You can professionally print hundreds of business cards for less than $20.

Hand out your networking card to friends, family, colleagues, the parents of your children's friends, your spouse's colleagues, friends of your parents, neighbors, and fellow residents of your apartment building. Don't hold back. Shyness is the enemy of the job seeker: hand out your card with wild abandon. Give them to fellow travelers on trains, planes, and buses. Pass them out at family gatherings and parties. Promote yourself at meetings of:

> ➤ Professional organizations: If you are a student or a career-changer, join professional organizations in your target field.

> ➤ Informal networking groups, such as meet-ups.

> ➤ Alumni organizations.

> ➤ Community and PTA groups.

> ➤ Political groups.

Break Out of Your Cubicle

If you're a current fed, stuff your networking Rolodex by joining workgroups, committees, and task forces and by signing on to detail assignments that will expose you to colleagues from other offices within your agency or from other agencies. Enhance your chances of being appointed to such groups by informing your supervisor of your interest in them.

Also, attend meetings of professional organizations in your field that are frequented by members of your target community. (For more on this, see Part IV of this book.) Stay in touch with new contacts by inviting them to lunch or other social outings and via e-mail.

If you want to branch out into a new field, look for opportunities within your current job that may provide pivotal experience. For example, I know of a human resources specialist who volunteered to write articles about his office's activities for his agency's newsletter and Intranet site. By doing so, he eventually qualified for a position as a writer in his agency's public affairs office.

You may also gain pivotal experience by volunteering with professional organizations and advocacy groups. As Janet Hanson, the founder of a billion-dollar investment firm and a networking guru, told *Elle* magazine, "Volunteering is one thing you don't have to ask permission to do. You can go beyond your job description—there are no boundaries, roadblocks, or glass ceilings."

For more ideas of how to raise your profile and amass résumé-stuffing experience, see Part IV.

Run a Cyber Campaign

Announce your availability to your network via a concise group e-mail with a relevant subject line. This e-mail should summarize your credentials, mention that you are looking for job leads related to your expertise, and link to your professional Web site, if you have one. Also, attach your résumé in PDF format as opposed to a Word file. (For more on PDF files, see Chapter 11.) Additionally, announce your job search on the list serves of professional organizations.

Craft your pages on Linkedin, Facebook, and other social networking sites to impress potential hiring managers who are increasingly likely to check out your online persona. This means that you should scrub your online profiles of any foul language as well as incriminating, unflattering, party animal-esque comments and photos. (*Hint:* That video of you rocking out in a mosh pit with blood-shot eyes, a lamp shade on your head, and um . . . er . . . revealing clothes won't win you any points with buttoned-down hiring managers who are evaluating your seriousness and dedication.)

Also, you would be wise to remove information about your political and religious beliefs because they may antagonize hiring managers of differing persuasions. *Warning:* Believe it or not, I have heard of many top contenders ultimately being rejected by hiring managers who discovered evidence of their unsavory behavior and strident, even scary, radical beliefs on their online profiles.

> **Hot Tip**
>
> **Essential Ammo for Your Networking Campaign.** One savvy networking method is to send your résumé and/or request informational interviews with managers at your target organizations. Many agencies post organizational charts on their Web sites. Alternatively, you may obtain the names and contact info (including e-mail addresses) of federal managers from the *Federal Yellow Book* and *Congressional Yellow Book*, which are available online for a fee. Also, you may be able to access *Yellow Books* for free at a public, college, or government library.
>
> Another approach is to download an up-to-date profile of almost any federal employer or federal manager for a minimal fee from http://www.leadershipdrectories.com.

While cleansing your online profiles, update them with your current contact information and with punchy, fast-read descriptions of your recent work history, credentials, awards, professional activities/contributions, and interests. (Show passion!) You may even consider adding endorsements from your professional contacts on your profiles.

Don't just passively rely on hiring managers to find you on social networking sites: Instead, use these sites to seek and cultivate inside contacts at your target agencies who may provide you with job leads as well as pre-interview intelligence about your potential interviewers and the culture at your target agencies.

Another idea: If you have time, use Twitter and Facebook to generate conversations with people in your field and to establish yourself as someone who is knowlegeable in your subject area. Consider, for example, tweeting about articles of interest and the latest research in your field.

Hot Tip

Listen to Derrick T. Dortch's radio/Internet show on federal careers—FedAccess—at http://www.federalnewsradio.com. Dortch also writes articles on federal jobs for http://www.WashingtonPost.com. Find them by entering his name into the Web site's search window.

Cold Calling

Another way to generate potentially pivotal contacts is to call and send your résumé to federal agencies that do the type of work that interests you. But be aware that cold calling may be a more productive strategy for landing jobs in agencies that belong to the excepted service than those that belong to the competitive service. Why? Because the relatively flexible hiring procedures followed by excepted service agencies enables them to snap up applicants on a spontaneous, ad hoc basis more easily than competitive service agencies can.

If you make cold calls or send out snail-mail queries, aim your efforts at a specific person. This is important because if you send your résumé to a nameless recipient, such as "To Whom It May Concern," it is unlikely to concern anyone. You can get a copy of your target agency's employee directory from its Web site or Public Affairs Office.

Incorporate zest, creativity, and peristence into your cold-calling strategy. A case in point: I know a specialist in computer mapping who had, some time before beginning his job search, called a manager at EPA to discuss with him a computer mapping issue that was relevant to both of them. Then, once the mapping specialist kicked-off his job search, he called back the EPA manager (who remembered him) and informed him how a mapping strategy that he had personally innovated might be useful to EPA. Their resulting conversation led to a presentation by the mapping expert before the manager and ultimately to an EPA job.

3

Fast Track into Management

Internships and Fellowships for Novices and Experienced Professionals

---

"That summer pretty much settled things. I think I knew from that point on that I was going to be a physicist."
—DEBORAH JIN, WINNER OF THE 2003 MACARTHUR FOUNDATION GRANT, ON HER SUMMER RESEARCH JOB AT GODDARD SPACE FLIGHT CENTER

"I'm trying to avoid the missteps of early success."

The best way to learn about a field is through a total immersion experience—similar to those provided by summer and year-round internships and student jobs for undergrads, grad students, recent grads, and lawyers and by fellowships for experienced professionals.

Federal internships, student jobs, and fellowships are available in virtually every discipline. So whether your passion is space exploration or more earthly concerns like information technology, economics, international relations, ecology, law, art, history, or practically any other subject, the federal government runs career-boosting internship(s) or fellowship(s) for you.

Internships and Jobs for Students and Recent Grads

Caught by that old catch-22? You can't find a job without experience, and you can't get job experience without a job? If so, an internship or student job might be for you. More than 60,000 students and undergrads, grad students, law students, and recent grads currently work summer and year-round federal internships and student jobs. Their programs are based all over the United States and overseas.

Although many congressional and White House internships are voluntary, dozens and dozens of federal internship programs offer excellent salaries. *That's right: you don't have to slave for free even if you're just starting your career!*

On the CD...

>   This book's CD features program descriptions and links to the Web sites of over 100 well-
paying, dynamic federal internship programs, student jobs, and special recruitment programs
for young professionals. The CD also features program descriptions and links to the Web
sites of dozens of fellowship programs for PhDs, experienced professionals, and current feds.
Programs that specially recruit for minorities, women, and people with disabilities are
flagged.

Almost every federal department and major agency runs its own internship program(s) and hires students and recent grads. A comprehensive directory of agency internship programs and jobs programs for students and recent grads is included in the CD accompanying this book. Also, some federal internships and student jobs programs specially recruit women, minorities, and people with disabilities. A separate directory of such programs is also included in the CD accompanying this book.

In addition to sponsoring their own hiring programs for students and recent grads, all federal agencies participate in a new, three-tier government-wide Pathways Program. The Pathways Program gives each new hire a two-year "on the job" tryout, enabling the individual to grow into the job and develop. At the end of the two-year tryout, a Pathways participant may be converted to a permanent federal job if she or he meets agency qualifications. (But Pathways does not guarantee permanent jobs.)

The three tiers of the Pathways Program are:

➤   **The Internship Program.** A program for current high school, college, and graduate-level interns. Interns may segue into permanent jobs after they have completed their degrees or other study.

➤   **The Recent Graduates Program.** A developmental program for recipients of degrees from trade and vocational schools, community colleges, or universities within the last two years. Veterans who are required to complete military service after graduating from college are given six years to apply for this program.

  Recent graduates would usually be appointed to GS-9 or lower positions. Graduates from science, technology, engineering, or mathematics programs could be appointed to GS-11 jobs if they have doctoral degrees, and to other scientific and professional research programs at the GS-12 level.

➤   **The Presidential Management Fellows (PMF) Program.** A highly selective leadership development program featuring mentoring, training, and rotational assignments for advanced-degree candidates and graduates. Applicants to the PMF program must apply within two years of earning an advanced degree.

Note that when making selections of candidates in any of the three Pathway Programs, agencies must give preference to veterans who apply under standard government rules. For more information about Pathways for Students and Recent Graduates, Google that phrase.

Take Note! _____

Summer Work Can Be a Launching Pad: Federal Internships Offer Experiences Beyond Filing and Phone Duties

By Lily Whiteman, Special to the *Washington Post*

SUNDAY, APRIL 30, 2006. If Shirley Murillo had settled for flipping burgers during her college summers, she probably would not be what she is today: a hurricane hunter at the National Oceanic and Atmospheric Administration who flies straight into the earth's deadliest storms to collect life-saving information.

So what did Murillo do during her summers to catapult her career into the clouds? She interned in the federal Significant Opportunities in Atmospheric Research and Science (SOARS) program in Boulder, Colo. She worked shoulder-to-shoulder with leading scientists in state-of-the-art labs analyzing real-time data on hurricanes as they plowed across the United States—experiences that "helped me realize that hurricanes were my passion," Murillo said.

The program, she said, also featured mentoring, networking with prominent scientists, and training in giving conference presentations that introduced her to the scientific culture. And because SOARS houses interns together in rent-free townhouses, pays generous stipends, and covers travel costs, the program offers an all-expenses-paid, around-the-clock immersion that interns describe as the scientific community's version of MTV's "Real World."

SOARS is just one of dozens of well-paying internship programs that are based in federal offices, labs, museums, courts, and parks around the country. In preparation for a huge retirement wave, federal agencies are currently rolling out these entry-level programs almost as fast as Starbucks is opening new cafes.

Like SOARS, most new internship programs feature advanced training and substantive project work. "Interns aren't here to fetch coffee or Xerox," said Raul Quintero, who spent a summer during his master's in public administration program interning at the Government Accountability Office, a watchdog agency. "We were given important projects, and we ran with them."

His projects included attending congressional hearings on border controls and reporting on them to agency executives, and writing chapters of a published report on flood control policies.

Quintero compares internships such as his to rent-with-option-to-buy leases because they can help interns and the agency decide whether to seal long-term deals with one another. His summer job led to his admittance into the agency's two-year professional development program, which grooms staffers for advancement.

But even internships that don't segue into permanent jobs can provide pivotal credentials, said Tomas Rivas, who will soon complete a year-long internship at the National Gallery of Art. He interned there after earning a master's in fine arts "because it's the best place to learn about exhibit design."

Now, he's confident that his experiences—which included single-handedly designing a house-sized, three-dimensional collage for the gallery's popular Dada exhibition—will help him land another job.

Another benefit of federal internships is their networking opportunities, said Scott Douglas, who completed the Health and Human Services Department's two-year Emerging Leaders Program. "I met people in many offices through the program's rotational assignments," he said. "The contacts—that was where the program had its magic."

Douglas is now a program analyst at the agency, and those contacts are still valuable. "If I haven't addressed an important issue before, one of my Emerging Leaders friends has. And I call them and get their take on it," he said.

Similarly, Tamara Singleton, a SOARS alumna who is now a PhD student at the University of Maryland, still sometimes benefits from SOARS guidance, even though her internship ended in 2004. "SOARS offers an ongoing relationship. Those scientific conferences can be big and intimidating. So I might e-mail my presentation to my SOARS advisers beforehand to get their feedback on it," she said.

If you want to become an intern, Singleton offers advice for writing successful applications: Study your target organization's Web site. Ask the program director how to contact previous interns, and interview those interns about their experiences. Then, convey in your application your program knowledge, enthusiasm, credentials, and commitment to taking advantage of opportunities offered.

Fellowships for PhDs and Experienced Professionals (Including Feds and Non-Feds)

Federal agencies and congressional organizations also offer dozens of well-paying fellowship programs for newly minted PhDs and seasoned medical researchers, journalists, economists, policy experts, teachers, and other types of professionals. These programs feature training, mentoring, lectures, career-building seminars, and social outings. (Fellows range in age from their 20s to 70s.) Some federal fellowships exclusively recruit nonfeds, but others are open to current feds. Some programs favor minorities.

While contributing to hot-button policy issues or conducting cutting edge research, fellows gain top-level experience and generate powerful networking contacts. Therefore, fellowship programs offer fantastic opportunities to pivot into new careers: after completing their programs, many nonfederal fellows land permanent jobs on the staffs of the federal agencies, congressional organizations, think tanks, lobbying groups, or consulting groups that sponsored their fellowships. Similarly, current feds may use fellowships to gain career-boosting experience that will help vault them up the federal career ladder. Alternatively, after completing federal fellowships during sabbaticals, some academics and industry professionals return to their home organizations.

> One of the best kept secrets in government is that there are tens of thousands of well-paying—not volunteer—internships available in the federal government.

A directory of federal fellowships for experienced professionals, which distinguishes between fellowships for nonfeds and fellowships for current feds, is included on the CD accompanying this book.

The Benefits of Internships, Student Jobs, and Fellowships

Through an internship, student job, or fellowship you can:

> ➤ **Earn a competitive salary.** Some internships and fellowships even provide housing, round-trip travel expenses to assignment locations, and tuition money during the school year on top of excellent salaries.

> ➤ **Have eye-opening experiences.** Meet people and learn about issues that are entirely new to you. These exposures may steer you onto fascinating career paths that you would otherwise have bypassed.

> ➤ **Get the real deal.** The best way to learn about an occupation is to work it. An internship or fellowship may show you whether your target career is all that it's cracked up to be, or whether you want to detour onto a different track.

> ➤ **Expand your mind.** Many internships and fellowships offer training.

> ➤ **Enhance your marketability.** Internships and fellowships provide expertise that is highly valued in private industry, nonprofits, and government. In addition, many programs segue into permanent federal jobs—like "rental with an option to buy" contracts. What's more, most internship programs and all fellowship programs are specifically designed to provide in-depth, substantive work experience and training that may fast-track participants into senior and management positions—not to assign participants busywork, such as coffee-fetching or Xeroxing.

➤ **Change the world.** Interns and fellows weigh in on important issues, such as environmental problems, medical research, international relations, and corporate finance.

➤ **Rub elbows.** Interns and fellows work shoulder-to-shoulder with distinguished scientists, economists, diplomats, business experts, writers, and other professionals who provide mentoring and references. In addition, many programs feature professional and social activities that introduce participants to like-minded peers.

➤ **Escape the cubicle farm.** Internships and fellowships are based in some of the world's most magnificent parks, forests, and marine sanctuaries and most dynamic museums, libraries, labs, and embassies.

➤ **Make a career switch.** Many experienced professionals use internships and fellowships to satisfy their itch to ditch their current careers and launch entirely new careers. For example, I know a New York City police officer who used the Government Accountability Program's Professional Development Program to launch a policy career. I also know a school teacher who used an internship program at a defense agency to start a career as a federal contract manager. He says he landed his position "by emphasizing my experience in front of a classroom as evidence of my leadership skills."

Types of Programs

Each internship, student job, and fellowship program has a unique design. For example, some programs operate year-round, some programs only operate during the summer, and some programs are part time. Other factors that vary among programs include salaries, types of assignments, training opportunities, opportunities for advancement, program duration, eligibility, and application requirements. Also, some programs are based in Washington, D.C., while others are located throughout the United States or overseas. So consider all appropriate programs described on this book's CD before focusing on particular program(s).

Housing for Out-of-Towners

If you're moving to a new location for a new professional opportunity, ask your employer for housing leads. Also, check the housing listings posted at local colleges and on online boards. And Google phrases such as *temporary housing in [name of your city]*.

If your internship is in Washington, D.C., Washington Intern Student Housing may help you find housing. See http://www.internsdc.com.

Write a Winning Internship or Fellowship Application

Here are some tips from hiring managers on how you can craft a winning application for an internship or fellowship.

Target Your Application

Hiring managers warn against using the same application for multiple programs and merely repeating your résumé in answers to essay questions. Why? Because, when reviewing your application, hiring managers will primarily look for evidence that you want to participate in *their* program, and would contribute to it and benefit from it. To provide this evidence, your application must address the requirements, emphases, and activities that distinguish each program.

To do so, your application should: (1) open with a purposeful statement, such as, "I am eager to contribute to this program because . . . "; (2) describe what types of projects you would like to work on as an intern or fellow (but also describe your flexibility); and (3) explain how your academic or professional experience, team-friendly approaches, and other credentials would enhance the program.

Stand Out from the Pack

Obtain the contact info for several alumni of each of your target programs. Then, contact these alumni and interview them about your target program's activities, what they learned from the experience, and how they contributed to program activities. Incorporate your resulting knowledge in your application. (Trust me, you will be the only applicant who will take the time and trouble to do this—and your energy and effort will impress hiring managers BIG TIME!)

Strutt Your Stuff

Identify your unique academic and professional credentials that qualify you for your target program and would enable you to contribute to the program.

Address Major Application Weaknesses

If there is an obvious important weakness in your background, explain it. For example, a hiring manager in the federal fellowship program sponsored by the American Association for the Advancement of Science advises, "If you are a scientist with a weak publication record, address this issue; don't let us just wonder about it because we probably won't give you the benefit of the doubt without being given a reason to do so."

Prepare Your References

Help your references advance your case by explaining to them why you want to participate in your target program, how participating in the program would advance your career, and why your background fits the program.

Be Persistent

If you are rejected from your target program, apply again.

* * *

An article that I wrote for the *Washington Post* about special recruitment programs that target young professionals appears on page 32. (Other *Washington Post* articles I wrote about federal careers are included in this book's CD.)

CHAPTER 4

Location... Location... Location

Working in Agency Headquarters Offices vs. Field Offices

"You know more of a road by having traveled it than by all the conjectures and descriptions in the world."
—WILLIAM HAZLITT, ENGLISH LITERARY CRITIC

As the saying goes, LOCATION, LOCATION, LOCATION. So what are the relative advantages and disadvantages of working in agency headquarters offices located in the Washington, DC, area vs. field offices located throughout the U.S?

These relative advantages and disadvantages are described in the tables below. (But note that these tables provide general overviews: conditions and opportunities vary from office to office, and impressions/perspectives about any particular office would likely differ among staff members, depending on their personal preferences and individual circumstances.)

Advantages of Gaining Field and Headquarters Experience

Each agency's ability to fulfill its mission largely hinges on cooperation between its headquarters office and field offices. Nevertheless, relationships between headquarters and field offices are sometimes strained because of the geographic distances between them, the differences in the pressures, constraints and cultures that influence their management, and the relatively limited opportunities available to headquarters and field staffers to get to know one another. As a result, in many cases, headquarters and field staffers do not really understand what the other does and why they don't do it better.

Therefore, an ability to promote cooperation and understanding between headquarters offices and field offices, and thereby strengthen relationships between them, is a particularly appealing selling point. You may generate this ability by gaining first-hand experience in headquarters and field offices via full-time jobs or detail assignments that would teach you about the inner workings of each type of office.

On Your Application . . .

If you are working to rise through management or the Senior Executive Service (SES), multi-locational experience would be a particularly important feather in your cap—particularly if you are aiming to lead an organization without having risen through its ranks.

If you apply for a federal job that would require you to relocate to a field or headquarters office, identify in your cover letter how your previous jobs in other locations/types of offices has prepared you to offer unique contributions to your target job. For example, your multi-locational experience would:

> Provide you with practical insights that would improve your effectiveness as a leader. As a current headquarters manager says, "The field offices are where the rubber hits the road; if you don't understand how these offices work, it is tough to get anything substantive done. I wouldn't trade my field experience for anything."

> Add to your likeability (hopefully, to know you is to love you!) and increase your credibility among the staffers whom you would lead; professionals of all stripes tend to respect and relate relatively well to others who have taken the time and trouble to walk a mile in their shows and thereby gain an appreciation for the obstacles they face and their achievements.

> Fill your Rolodex with nationwide contacts with whom you can exchange otherwise unavailable advice and insider information.

➤ Help you maximize the effectiveness of any management changes you might make. After all, you can't really fix an organization without understanding it from the inside out.

➤ Enable you to improve liaison activities between field and headquarters offices by encouraging and managing interactions/ information exchanges between their contacts at both locations.

In particular, feds who transfer from a headquarters office to a field office would be specially prepared to:

➤ Help demystify the personalities of headquarters managers (including political appointees) and interpret their actions for field staffers.

➤ Explain to field staffers how political pressures in headquarters may delay or suspend decision making on issues impacting field offices, slow the development of new regulations, and stall responses from headquarters to field requests.

➤ Promote the enforcement of regulations in the field by identifying and explaining to field enforcers how to avoid traps that may inadvertently have been written into regulations issued by headquarters.

➤ Generate positive press coverage of field activities in the national press by informing national press contacts of relevant local achievements that may have national implications.

In particular feds who transfer from a field office to a headquarters office would be specially prepared to:

➤ Teach headquarters staffers about the budgetary and staffing constraints/challenges and cultural morays in the field that may influence the effectiveness of field offices, as well as explain to headquarters the achievements of field offices that may have been overlooked by headquarters.

➤ Use their knowledge of field operations and contacts with field staffers to provide leadership and guidance during emergencies and crises, such as natural disasters that are often managed from the bottom up.

➤ Advise headquarters staffers how to craft regulations, programs, and policies that realistically accommodate conditions in the field and minimize ambiguities that hamper enforcement.

➤ Generate positive press coverage of headquarters activities in the local press by informing local press contacts of relevant headquarters achievements that will impact the activities of field offices.

➤ Improve liaison activities between field and headquarters offices by encouraging and managing interactions/information exchanges between their contacts at both locations.

If you apply for a federal job that would require you to relocate, also state in your cover letter why you would be willing to relocate. Your expressed reason should address substantive opportunities offered by your target job—even if your reasons are otherwise.

Working in Headquarters		
Characteristic	**Potential Advantages**	**Potential Disadvantages**
Mission Headquarters offices design and issue programs, policies, priorities, and legally binding regulations; monitor the implementation and enforcement of these directives by field offices; help Congress hammer out legislation; respond to oversight inquiries from Congress; manage agency budgets; issue grants; interact with the national press; and conduct outreach and education activities.	• Decisions made in headquarters frequently influence the health and welfare of huge numbers of people—sometimes with life/death consequences), the fate of large sums of tax dollars, and the future of precious natural and human-made resources. Contributing to such important and far-reaching decisions may be gratifying for headquarters staffers. • Policy wonks who revel in the abstractions and details of programmatic alternatives and enjoy working in power vortexes run by senior-level managers and political appointees may be particularly well suited to working in headquarters offices.	• Because of the potential importance of headquarters decisions and the watchful eyes of the White House, Congress, and the national press on headquarters activities, headquarters officials tend to act cautiously and slowly; many layers of approval are often needed before headquarters staff take action. *Read:* bureaucracy and frequent meetings. • Headquarters staffers generally have only limited one-on-one contact with the people, places, and things that are impacted by their activities, and may feel as if they are operating in a bubble that is removed from the real world.
Office Atmosphere	• Headquarters staffers located in Washington, DC, are ideally located to attend important and informative conferences, lectures, and trainings. • Headquarters jobs may offer opportunities to mingle and work with dynamic staffers from non-profits, think-tanks, various government organizations, and other types of stakeholder groups—opportunities that may yield social and/or professional opportunities.	• Washington, DC, tends to attract motivated go-getters who may be vulnerable to "Potomac Fever"—a potentially contagious syndrome that may promote competitive, rather than collegial, working environments. • Some high-level headquarters positions require long working hours. (Nevertheless, many headquarters staffers are able to stick to 40-hour weeks.) • Because political appointees have relatively little job stability and their actions are constantly scrutinized, they are often under considerable pressure. Therefore, working for them may, depending upon individual circumstances, be stressful.

Characteristic	Potential Advantages	Potential Disadvantages
Promotion Potential for Employees	• Headquarters staffers who address controversial issues and/or are able to "hitch their wagons" to headquarters-based rising star executives and political appointees may climb the career ladder faster than feds who have comparable seniority and skills but work for more obscure field-based managers. • Because headquarters offices are relatively large, frequently employ relatively large numbers of senior-level professionals, and are clustered geographically together in the D.C. area, headquarters staffers usually have more opportunities to rise into senior-level positions and/or lateral into other jobs in their own or other agencies than do field staffers. • Headquarters staffers who interact with political appointees, Congressional staffers and senior-level managers have more opportunities to learn about the inner workings of the highest levels of government from first-hand experience than do field employees.	• Because headquarters offices are relatively large, staffers who work in relatively obscure offices in headquarters that do not address attention-grabbing, hot-button issues may feel isolated and suffer from the "small fish in a big pond" syndrome.

Working in Field/Regional Offices		
Characteristic	**Potential Advantages**	**Potential Disadvantages**
Promotion Potential For Employees	• In some cases, field staffers may be able to make decisions faster than headquarters staffers because: (1) the activities, crises, and emergencies that they manage often demand quick responses; and (2) field staffers generally need fewer approvals to make decisions than do headquarters staffers. A public affairs officer who started his current headquarters job after serving in several field offices observed, "Field staffers don't have to ask 'Mother may I?' before making decisions or talking to the press as often as do headquarters employees." • Because field offices are relatively small, they may—in some cases—offer more collegial, more informal, less competitive, and less hierarchical working environments than do headquarters offices. READ: less bureaucracy and fewer meetings. • Field staffers generally work "in the trenches" on projects that: (1) involve more direct contact with the people and resources that are targeted by their agencies' activities; and (2) require more expert knowledge about the progress and problems involved in completing local projects than do headquarters staffers. • Field staffers frequently form strong relationships with particular local reporters because circumstances often require them to regularly interact with one another and to address issues that require expert knowledge of the ins-and-outs of local projects.	• Most field staffers are given only very limited or no opportunities to contribute to the design of national programs, policies, and regulations.

Characteristic	Potential Advantages	Potential Disadvantages
	By contrast, headquarters staffers tend to interact with a relatively large pool of national reporters on broad issues—circumstances that tend to produce relatively superficial relationships.	
Office Atmosphere	• The culture of each field office is determined by: (1) the size, demographics and educational levels of its staff; (2) the office's level of collegiality and hierarchy; and (3) the prevailing culture, history, political views, geography, and recreational opportunities in the area. As a result, the preferences of any particular fed for a field vs. headquarters office will necessarily hinge on his/her own personality and career options as well as on the unique atmosphere of each field office. As one example: I know a supervisory GS-15 who recently transferred from a high-pressure managerial job in Washington, DC, to a managerial job in a San Francisco field office. Because she enjoys the relatively calm, California-esque atmosphere of her new office and loves the Bay Area, she is much happier in her field job than she was in her headquarters job.	• Field offices that are not located in relatively large cities tend to be more isolated than headquarters offices and field offices that are located in relatively large cities. Therefore, positions in those isolated field offices usually offer their staffers fewer opportunities to interact with staffers from other governmental and non-governmental organizations.
Promotion Potential for Employees	Because of the relatively small size and relatively flat organizational structures of many field offices and the potential urgency of decision making in the field: • Entry-level and mid-level feds in field offices may be given more career-boosting responsibilities and opportunities to gain leadership experience than headquarters-based feds who have comparable experience.	• Some field offices employ only limited numbers of senior-level professionals in some occupations. Therefore, depending on the field office and occupation at hand, some feds who work in field offices may have to lateral into different types of jobs or transfer to other field or head-quarters offices in order to advance into management.

(continues)

	Working in Field/Regional Offices	
Characteristic	**Potential Advantages**	**Potential Disadvantages**
	In other words, under some circumstances, field staffers may benefit from being "a big fish in a small pond." • Under some circumstances field staffers may form strong professional bonds with high-level managers in their offices, and then have opportunities to ride the coattails of those managers as they move up and throughout government.	• Because field offices are, by definition, geographically and managerially distant from their headquarters offices (which determine agency budgetary priorities) and Congress (which determines agency budgets), field offices may have relatively few opportunities to justify their work to Congress and headquarters offices. • Therefore, during economically lean times, field offices may be more vulnerable to budget cuts and cost-saving plans that involve consolidating offices than headquarters offices.

CHAPTER

5

Into the Capitol Hill Power Vortex

Working for Congress

"If you want a front row seat to history, you want to work for Congress."
—SENATE STAFFER

"But how do you know for sure you've got power unless you abuse it?"

If your pulse quickens the closer you get to power, if you're a political junkie, if you enjoy political horse races, consider working for Congress.

What Does Congress Do?

While federal agencies carry out and enforce laws, Congress writes them. Congress also researches and holds hearings on issues it legislates, oversees federal agencies, confirms the political appointees who run those agencies, and establishes foreign policy. In addition, Congress investigates various government activities, as in *What did you know and when did you know it?*

Ka-CHING! Congress holds the nation's purse strings: It doles out foreign aid and approves the federal budget. Congress decides, for example, how much money goes to scientific and medical research and how much goes to defense every year. And generally, only Congress, not the president, can declare war.

What Do Congressional Staffers Do?

Congressional staffers help the members of Congress do their jobs: they write and track legislation, research and strategize policy alternatives, plan the appearances of members of Congress, write their speeches, negotiate compromises, communicate with the press, meet with lobbyists, and respond to constituents' concerns.

Congressional staffers also organize hearings on hot-button issues. In fact, the next time you see footage of congressional hearings on the news, look for the people who occasionally whisper in the ears of members of Congress and pass them notes: they are congressional staffers. The fast-paced, high-visibility schedules of congressional staffers was brought home to me by one of my clients—the press secretary of a member of Congress—when I asked her to describe a typical workday. She responded by telling me that she had helped her boss prepare for three televised interviews and an appearance on a cooking show, plus she wrote four press releases. (Whew!) All in one day.

Congressional versus Agency Jobs

Congressional staffers (also known as "Hill staffers") work in the nation's power vortex. Indeed, many Hill jobs provide prime opportunities to influence members of Congress and thereby influence history. One Senate staffer remembers: "After having one conversation with my boss—a Senator—I convinced him to insert a line into a bill that for the first time declared Tibet an occupied territory, which was a major historical milestone. That's all it took—one conversation. No bureaucracy."

But despite the power that may accompany Hill jobs, Hill careers involve some relative disadvantages. For one thing, only about 30,000 staffers work on the Hill (and a relatively small number of staffers work in the district offices of members of Congress), so Hill jobs account for only a very small percentage of the federal workforce.

Another disadvantage of Hill jobs is their lack of job security. Instead of following civil service or uniform personnel regulations, each House representative, senator, and congressional committee hires and fires based on its own criteria. In addition, whenever members of Congress voluntarily or involuntarily leave their jobs, their staffs usually lose their jobs as well. This means that networking and maintaining contacts are very important for survival on Capitol Hill. But the high turnover on the Hill also means that there are frequent openings.

In addition, because the activities of Hill staffers revolve around Congress's legislative sessions, work schedules are relatively rigid and workdays are long. Also, Hill offices tend to be more cramped and require more formal dress than agency offices.

Other differences between congressional and agency jobs are summarized in Table 5-1.

Types of Congressional Jobs

Congress hires lawyers, economists, communications experts, experts on various policy issues, IT professionals, procurement managers, administrative assistants, and many other types of professionals. For descriptions of common types of political jobs in Congress, see http://www.congress.org and the Web site of Opportunities in Public Affairs at http://www.opajobs.com/jobresources_guide.php.

There are basically three types of congressional employers: (1) members of the House of Representatives; (2) members of the Senate; and (3) congressional committees that address specific issues. For links to the Web sites of all members of Congress and all congressional committees, go to htt://www.thomas.gov. See Table 5-2 for a comparison of the pros and cons of working for the three types of congressional employers.

How to Land Capitol Hill Jobs

Finding Openings

Capitol Hill jobs are not posted on USAJOBS. You can find them by using the congressional resources listed in Chapter 2. Some additional strategies recommended by Capitol Hill hiring managers:

1. **Be a campaigner.** When you work on political campaigns, you will probably cultivate key Capitol Hill contacts. And if your candidate wins, you will have an excellent chance of getting hired onto his or her staff. Find openings on campaign and Hill staffs by contacting the Democratic and Republican National Committees, the Democratic and Republican Congressional Campaign Committees, or the Democratic and Republican Senatorial Campaign Committees. (Google these organizations to find their Web sites.)

2. **Do internships.** Hill internships for students and recent graduates of graduate-level programs and law school provide valuable experience and references, and frequently segue into permanent jobs. For information on well-paying internships, see Chapter 3 and the list of internships included in the CD accompanying this book.

TABLE 5-1	Working for Congress Versus Federal Agencies	
	Congressional Staffers	**Agency Staffers**
Proximity to Power	Almost all staffers have some interaction with Members of Congress. They may also enjoy occasional power perks, like a ride on *Air Force One.*	The further up the agency career ladder staffers climb, the more likely they are to work directly with political appointees.
Involvement with Politics	Congressional staffers impact politics and are greatly impacted by it.	Most agency employees are far from politics and are not significantly impacted by it.
Impact on National Issues	Congressional aides help determine what national laws say and how members vote on them. They may do so by working directly with Members without confronting multiple layers of bureaucracy.	Staffers manage large budgets, enforcement and research programs, high-profile events, reports, investigations, and other decision-making tools. But to impact national policy, agency staffers must usually work through multiple layers of bureaucracy.
Salaries	Significantly less than agency salaries And most congressional internships are volunteer. (Nevertheless, many organizations place salaried interns in Congressional offices via internship programs that are listed in Chapter 3.)	Significantly higher than Hill salaries. And almost all agency internships are salaried. See Chapter 3 for agency internships.
Work Hours	Many Hill staffers work long hours with relatively inflexible schedules.	Most feds work a 40-hour week. Many have flexible schedules and/or telecommute part of the week.
Job Security	Very little. Congressional staffers can easily be fired. When Members leave their jobs, their staffers frequently do also. When the majority party shifts, Committee staffers may lose their jobs.	Unbeatable. Layoffs and firings are rare.
Location	Almost all jobs are based in D.C. (Although members of Congress do have small staffs in their districts.)	Jobs are based throughout the United States and overseas.
Importance of Political Experience to Your Application	Everything is partisan on the Hill. So only apply for jobs that jive with your beliefs. Also, emphasize your political passions and experience. If, for example, you worked for the Democratic or Republican National Committee, say so.	Federal agencies are supposed to be partisan-free zones. So if you brandish your politics, you risk alienating hiring managers who have opposing beliefs. If, for example, you worked for the Democratic or Republican National Committee, don't mention it, if possible.

3. **Do fellowships.** Hill fellowships for recent graduates of PhD programs and experienced researchers, academics, policy wonks, and teachers provide many of the same advantages as internships but are designed for senior-level professionals. For information on well-paying fellowships, see Chapter 3 and the list of fellowships included in the CD accompanying this book.

TABLE 5-2	Comparisons of Capitol Hill Employees		
	House	**Senate**	**Congressional Committees**
Size of Staff	Smaller than Senate staffs.	Larger than House staffs. Senators from states that have bigger populations have larger staffs.	Depends on the Committee.
Prospects for Finding Openings	There are more House offices than Senate offices. So it may be generally easier to find House openings than Senate openings.	Senate staffs are generally larger than House staffs and so any particular office may have openings at any time.	Depends on the Committee.
Focus of Office	Offices answer the requests of constituents and interest groups, manage Members' activities, research policy issues, and contribute to legislation. Committee and subcommittee chairs have the most influence.	Offices answer the requests of constituents and interest groups, manage Members' activities, research policy issues, and contribute to legislation. Generally, the typical Senator has more influence than the typical House member.	Little grunt work and constituent work. Each congressional committee researches, holds hearings, and reports on a particular issue. Therefore, committees tend to hire subject matter experts with advanced degrees.
Type of Experience Offered by Jobs	Because House staffs are relatively small, they are generally more stretched than Senate staffs. Therefore, assignments tend to be less compartmentalized and less rigid, and tend to offer more opportunities for gaining diverse and high-level experience than jobs on Senate staffs.	Jobs in Senate offices tend to be more specialized and so tend to offer narrower areas of experience than jobs on House staffs.	Each committee offers experience in the particular topics that it addresses.
Salaries	Usually lower than Senate salaries.	Usually higher than House salaries but lower than committee salaries.	Usually higher than House and Senate salaries. See Chapter 16 for more info on Congressional salaries.

4. **Go with the home team.** Many members of Congress give priority treatment to applicants from their own states. So, contact the senators and representatives from your home state and the state(s) where you went to school. If such offices are not currently hiring, ask them for leads.

5. **Work your issues.** Contact members of Congress and congressional committees that take a strong stand on issues that you have studied or worked on before.

6. **Network.** Participate in alumni events and contact fellow alumni who work on Capitol Hill. Also, attend D.C. happy hours and meetings of professional associations and advocacy groups because you will almost certainly meet Hill staffers at these

events. Before each event, practice describing your credentials and interests concisely and energetically. Then when you arrive, work the room—don't just hang with your friends.

7. **Find mentors.** Milk your Rolodex for direct or indirect Hill connections and seek them out. When you consult mentors, make it easy for them to help you; provide them with your résumé and concisely explain to them your interests and goals. Send a thank-you note and/or gift to those who extend themselves for you, and keep them posted on your progress.

8. **Play leap frog.** Look for jobs with D.C. associations, nonprofits, and lobbying groups; such positions will arm you with pivotal Hill contacts.

Application Tips

Here are some more suggestions, especially pertaining to your applications for these positions.

1. **Do the reading.** Subscribe to *The Hill* and *Roll Call* or read these publications online. For an excellent article on Hill jobs, Google the *Washington Post* on the term *Help Wanted on the Hill.* Also read the *National Journal*'s "The Hill People" issue, which is published every four years. This issue features profiles of key congressional aides that will provide important background information on key players in your target offices, help you prepare for interviews, and enlighten you about Capitol Hill culture and various potential career tracks.

2. **Do the research.** Before applying and interviewing for jobs with members of Congress or congressional committees, review their Web sites, hearings in which they participated, and look them up in *The Almanac of American Politics.* Also, review their voting records and read about the legislation they have sponsored. You can access a database of every congressional vote since 1991 by Googling these terms: *Washington Post* and *U.S. Congress Votes Database.* Also, be prepared to explain to interviewer(s) why you want to work on the Hill.

3. **Target the right people.** Address your application to your target office's top manager; in many offices, this is the staff director or chief of staff. Get the names and titles of top managers in congressional offices by calling these offices or by retrieving them from the *Congressional Yellow Book,* which provides the names, titles, and contact info (including e-mail addresses) of staffers in each congressional office.

4. **Target your applications.** In your applications and interviews, emphasize any previous Hill experience you have, including internships, or campaign or advocacy experience. Also explain why you want to work in public service in general and in your target office in particular. In addition, emphasize your leadership skills, coursework in politics or government, substantive knowledge of issues addressed by your target office (such as economic, public health, or defense issues), skill in conveying such issues to laymen, ability to meet deadlines in high-pressure environments, and multi-tasking skills.

5. **Use good timing.** The months following an election are particularly promising because that's when new members of Congress create their staffs. In addition, turnover is also high in the fall after summer interns leave. Nevertheless, there is regular turnover throughout terms. Also, keep in mind that during congressional

recesses and days surrounding weekends, votes are usually not held. Therefore, during these periods, congressional offices are usually relatively relaxed and would therefore probably be particularly inclined to give your bid for employment attention.

6. **Do walk-ins.** If you visit or live in D.C., personally visit your target offices. If possible, make an appointment before your visit with the office's hiring manager. But if this is not possible, drop into your target office(s) without an appointment(s). When you arrive at each office, ask to speak to the hiring manager, inquire about job openings in his or her office, ask for other leads, and give the hiring manager your cover letter (addressed to him or her) and your résumé. Dress in business attire for such visits.

7. **Persevere.** Follow up and follow through on all your applications and leads. Brad Fitch, a former Hill Chief of Staff, told *Roll Call* that job hunting on Capitol Hill is mostly about "polite persistence . . . and don't take it personally."

Stand Out from the Pack

1. **Use connections.** Work your Rolodex to find any Hill connections that may be lurking within your circle of family friends, neighbors, professors, colleagues, and others. Ask your Hill contacts to alert your target Hill employers of your impending applications and/or to write a short letter introducing you accompanied by your résumé. To survive mail screens and reach the desk of a senior staffer, an introductory letter should identify the writer's personal connection with the senior staffer it addresses by saying something like the following:

> Dear *[Name of senior staffer goes here]*:
>
> How are Alice and the kids? I am sure that you are very busy because I read in the news that you are doing X, Y, and Z.
>
> I'm enclosing the résumé of [your name goes here]. She/he has an impressive background in X, and I wanted to give you a heads-up that she/he will contact you soon about her/his search for a [titles of your target jobs go here] position. I would greatly appreciate if you would give her/his application your personal consideration.

2. **Stand out for the right reasons.** Forget gimmicks like résumés printed on pink paper rimmed by blinking disco lights. Why? Because such gimmicks may get you noticed but probably won't get you hired in government. Instead, stand out from the pack by doing more than the pack. How? By, for example, including in your applications writing samples and glowing written references from previous employers or professors, even if they're not requested.

   Also, craft your cover letter to convey zest. For example, I know a 13-year veteran of senior Hill jobs who landed his first Hill job with the help of a cover letter that opened with this text:

> If you want to communicate your message in new and different ways, I would be eager to develop innovative communications strategies for your office. (However, if you're looking for a Press Secretary who will just track press clippings and write standard press releases, please don't consider me.)

3. **Make an offer they can't refuse.** At the beginning of an election year, write to a member of Congress who is running for reelection and say something like:

> Dear Senator X:
>
> I understand that you're running for reelection, and so some members of your office staff may currently be detailed to your campaign. If your Senate office is now short-staffed, I would like to offer my assistance. I am available to join your Senate staff on a very cost-effective basis. I offer expertise in X, Y, and Z.
>
> Please note that I would not request a commitment to continue working for you after the election. (But I would hope that if you are satisfied with my work, you would want to keep me on.)

How to Move Up

Hot Tip

Communicating with Congress. Snail mail to congressional offices is often severely delayed and damaged by security screens. Therefore, it is generally better to communicate with congressional offices through e-mail than snail mail, when possible.

If you're a recent grad, set realistic goals; don't expect to instantly become a Capitol Hill power broker. In the Hill's highly competitive and political environment, you will probably have to prove your loyalty and diligence by working your way up through the ranks.

As Fitch told *Roll Call*, "I spent a lot of time in the basement of Rayburn [a congressional office building] with an autopen." The key to getting past this phase is to stay aggressive, he said, and not miss any opportunities that may present themselves.

More tips from veteran Hill staffers on how to move up from the basement:

➤ Show humility and deference to senior staffers and use every Hill job to learn how Congress works.

➤ Stay on good terms with all of your managers and colleagues, particularly your office's staff director. If you don't regularly interact with him or her, occasionally submit progress reports on your projects, even if they are not requested.

➤ Approach one of your office's legislative assistants who addresses your areas of interest and volunteer to help him or her with some projects.

➤ When you start looking for your next Hill job, remember that many positions are filled via connections. So maximize your chances of landing such inside jobs by regularly reminding your Hill contacts about your search.

➤ Read *The Hill's* "Onward and Upward" columns, which features profiles of successful Hill staffers; reviewing descriptions of their experiences may give you ideas about how you may similarly succeed on the Hill. Find these columns by entering the phrase *onward and upward* into the search window at http://www.thehill.com.

➤ Obtain the Congressional Management Foundation's *Congressional Intern Handbook* from http://congressfoundation.org. The *Handbook* is a nuts-and-bolts guide to the culture of congressional offices and how to excel in them.

CHAPTER

6

Those !@#! Vacancy Announcements

"Adventure isn't hanging on a rope off the side of a mountain. Adventure is an ATTITUDE that we must apply to the day to day obstacles of life-facing new challenges, seizing new opportunities, testing our resources against the unknown and in the process, discovering our own unique potential."
—JOHN AMATT, MOUNT EVEREST CLIMBER AND WILDERNESS EXPEDITION LEADER

So, you've found a juicy job opening(s), and you're rarin' to throw your hat into the ring and apply, right? Well, not so quick. First, you've got to figure out if you can and should apply for the opening. And to do that, you must decipher those dense announcements of federal jobs called "vacancy announcements"; this task is commonly associated with a syndrome called *docutrauma*.

You can prevent docutrauma by reading this chapter. This chapter explains everything you need to know in order to understand and use vacancy announcements, including:

> ➤ How to find the information you really need from them

> ➤ How to decide which openings to pursue

> ➤ The various hiring mechanisms used by federal agencies

> ➤ The basic components of federal job applications

> ➤ How to apply for executive jobs

 **Caution**

Sometimes a single federal opening is advertised with two vacancy announcements: (1) one vacancy announcement that is open to all applicants, including nonfeds and current and former feds; and (2) another vacancy announcement that is open only to current and former feds.

If you are a current or former fed without veterans' preference, be sure to apply to the announcement that is for current and former feds. (See Chapter 10 for more on this.)

How to Read Vacancy Announcements

Vacancy announcements are flat-out confusing, boring, and long-winded. And those are the user-friendly ones!

But even many of the most dynamic federal jobs are announced in seemingly impenetrable announcements. So you shouldn't judge a job by its vacancy announcement. In other words, don't abandon a juicy job opening that meets your salary and geographic requirements just because its announcement was written in verbose bureaucratese.

And don't be intimidated by the length of vacancy announcements. Much of their hulk and bulk is generated by legal filler to satisfy regulations that probably don't concern you.

Steps for Reading a Vacancy Announcement

Once you find a vacancy announcement that piques your interest and meets your salary and location criteria, decide whether you should apply by:

1. Checking the location of the job.

2. Checking whether you fulfill the "Who May Apply" criteria. Some openings are open to *all* U.S. citizens. But others are restricted to current and former feds or the hiring agency's current employees. (Most current feds have what is known in government lingo as "status" or "competitive status"; most former feds have what is known as "reinstatement eligibility.") Most federal jobs are open only to U.S. citizens.

3. Ensuring that you can meet the application deadline, known as the "closing date." A few caveats about closing dates:

➤ Applications submitted via online application systems are usually due by midnight Eastern Standard Time of the closing date. To meet such deadlines, you must hit the "submit" key of your electronic application by midnight of the closing date.

➤ If paper applications are accepted for your target opening, the closing date may identify the deadline for postmarking or the deadline for the agency's receipt of the application. Check with your target opening's contact person if you are unsure which deadline your closing date identifies.

➤ Under some limited circumstances, late applications from active military or veterans are accepted. For more info, type *filing late applications* and *veterans* into the search window at www.opm.gov.

4. Evaluating the "Salary" section of the vacancy announcement. (See Chapter 16 for salary guidance.)

5. Checking the "Series and Grade" section of the vacancy announcement to evaluate the position's promotion potential. Note that when you reach the top of a position's series and grade, you can only move up by landing a more senior position or by convincing your boss to upgrade your current job—a lengthy process.

6. Checking whether you want the job and meet its requirements. Do so by evaluating its job description as well as all requirements identified in the "Qualifications and Evaluations" section of its vacancy announcement and all application questions. If you can't fulfill all, or almost, all of your target job's requirements with your education and/or work experience, your time would be better spent applying to other openings. The reality is that most federal openings draw dozens of applicants, or more. And so if you don't meet all of your target job's requirements, somebody else probably will—and that somebody else will likely get hired.

7. Reading the vacancy announcement and crossing out any information that is irrelevant to you.

8. Verifying that you meet any background, licensing, physical or medical requirements, or other conditions of employment specified for the job.

9. Listing everything you have to do and submit in order to apply for the job. Gather this information from the "How to Apply" section of the vacancy announcement, as well as from other sections of the vacancy announcement that specify additional requirements.

10. If you have questions about an opening and/or are unsure about whether to apply for it, get the contact info for the job's hiring manager from the Human Resources contact person identified on the job's vacancy announcement. Then call the hiring manager and discuss your concerns (and ask for additional leads).

Ways That Federal Jobs Are Filled

There are two major ways that the federal government fills jobs: through competitive appointments and through noncompetitive appointments. (In government lingo, an "appointment" is a job.) It may be helpful for you to quickly familiarize yourself with the basics of how competitive and noncompetitive appointments work so that you will understand the associated terminology included in most vacancy announcements.

Take Note! _____

The Real Deal on Preselected Jobs

Granted, some federal jobs are initially targeted to selected candidates, though no stats are available on this phenomenon. But I know that a large percentage of desirable jobs at all levels, even executive positions, are NOT preselected because: (1) I have coached hundreds of professionals into them; and (2) along the way, I have landed a few such jobs myself.

And even if you do apply for a preselected job, you may land it anyway. This may happen if: (1) the preselected applicant accidentally misses the application deadline or, for one reason or another, does not apply for the preselected job after all; or (2) preselection attempts are thwarted by the checks and balances built into federal selection processes, as well as by the weight given to veterans' preference. Both of these situations happen more often than you would think!

Many job seekers wrongly believe that any federal job that is open for two weeks or less is preselected. According to this myth, the short window of opportunity for applying reflects the hiring agency's effort to minimize its processing of doomed applications. But the presumed two-week red flag is really a red herring. In fact, many agencies keep *all* of their vacancy announcements open for only two weeks to speed their hiring process and/or to minimize an expected flood of applications. (Too bad that the federal government's reputation for sluggishness is so entrenched that its quick-response policies are apparently almost enough to spawn conspiracy theories!)

The truth is that there is simply no sure way to identify preselected jobs from their vacancy announcements. (A vacancy announcement will not surrender its secrets easily!) Nevertheless, a vacancy announcement that describes responsibilities so specific that they could only be fulfilled by one or two people in the world is more likely to be preselected than one that describes reasonably broad responsibilities. And because agencies are unlikely to pay to advertise preselected jobs, it is safe to assume that those advertised in fee-based publications are not preselected. In addition, any opening that has been filled without any interviews is suspect.

Conversely, a vacancy announcement that advertises multiple openings is less likely to be preselected than one that announces a single opening. But the chances of being thwarted by preselections are too remote and vacancy announcements for multiple openings are too few for either of these phenomena to be the sole basis for any sensible job search. Bottom line: **You should apply for every opening that would be a good fit for you.**

Competitive Appointments

A competitive appointment is a federal job that is filled through an open competition designed to identify the best qualified applicants. In an open competition, applicants are rated and ranked depending on their qualifications and veterans' preference. Then, based on interviews or other criteria, the selecting official selects one of the best qualified applicants. For more info on competitive appointments, see Chapter 8.

Noncompetitive Appointments

Some federal jobs are filled through noncompetitive appointments. When an agency fills a job through a noncompetitive appointment, it bypasses requirements to hold an open competition and to award the job to the most qualified candidate.

Instead, the agency uses special, streamlined procedures to hire an applicant who meets or exceeds the job's basic qualifications and meets certain, other specified criteria that allow the applicant to bypass competitions. In other words, to qualify for a noncompetitive appointment, an applicant does not have to beat the best qualified applicant; she or he only has to meet the minimum qualifications and fall into one of these categories:

➤ **Veterans.** Veterans are eligible for noncompetitive appointments to federal jobs under the Veterans' Employment Opportunities Act of 1998 (VEOA), the 30 Percent or More Disabled Program, or the Veterans Recruitment Appointment. For more information about these and other special hiring opportunities for veterans, see Appendix 1.

➤ **People with Disabilities.** People who have severe physical, cognitive, or emotional disabilities may receive noncompetitive appointments to certain positions under Schedule A Appointments. For more information on this topic, see Appendix 2.

➤ **Displaced Federal Employees.** Federal employees who have been laid off or whose jobs have moved are eligible for noncompetitive appointments to some federal jobs through the Interagency Career Transition Assistance Program (ICTAP) and Interagency Career Assistance Plan (ICAP). (A federal lay-off is called a RIF—short for "reduction-in-force.")

➤ **Returned Peace Corps Volunteers (RPCVs).** RPCVs may receive noncompetitive appointments during the first year after completion of their Peace Corps assignment. See "Resources for Returned Volunteers" at http://www.peacecorps.gov/index.cfm.

➤ **Applicants to Internships and Student Jobs Programs.** Participants in many internships and student jobs programs covered in Chapter 3 are hired noncompetitively.

➤ **Current and Former Feds.** Current federal employees may be transferred to other federal jobs at their current grade without competition. Former feds who have reinstatement eligibility may be noncompetitively hired into jobs that are of equal or lower grades than their previous jobs.

Why do federal agencies frequently opt to fill some jobs through noncompetitive appointments rather than through competitive appointments? In most cases, agencies opt to hire applicants through noncompetitive appointments iin order to help meet their obligations to hire certain numbers of the types of employees listed above. In addition, noncompetitive appointments are much faster and easier for the hiring agency to process than competitive appointments.

Finding Noncompetitive Openings

Each vacancy announcement posted on USAJOBS lists the types of noncompetitive appointments that can be used to fill the opening. Therefore, you can use the name of a noncompetitive appointment in a keyword search of vacancy announcements posted on USAJOBS to find those that meet your requirements.

Some federal jobs that can be filled through noncompetitive appointments are not advertised. To find them, contact your target agency's Selective Placement Coordinator. These coordinators, which are located in each agency's human resources or EEOC office, stay current on noncompetitive hiring and match eligible applicants with openings. To find these coordinators, type *Selective Placement Coordinators* into the search window at http://www.opm.gov/. You may also find Selective Placement Coordinators by Googling that phrase along with the name of each of your target agencies.

If You Apply for a Noncompetitive Appointment

1. Specifically state your request for a noncompetitive appointment in your cover letter, and carefully answer short-answer questions in applications about noncompetitive appointments.

2. Answer all application questions just as carefully and completely as you would if you were requesting a competitive appointment. Even though you don't necessarily have to be the most qualified candidate to land a noncompetitive appointment, the hiring agency is not required to hire applicants who qualify for noncompetitive appointments; they do so at their own discretion. So the better your application is, the better your chances of receiving an offer.

The Meat of Most Applications

The vacancy applications of most white-collar federal jobs require applicants to submit some combination of the following components:

> **A Federal Résumé.** As covered in Chapter 11, résumés for federal jobs must include more types of information than résumés for other sectors.

> **A Cover Letter.** As discussed in Chapter 13, a cover letter may, by itself, shape a hiring manager's first, and most important, impression of you. Craft your cover letter for success by using it to concisely summarize your most impressive, relevant credentials (i.e., hit hiring managers with your best shot), and to convey enthusiasm and zest. In addition, remember that cover letters serve as writing samples, so design yours to be letter-perfect. Remember: You have only a precious few opportunities to impress hiring managers; if you succumb to the temptation to skip cover letters altogether, you will sacrifice an important opportunity to prove your mettle.

> **Short-Answer Questions about Your Credentials.** These questions are usually formatted as yes/no, check-the-box, or tiered response questions that ask for self-ratings on your skills. For example, a short-answer question about oral communication might ask you to judge your experience presenting information to others, using five multiple-choice ratings ranging from "I have not had any education, training, or experience performing this task" to "I am regularly consulted by others as an expert in this task."

The more types of experience and the more high-level experience you claim on short-answer questions, the higher your rating in the competition will be and the more likely you will be to get an interview. Bottom line: if you can't give yourself a top rating on all, or at least almost all, of the short-answer questions in an application, you should probably set your sights on another opening. (See Chapters 8, 10, and 12 for more guidance on short-answer questions in online systems.)

> **Take Note!** _____
>
> *No More Civil Service Test*
>
> The civil service test no longer exists, and very few types of federal jobs are now screened with tests. (Despite implying otherwise, the term "competitive examination," which is government lingo for a standard job competition used to fill competitive appointments, does not involve tests or exams.)

➤ **Essay Questions.** Most agencies have phased out essay questions—known as KSAs or ECQs—from initial applications. However, some applications require people to support their responses to short-answer questions by providing "mini essays" citing their relevant experience/credentials, and some agencies still use essay questions to eliminate applicants in a second screening and/or for applications for executive jobs.

See Chapter 12 and the CD accompanying this book for more guidance on writing winning mini essays and KSAs.

Applications for Senior Appointments

The senior executive service (SES) is the federal government's corps of big enchiladas, top brass, and high muckety-mucks. There are about 6,000 career, nonpolitical executives in the SES.

You need two things to land an SES job:

1. An offer for an SES job from a federal agency

2. Certification for membership in the SES from the Office of Personnel Management (OPM)—the federal government's main personnel office

> ⚠ **Caution** _____
>
> **Follow Directions.** Believe it or not, most federal job applications are rejected simply because they're late or omit required information.
>
> This means that just by making your application deadlines and following all application instructions, you will beat out most of your competition. Apparently, the saying that "90 percent of life is just showing up" is as true in federal job applications as in life.
>
> Unfortunately, if your application is problematic, the hiring agency probably won't notify you of the problem or give you a second chance. So keep your application out of the circular file by following all directions in the "How to Apply" section of vacancy announcements and by conquering potential online glitches described in Chapter 10.

Avenues into the SES

There are two ways to fulfill the two SES prerequisites:

1. **The Direct Route.** You may apply for an SES job just like other jobs—by submitting an application in response to an opening advertised on USAJOBS or an agency Web site. But there's one extra step: Once selected for an SES job, you must apply to OPM for SES certification.

   OPM will evaluate your application for SES certification based on your résumé, answers to short-answer questions, and perhaps also essays explaining your experience in five executive core qualifications (ECQs): (a) leading change; (b) leading people; (c) results driven; (d) business acumen; and (f) building coalitions. As soon as you receive the SES certification from OPM, you will be permitted to start your new SES job.

2. **The Indirect Route.** You may apply to a federal SES prep program, known as a Candidate Development Programs (CDP). A CDP would give you experience in the ECQ areas. At the end of the program, you submit your application for SES certification to OPM. Once you receive this certification, you can land an SES job by (a) being selected straight into an SES job without competing against other applicants, or (b) by winning a competition involving the same type of rating and ranking of applications that are used to fill other federal jobs.

Types of CDP Programs

The CDP programs last anywhere from 14 months to 2 years and provide classroom training, mentoring rotations, seminars, and experience in group projects. There are two main types of CDP programs. One type of program is OPM's CDP (see http://www.opm.gov/fedcdp). This is a small program that only accepts a few dozen participants at a time. Another type of CDP programs are those run by federal departments. These programs are usually open only to their own employees. Most departments post information about their CDP programs on their Web sites.

A Few Pointers for Applying to the SES

1. The CDP programs and SES jobs are very competitive, and applying for them can be very time-consuming. So apply only if you truly have advanced credentials and are willing to devote a considerable amount of time to your pursuit.

2. Federal agencies are currently working to increase the diversity of the SES. This means that if you are a member of a minority or are a woman, this is a great time to apply for the SES.

3. When preparing your applications, use the résumé preparation guidance in Chapter 10 and the essay-writing guidance in Chapter 12.

4. If you are a current fed, your agency's SES training specialist can provide you with strategic advice and advice on preparing winning SES applications.

5. The CDP programs accept applications only during limited windows of opportunity. So check these dates on program Web sites and plan accordingly.

6. SES pay varies by agency. Agencies whose performance appraisal systems have been approved by OPM pay better than agencies whose systems have not been certified. To identify SES salaries by particular agencies, type *agency appraisal system certification and recertification* into the seach window at http://www.opm.gov. Also, SES bonuses vary by agency. You can look up your target agency's bonus history in OPM's *Fact Book*. Find it by Googling OPM together with *The Fact Book*.

7. More info about the SES is provided in Chapter 18 and posted online at http://www.opm.gov/ses.

7

The Basics of Security Clearances

More than 2.8 million federal employees (including military employees), and at least 1 million contractors and consultants, currently have security clearances.

Hot Tip _____

Strut Your Stuff. A federal security clearance is valid for two years after leaving a job requiring a security clearance. Because your ability to obtain a security clearance would testify to your trustworthiness and sense of responsibility, brandish on your résumé any security clearances you have held, even if they have expired.

All applicants who accept offers for federal jobs, and some applicants who accept offers for federal contracting jobs, must undergo a basic background investigation that—with some variation according to the particular opening at hand—is designed to ensure that the applicant has no glaring deal-breakers in his or her background, such as outstanding legal and credit problems. Such background investigations are designed to ensure, among other things, that each selected applicant is trustworthy, responsible, not vulnerable to bribery or blackmail, and unlikely to betray the United States.

More and more jobs with federal agencies and federal contractors currently require security clearances that involve much more exhaustive investigations than basic background investigations. A security clearance is an authorization from the federal government to a fed or federal contractor to access classified materials needed to do a particular job.

You cannot apply for a security clearance by yourself. To apply for a security clearance, you must work for a federal agency or a federal contractor that requests a security clearance for you because your job requires access to classified information.

Types of Security Clearances

The main types of clearances are:

➤ **Confidential.** Provides access to information or material that may cause damage to national security if disclosed without authorization.

➤ **Secret.** Provides access to information or material that may cause serious damage to national security if disclosed without authorization.

➤ **Top Secret.** Provides access to information or material that may cause exceptionally grave damage to national security if disclosed without authorization.

In addition, some classified information and materials are so sensitive that they warrant extra protection and more restrictive access/control measures than those applied to even Top Secret information. Such information is known as Sensitive Compartmented Information (SCI) or Special Access Programs (SAP), and one needs special SCI access or SAP approval to access such information. For example, a SAP may impose particularly stringent investigative or adjudicative requirements, specialized nondisclosure agreements, special terminology or markings, and exclusion from standard contract investigations.

Security Clearance and Job Applications

Some federal and federal contracting openings are open only to applicants who already have security clearances. But other openings are open to applicants who don't have security clearances but would be expected to qualify for them. (In government lingo, such applicants are called "clearable.") Job offers to clearable applicants are usually made on a contingency basis—that is, the job offer will not be final until the applicant passes a security investigation, and the job offer will be rescinded if the applicant fails the investigation.

In some cases, applicants who receive contingency offers must wait until their security investigations have been completed before starting their new jobs; in other cases, applicants may be allowed to start their jobs before their investigations have been completed.

If you receive a contingency offer, remember that your new job will not be a done deal until you receive your security clearance. After all, even if you consider your record squeaky clean, your job offer may be rescinded if your investigation unexpectedly reveals snags in your background or if your target office gets hit by problems unrelated to your background, such as the development of unanticipated budget woes. So, if you receive a contingency offer, resist the temptation to open your window and shout out to the world, "I got the job!" until you pass your security clearance and the contingency aspect of your offer is removed.

What Investigations Entail

The higher a job is up the security-clearance ladder, the more exhaustive its associated background investigation will be. But all investigations for security clearances require applicants to complete Standard Form 86 (which is accessible from http://www.opm.gov/forms/html/sf.asp) along with some combination of the following: interviews with the applicant, the applicant's current and former friends, neighbors, colleagues, bosses, psychologists and psychiatrists; medical examinations to ensure the applicant's medical and mental fitness; checks of the applicant's travel history, foreign contacts, current and previous residences, academic records, military records, credit history, court and police records, employment history (too many terminations?); and a polygraph test.

Be aware that contacts that you reveal to investigators may, in turn, direct investigators to other people who have interacted with you. So you might not be able to anticipate all of the people that will be interviewed during your investigation.

Ultimately, an adjudicator will weigh 13 guidelines to decide whether you will receive a security clearance. For more information about these adjudication guidelines, Google the term *Adjudicative Guidelines for Determining Eligibility for Access to Classified Information.*

> ### Hot Tip
>
> **Finding Openings.** You may identify some employers that are seeking clearable or cleared applicants by searching http://www.USAJOBS.gov using the term *security clearance.* Also, check the employment sections of the Web sites of agencies that belong to the financial management, scientific research, homeland security, diplomacy, defense, auditing, law enforcement, and intelligence communities—many of which do not advertise their openings on USAJOBS.
>
> And note that many agencies in these communities do not advertise some of their openings at all, so inquire about their unadvertised openings with their Offices of Human Resources. Another hint: Look for openings on http://www.ClearanceJobs.com.

Why would anyone, including possibly you, ever agree to subject themselves to such intrusive investigations? Because depending on your target job and employer, you might need a security clearance to advance. Also, feds and contractors possessing clearances of Secret and above are generally more marketable and generally earn significantly higher salaries than their counterparts whose jobs don't require security clearances.

What Jobs Are We Talking About?

What types of jobs require clearances? Jobs with federal contractors and agencies addressing financial management, scientific research, homeland security, diplomacy, defense, auditing, law enforcement, and intelligence are most likely to require security clearances. (Find these agencies in the A-to-Z list of agencies posted at http://www.usa.gov.) Indeed, virtually everyone who works for the FBI—even administrative assistants—must pass security clearances.

Also, certain types of jobs that exist throughout the federal government are particularly likely to require security clearances—such as human resources personnel who access staffers' personnel information, accountants who access confidential financial information, auditors who access legal information, and IT professionals who access secure systems, to name just a few.

> **Hot Tip**
>
> **Warning.** Even small, seemingly petty, outstanding debts and outstanding payments on loans (including student loans and mortgages) may doom security investigations for applicants who have ignored them and failed to assume accountability and responsibility for them by, for example, failing to even start a payment plan for them.

Tips on Passing Investigations for Security Clearances

Here are some ways to make the process of clearing security easier:

➤ Prepare for your security investigation. Such preparation should include completing Standard Form 86 (which can be obtained as instructed above) and determining what kind of impression your completed form would likely make on investigators.

➤ Google the name of your target agency with the term *security clearance* to learn about the agency's particular clearance policies.

➤ Obtain your credit reports from all companies that produce them, and immediately correct any mistakes and genuine credit problems cited by them. Also, obtain all documents related to any court history you may have or any brushes with the police you may have had. (But don't worry about parking tickets.)

➤ If you have been treated by psychologists or psychiatrists, warn them that they will probably be interviewed by your investigators, and ask them what they would say about you to them.

➤ Scrub your online profiles and Web sites of any potentially incriminating, unflattering, inflammatory, or controversial behavior broadcasted by them about you.

➤ Once your security investigation begins, tell the truth throughout the process; lying about your potential liabilities may hurt you more than will your actual liabilities.

➤ Document every phase of your security investigation. For example, write down the names, titles, contact information, and any other relevant information about all investigators or polygraph examiners who interact with you throughout your investigation, and what you discussed with them during these interactions. Also, take notes during your interviews with investigators.

➤ Immediately after your interviews or polygraphs are completed (while these interactions are still fresh in your mind), note any biases or prejudices that may have been shown by your interviewers or polygraphists, and any questions or statements they may have said that were inappropriate or made you feel uncomfortable. You may need this information if you are ultimately denied a security clearance and opt to appeal it.

➤ If your investigation includes a polygraph test, be sure to discuss with your polygraph examiner any issues that are bothering you before you start your polygraph test. If the results of your polygraph test are problematic, keep in mind that some agencies allow applicants to take two or sometimes even three polygraphs. But this is not always the case, so the failure of a polygraph may trigger a cancellation of a conditional offer. If this happens to you and you really have been truthful, immediately appeal the decision and request to take another polygraph.

➤ The emphases of polygraph exams vary among agencies. For example, some agency's polygraphs emphasize lifestyle questions, involving potential drug and alcohol abuse, criminal records, and problems with personal finances. By contrast, the polygraphs of agencies focusing on intelligence may emphasize factors signaling a potential willingness to spy on the United States, such as an extensive travel history, experience living overseas, and the character of the applicant's overseas relatives and friends (although international experience and foreign language skills are generally considered pluses).

Mitigating Your Liabilities for Security Clearances

A reassuring fact: Few (if any) people have perfect pasts. Virtually everyone has made mistakes or misjudgments at one time or another in their lives. So don't necessarily assume that any of your past mistakes would doom your application for a security clearance.

Differing Clearance Policies

Various factors would likely influence the importance of your mistakes or liabilities to investigators, including the particular clearance policies of your target agency. For example, the FBI generally considers marijuana use in the past three years, or use of illegal drugs in the past ten years, as automatic deal busters. By contrast, the CIA generally only requires applicants to have refrained from using illegal drugs within the previous 12 months (but does evaluate drug use prior to the previous 12 months).

Therefore, if you previously occasionally smoked marijuana and you most recently smoked marijuana two years ago, your marijuana use would probably disqualify you from receiving an FBI security clearance but not necessarily from receiving a CIA clearance.

"I was afraid I was lying to myself, but, thank God, I passed the polygraph."

© J.B. Handelsman/*The New Yorker* Collection/www.cartoonbank.com.

Your Personal History

Once investigators complete a security clearance investigation, an adjudicator weighs the applicants' results against 13 guidelines in order to decide whether the applicant warrants a security clearance. (For more information about these 13 guidelines, Google the term *adjudicative guidelines for determining eligibility to access to classified information*.) The adjudicator would also be required to take into consideration any illnesses, job losses, or other special circumstances relevant to the applicant's case.

So suppose you are applying for a security clearance, and you have had difficulties with financial matters, substance abuse, unsavory associations, psychological/psychiatric setbacks, or other issues? Under some circumstances, you may be able to mitigate your potential liabilities to investigators and an adjudicator in two ways: through accountability and through time.

This means that your liabilities might not be held against you if: (1) You have assumed accountability and responsibility for them; (2) you have already corrected them; (3) you are diligently following a plan to correct them; or (4) sufficient time has passed since your transgressions occurred to assure investigators of your current integrity.

Some examples of how such mitigation might work are:

> Suppose you are applying for a CIA clearance, and the last time you experimented with drugs on an occasional basis was two years ago. Because the CIA does not necessarily consider experimental, occasional marijuana use that occurred more than one year ago as an automatic deal buster, you might be able to mitigate concerns about your drug use by explaining to investigators that you only smoked marijuana infrequently in college and, since graduating, you have completely stopped doing so. You might thereby convince your investigators that you will not use marijuana again and your past use should not cast doubt on your current reliability, trustworthiness, and good judgment.

> Suppose your clearance investigation reveals that you used to be a problem drinker. You may be able to mitigate concerns about your drinking by proving to investigators that you successfully participated in an alcohol-treatment program some time ago, and since then you have lived an alcohol-free life, have received a favorable prognosis by a duly qualified medical professional or a licensed clinical social worker from a recognized alcohol treatment program, and have changed your friends and other relevant lifestyle habits accordingly.

> Suppose your clearance investigation reveals that you were once treated for depression by a psychologist or psychiatrist. You may be able to mitigate concerns about your mental health by explaining (with supporting corroboration from your psychologist or psychiatrist) that your depression was an understandable response to the death of a close loved one, the result of a divorce, or a reflection of some other traumatic event, and by proving that your treatment led to your successful emotional recovery without relapse.

> Suppose your clearance investigation reveals that you have had, or currently have, financial problems, such as a bankruptcy or outstanding debts or loan payments. You might be able to mitigate concerns about your financial status by showing evidence of some combination of the following: (1) the underlying conditions that caused your financial problems were largely beyond your control (e.g., loss of employment, a business downturn, unexpected medical emergency); (2) you have conquered the conditions that caused your financial problems; (3) you have a reasonable basis to dispute the legitimacy of the past-due debt at issue and you provide evidence that you have taken appropriate actions to resolve the issue; and/or (4) you have taken responsibility for your financial problems by receiving counseling from a certified credit counselor, and you are either paying back your outstanding debts or are diligently following a payment plan that will eliminate those debts and get you back into good financial standing.

➤ Suppose your clearance investigation reveals that you have associated with people who are involved with illegal activities, such as those related to drugs, theft, weapons, autocratic regimes, organized crime, or terrorism. You may be able to mitigate concerns about your unsavory connections by showing that a significant amount of time has passed since you were in contact with your criminal associates and that you have since changed your circle of associates, your lifestyle, and, if relevant, your residence, accordingly. The more documentation you can provide about your split with the past, the better.

➤ Suppose that your house is in foreclosure. You may be able to mitigate this problem by consulting a certified credit counselor; by showing that you have started and are keeping up with a payment plan; and explain that you are taking whatever other steps are necessary for you to assume responsibility and accountability for your foreclosure.

For example, a recent applicant for a secret security clearance had long held a confidential-level clearance, but she and her husband fell behind on payments on an investment property, and the lender eventually foreclosed on it. The administrative judge in her case noted that the applicant otherwise paid her bills on time and was willing to sell her home if necessary to satisfy a leftover claim from the foreclosure, and so the judge ruled in her favor.

One strategy for applicants who are at risk of foreclosure is to consider doing a short sale, in which the lender accepts less than the full value of the mortgage, as a way of minimizing damage to a credit report. Also, note that, under some circumstances, adjudicators may give special consideration to service members who show foreclosures on their credit reports.

About Polygraph Tests

A polygraph test is used by some federal agencies to determine if an applicant is providing honest or deceptive answers to questions about their background. The polygraph test works by monitoring changes in the applicant's heart rate and other physiological responses while being questioned by an examiner.

Polygraph tests remain controversial because, among other things, the answers of a nervous but truthful person may register in a polygraph test as deceptive. Because of such potential flaws, polygraph tests are not currently admissible in court. Nevertheless, many agencies addressing financial management, scientific research, homeland security, diplomacy, defense, auditing, law enforcement, and intelligence continue to use them in some security investigations.

Ask to Retake the Test

If you take a polygraph that produces problematic results, be aware that agencies sometimes allow applicants to take two and sometimes even three polygraph exams. But this is not always the case.

If you fail a polygraph test, your target agency will not necessarily inform you of your failure, either at the end of the exam or later—even though a failed polygraph will almost certainly immediately end and doom a security investigation. So if you don't receive follow-up on your investigation results from your target agency within about two weeks of taking a polygraph test, inquire about your polygraph results and the status of your investigation.

If your target agency does ultimately inform you that your application for a security clearance was denied because you failed your polygraph, request a redo of the polygraph. (Note that some agencies that allow polygraph redos do not necessarily provide this option to applicants unless they are specifically asked about it.)

File a Request for Reconsideration

If you are ultimately denied a security clearance, your target agency might only inform you of your denial with a vague explanation, such as, "We have determined that you would not be a good fit with our agency." If you are informed as such, ask for a specific reason for your denial. Also, request an opportunity to appeal your rejection and an opportunity to redo your polygraph, if you even suspect that your polygraph results were the deal breaker. Support your request by citing any factors that may mitigate your liabilities and reasons any problematic polygraph results may have produced false negatives (i.e., your answers were true but registered as false).

Note that it is important to file a request for reconsideration even if you already know that your request will be denied. Why? Because if your well-justified request for reconsideration is on record, your target agency's clearance denial will not be the last word on your worthiness for a security clearance, and your discussion of your mitigating factors will counter your target agency's denial.

If your target agency refuses to disclose why you failed your security investigation and will not reconsider your application, you may request your target agency's file on your security investigation through a Freedom of Information Act (FOIA) request. But while some agencies would probably respond positively to your FOIA request, others, such as the CIA, would be unlikely to do so.

Maintain Your Clearance Status

If you receive a security clearance, be sure to maintain a clean record—free of debts, drug abuse, associations with unsavory connections, data breaches, and other potentially incriminating blemishes. Also, be sure that you understand and follow restrictions on such issues as: (1) use of e-mail and social media; (2) types of information and documents that you are permitted to discuss and share with others; and (3) types of electronic and hard-copy documents and communication devices that you are permitted to take out of your office and the types that you must leave in the office.

Warning: Violations of such rules have triggered the cancellations of many security clearances and ended the careers of many cleared feds, even in cases in which the cleared feds did not know that they had broken the rules. What's more, it is also important to stay clean while you are holding a security clearance because you may have to submit to occasional polygraphs or drug tests to maintain your clearance, and you may be required to undergo additional investigations if you need to obtain higher levels of security clearances down the line.

For More Information…

➤ "Google" the term *federal security clearances*. Also, enter that term into the search window at http://www.opm.gov.

➤ Listen to Derrick T. Dortch's radio and Internet show *Fed Access* on Federal News Radio; Dortch's shows play on 1500 AM on your radio dial in the Washington, D.C., area and are archived for listening anytime/anywhere at http://www.federalnewsra-dio.com/?nid=211. Dortch is a federal career coach with special expertise on security clearances, a topic he frequently covers in his shows.

➤ Consult a federal career coach or an attorney with expertise on security clearances if you need advice on selecting target agencies whose security policies would accommodate your background, preparing required documents for security clearances, practicing for clearance interviews, appealing the results of a polygraph exam or a clearance denial, or determining how long you should wait to reapply for a security clearance.

CRANKING OUT
YOUR APPLICATION

"Hiring managers don't hire people; they hire applications."

Your application represents you to hiring managers. It is you on paper. It is your brain on paper. It is the only version of you that hiring managers will see when they decide whether to invite you to an interview or whether to toss your application into the circular file.

This means that in the selection process, it doesn't really matter how qualified you are for your target job. It only matters how qualified your application "says" you are, and how clearly and persuasively it says so. In other words, if you don't include all of your relevant qualifications and describe them in clear and persuasive terms, you will risk getting beaten out by less qualified applicants who convey their qualifications more skillfully.

With advice straight from federal hiring managers, Part II will teach you how to identify your key qualifications and format and phrase them for a quick, clear, and persuasive read—whether you are preparing a hard-copy or online application.

CHAPTER

8

Think Like a Hiring Manager

How Applications Are Screened

"I want to hire someone who really wants the job. If an applicant doesn't want the job enough to spend some time tailoring their application to the opening, then they don't want it enough to deserve to be hired."
—A FEDERAL HIRING MANAGER

Many job seekers use the mass-mailing approach to apply for jobs: they send out the same, generic application to every federal job and private-sector job that they can get their hands (or mouse) on. Although the mass-mailing approach is the easiest method, it's also the least productive method. Don't be a mass mailer!

Why not flood the world with your applications and résumés? Because many federal job openings draw dozens of replies—even more than 100 applications. If you fail to tailor your application to your target job, there is bound to be a gap between what the job requires and what your generic application says you offer—a gap big enough for an army of competing applications to plow through. And if your application fails to cater to the federal government's unique hiring process, it will almost certainly be overshadowed by more accommodating applications.

Here's another way to think about it: Your application for a job is really a letter to hiring managers explaining why they should hire you. Just as you probably give more attention to incoming letters that are personally addressed to you than to your junk mail that is addressed to the entire world, hiring managers pay more attention to applications that are addressed or targeted to them than to generic employment pleas addressed to the entire world.

Yes, it does take more time and effort to tailor applications to job openings than to send out mass mailings. But your chances of hitting employment pay dirt will be much better if you devote your limited time to targeting fewer applications than to carpet-bombing the federal airwaves with large numbers of generic applications that will all miss their mark.

Take a moment to think about all of the blood, sweat, and tears that you've already devoted to your career. Isn't your career worth a few more make-or-break hours of work? Don't scrimp on the last few hours of labor required to tailor each application—hours that could keep it out of the circular file and guarantee its place in the contender file.

In order to tailor your applications to your target jobs and the federal selection process, you must understand how the federal selection process works and its special demands— as explained in this chapter.

Selection the Old-Fashioned Way: Peer-Review Panels

Agencies that have not automated their screening processes rate applications through these steps:

1. Screen for Basic Qualifications

During the screen for basic qualifications, a human resources staffer compares each application to the "basic qualifications" defined in the job's vacancy announcement. Applications that meet basic qualifications survive; those that don't are kicked out of the competition.

Think of the basic screen as almost a laugh test: if you can't imagine a hiring manager saying that you're qualified for the opening with a straight face, your application won't survive this hurdle.

2. Rating via a Panel Screen

All applications that meet basic qualifications are rated by a panel of subject-matter experts—usually agency employees whose jobs are similar to the opening. Nevertheless, because every federal job is somewhat unique, panelists are not always thoroughly versed in the ins and outs of jobs that they screen.

Most panelists don't volunteer to serve on panels. Rather, they are usually drafted onto panels by superiors. (I have frequently been told by hiring managers that I may be the only person in Western civilization to ever volunteer to serve on selection panels; I frequently do so to gain insights into how to impress hiring managers.)

How do panelists rate applications? Each panelist usually receives a thick stack of applications—so thick it makes a huge THUD when dropped. Panelists rush through this application stack because of:

> ➤ **The Tediousness of the Task.** Most job applications are remarkably similar to one another and are well . . . um . . . er . . . boring. After all, the typical opening draws umpteen vague, faceless applications from applicants who are looking for "a challenging and rewarding position that provides opportunities for growth" and are "convinced that I am a perfect fit for the opening." They also generate gazillions of application essays formatted with minuscule margins, tiny fonts, and monotonous mile-long paragraphs that would dwarf the Empire State Building. Panelists are supposed to read all of them. Some fun.

> ➤ **The Time Crunch.** Hiring managers invariably run behind schedule; in many cases they procrastinate hiring responsibilities for so long that by the time they finally do attack their piles of applications, they were supposed to have finished reviewing them by the day before yesterday. So how much time do hiring managers usually devote to each application? Sorry, I don't want to be the bearer of bad news. Hint. See Chapter 11 for crafting your résumé to pass "the 20-second test."

> ➤ **The Heavy Workloads of Panelists.** Panelists are good people. They take their panel assignments seriously. But they are busy—always. And like most jurors, they regard their stints on peer review panels as unwelcome interruptions from their "real work," which is piling up in their absence.

During the panel screen, each panelist scores each application based on the point value of answers to short-answer questions and the quality of all other components of the application. (See Box for more info on short-answer questions.) Then, all panelists' ratings are tallied to give each applicant a total rating on a scale from 1 to 100 points.

3. Rating and Ranking Applications

After being rated by panelists, applicants are divided into two tracks depending on whether they are currently or ever have been a fed. The rules governing the ranking of applicants in each track differ. Here's how:

> ➤ One track is for all applicants, including outside applicants without any federal experience. Applicants on this track are, as warranted, rated, and ranked on the quality of their applications, and then given points for veterans' preference—a system of points awarded to certain types of veterans based on their military service. When rated and ranked against other applicants, veterans with veterans' preference frequently "float to the top" because of their extra points. Therefore, veterans' preference can be a deciding factor in hiring competitions.

> ➤ Another track is for current and former feds who are said to have "status." Applicants on this track cannot count their veterans' preference. Therefore, when applicants on this track are rated and ranked, feds without veterans' preference cannot be outranked by applicants with veterans' preference.

4. Generating "the Certs"

After applicants on each track are rated and ranked, top scorers on each track are added onto a certification list of "best qualified candidates." In government lingo, these surviving applications have "made the cert." Applications that don't make the cert are (sniffle, sniffle) rejected.

The number of applications that makes each cert varies according to the hiring agency's rules. But anywhere from three to ten applications are included on most certs.

5. The Final Cut

The certs are submitted to the selecting official—usually the future supervisor of the new employee (or a member of his or her staff). But note that the selecting official for any particular job is not necessarily in the same profession as the applicants he or she is screening. For example, a department head who is an accountant could serve as the selecting official for an opening in his or her department for a communications expert.

The selecting official reviews all applications on the certs, and depending on agency policy, may decide to interview all, some, or none of them. (See Chapter 10 for instruction on how to craft your résumé for the type of fast-read review it is likely to receive from hiring managers.) Phone interviews are allowed.

What types of applications tend to do best in this type of contest? These are applications that cater to a rushed, distracted, and not necessarily expert manager by concisely conveying impressive, relevant credentials in reader-friendly language that does not assume specialized knowledge. (More on this late in this chapter.)

Once the selecting official finishes interviewing applicants and checking references, he or she picks the winner of the competition, who is then offered the job. If the winner rejects the offer, another qualified candidate is usually offered the job.

If an outside applicant with no federal experience is picked, that individual usually must serve a probationary or trial period, which usually lasts one year. If a current or former fed with status is hired, the individual does not have to serve a probationary period.

Taking the "Human" Out of Human Resources

Some agencies still accept only paper applications. But more and more federal agencies have automated their selection processes—and some federal agencies allow applicants to choose for themselves whether to submit a paper or an online application.

If your target agency gives you a choice between submitting a paper application or an online application, choose the paper option. Why? Because:

➤ Most online applications don't recognize and accept modern text formatting features, like boldface and bulleted lists. Therefore, applications created on these software systems invariably print out as dense slabs of tiny, featureless text. Reading page after page of such texts is about as much fun as reading the phone book. By contrast, well-formatted paper applications are considerably more eye-catching and memorable. Therefore, hiring managers tend to give paper applications more attention than online applications.

➤ Some online software applications do not have spellcheckers and so are prone to errors and typos that can—by themselves—doom an application. By contrast, spellchecked paper applications that can easily be printed for proofreading are more likely to be error free.

The raw reality is that, in most cases, when time-pressured hiring managers confront piles of applications that include concise, well-formatted paper applications, as well as dense, hard-to-read online applications, the online applications sink to the bottom of the pile—perhaps never to be exhumed. Such burial does not bode well for the hiring prospects of their authors.

As one hiring manager said, with rolling eyes, "PEEE-UUUU! I hate those online applications. Page after page of long, unbroken paragraphs in tiny print remind me of the warning inserts that come with prescriptions. Nobody reads them because they are unreadable!"

How Online Applications Are Screened

Online applications usually feature the following components: résumés, essay questions, and short-answer questions that ask applicants to describe their experience via true/false, check-the-boxes, and tiered-response answers. (See Take Note! on pages 80–81.)

Each potential response to each short-answer question is worth a certain number of points; the more types of experience and the more senior-level experience each answer reflects, the more points it earns. So interpret your experience liberally and give yourself the highest rating you possibly can on each short-answer question.

Here's how online applications are screened by electronic hiring systems:

1. **Generating the Certs.** Computers—instead of people—rate each application based on its responses to short-answer questions (see the box on pages 80–81 for more information on short-answer questions) and veterans' preference, and then list the top scorers on the certs.

2. **Checking the Certs.** Human resources staffers verify that the short-answer questions in each application on the certs are supported by the applicant's résumé and essays. Unsupported applications are rejected. Applications on each cert that pass this screen are forwarded to the selecting official.

3. **The Final Cut.** The selecting official reviews top-scoring applications on the certs (usually quickly), interviews his or her top picks, and then makes the selection decision, just as selecting officials do in traditional hiring processes.

Does the speed and superficiality of this system seem brutally harsh to you? If so, that's because it is. But selections in the private sector are even more brutal than the federal ones. Why? Because federal agencies are required to review all complete applications that make the deadline. They are also required to fill positions based on the qualifications of applicants, not on their own personal preferences or nepotism.

This is not true in the private sector, where applications can be filed directly in the circular file without ever being reviewed by a person or machine, and where hiring managers are free to base their hiring decisions solely on nepotism or other subjective criteria.

What Makes a Successful Application

Whether you're applying for an entry-level job or an executive job, your hiring manager's main goal is to hire the zero-risk applicant who will solve the stated problems, not create new ones. And because it's relatively difficult to fire feds, your hiring manager is probably particularly scared of hiring the wrong applicant—one who looks great on paper but fritzes out once hired.

Proving That You're the Zero-Risk Applicant

How can you prove that you're the zero-risk applicant who will solve problems, not create them? The first principle of application preparation is that the short-answer self-rating questions on the applications are critical to your success.

If you don't give yourself top scores on all the short-answer questions, you almost certainly won't earn enough points to make the cert. (See the box on pages 80–81 for more information on short-answer questions.)

The Good, the Bad, and the Ugly. The bad news is that most job openings draw dozens of applications. But the good news is that most applications present irrelevant qualifications in rambling, typo-filled texts. So if you submit a targeted, concise, polished application, you will almost certainly stand out from the pack.

Also, remember that to be successful (that is, to make the cert and win over interviewers), even electronically screened applications must eventually impress harried, time-pressured human resource officials and interviewers who want a quick, easy, impressive read.

But hiring managers don't read applications like they read suspense novels, savoring every word while sipping wine and cuddled up by a cozy fire. Instead, they race through applications solely to get through the pile, dismiss applications, and whittle down the pile to a few choice candidates so they can get back to their "real work." And believe me, they use any plausible reason to eliminate applications, down to grammatical errors and typos.

So make your application an easy, instantly impressive read. Do so by crafting your application to do the following:

> **Be eye-catching.** Your application should be concise, formatted to support skimming, and crafted to make your key credentials leap off the page and into hiring managers' brains like a verbal grasshopper. After all, hiring managers skim piles of applications

fast, not word for word as if they were sitting by a fire, sipping wine and reading a suspenseful John Grisham novel. So to keep the attention of hiring managers, craft your application for a fast, easy read with language that sticks in their mind like Velcro.

➤ **Be concise.** Instead of aiming for a specific résumé length, describe your most impressive credentials succinctly. Format the names of your employers, your job titles, and your degrees to stand out. Confine each job description to a few quick-read, achievement-oriented bullets. And break up your answers to essay questions by writing in short paragraphs and using bullets and headings. (More on this later.)

➤ **Present yourself as an experienced veteran of your target position.** Prove that you've already done your target job and done it well by describing your credentials and success stories that parallel the requirements of your target job and by providing objective validation of your successes, as explained in Chapter 9.

➤ **Be understood by nonspecialists who are not familiar with your field and know nothing about your current organization or projects.** You can make sure that your application will be understood by hiring managers by soliciting feedback on it from friends, colleagues, and relatives before you submit it. Remember that hiring managers are plucked from the masses to serve on hiring panels. This means that today's cube neighbor is tomorrow's hiring manager; yesterday's hiring manager is today's cube neighbor. Therefore, today's cube neighbor can help you preview what tomorrow's hiring manager will think of your application.

➤ **Wake up hiring managers by showing your enthusiasm and zest.** Most applicants believe that federal job applications should read as dryly and bureaucratically as the tax code. Wrong! A job application that exudes life will wake up hiring managers, will stand out from the pack, and show that you are an energetic go-getter who requires minimal supervision. (Look, Ma! No cattle prodder!) So mention in your cover letter and application why your work is important or inspiring.

➤ **Be polished and error-free.**

> **Hot Tip**
>
> **Become an Insider.** As the saying goes, "It takes one to know one." So if you really want to understand how hiring managers think, become one. To do so, tell your boss, human resources office, or managers who are currently hiring that you would like to serve on hiring or interviewing panels. They will probably welcome your help. And, in return for your efforts, you will be paid in spades with career-boosting insights on how job applications are evaluated and how job seekers present themselves to prospective employers.

This Part of the book—Cranking Out Your Application—will teach you more about how to craft applications that meet all of these requirements.

Take Note!

Acing Short-Answer Application Questions

Some applicants see a federal job application and fear they'll be hit by the full force of the government's power—including visits from armed marshals and IRS audits—if their application provides anything less than a full confession of all of their professional mistakes, weaknesses, and liabilities. But remember: As long as your application answers are honest, you are well within your rights, and are well advised to keep your faults to yourself and to evaluate your credentials leniently and liberally.

After all, cold, callous soulless government computers and harried hiring managers won't give you credit for candor—only for your winning experience. So your answers to application questions should represent the highest level of experience, the biggest influence, the most responsibility, and the most seniority possible.

If appropriate, give yourself credit for experience that is comparable to, but not exactly like, the type of experience cited in the question. For example, suppose a short-answer question asks you whether you have taken a class in a certain subject but you have gained comparable knowledge through life experience rather than through a class: you would be wise to answer the question with a "yes."

To help you claim all of the credit you deserve on application questions, here are three examples of such questions with explanations of their winning answers.

Example of a Check-the-Boxes Question

1. I have independently written, without supervision, the following:

   ❑ Newsletters.   ❑ Magazine articles.

   ❑ Technical and/or status reports.   ❑ Nontechnical correspondence.

   ❑ Congressional testimony.   ❑ Fact sheets and/or brochures.

   ❑ Briefing packages.   ❑ Position papers.

   ❑ Policy analyses.   ❑ Press releases.

   ❑ I do not have any experience represented by the above choices.

As is usually the case with check-the-boxes questions, a winning answer to this question would feature checks next to all of the options except the option reflecting no experience. Why? Because each answer choice to a check-the-boxes question usually describes a type of experience that is required by the opening. So, to be a top contender for the associated opening, you should be able to claim to have all, or at least most, of the types of experience cited in the question.

When you answer short-answer questions, always interpret the language in the question broadly. For example, consider the term "fact sheet" in the above answer list. Almost any type of concise, reader-friendly document that contains facts may qualify as a "fact sheet" even if it was not named as such. Similarly, policy analyses that you wrote in school—not just those you wrote on a job—may qualify as "policy analyses."

Example of a Yes/No Question

2. Have you supervised employees?

   ❑ Yes   ❑ No

You could legitimately answer yes to the question if you supervised employees in any previous job, no matter how long ago you did so, or if you supervised employees as a manager of contractors, a lab scientist, or a team leader without serving as a first-line supervisor.

Example of a Tiered-Response Question

3. Select the response that describes your highest level of experience analyzing operational problems or issues and recommended solutions:
   ❑ I recommended and implemented a solution that permanently resolved a systemic operational problem or issue.
   ❑ I have successfully implemented solutions that I recommended to resolve systemic operational problems or issues.
   ❑ I have recommended solutions to system operational problems or issues.
   ❑ I have identified and gathered information addressing an operational problem. I have not performed this job function on my job.

The correct answer to tiered-response questions is always the option that represents the largest number of high-level activities involving more responsibility and impact, greater reach, broader influence, and deeper technical knowledge than other available options. So which is the correct answer to this tiered-response question?

The correct answer to this question is the second option because it involved: (1) implementing solutions to multiple systemic operational problems or issues (not to just one problem); (2) recommending solutions to multiple systemic problems (not to just one problem); (3) repeatedly resolving systemic operational problems or issues (not just identifying and gathering information about a single operational problem or issue); and (4) successfully recommending and implementing solutions (not just recommending and implementing solutions).

Note that, in rare cases, applications ask applicants to support their answers to short-answer questions with "mini essays" about their relevant experience/credentials. If your application requests such mini essays, use the worksheets (provided in Chapter 15) for telling impressive success stories and to help generate impressive answers.

Warning. If you make the cert, human resources specialists will cross-check your answers to short-answer questions against your résumé, and will reject your application if it doesn't check out. So craft your résumé accordingly.

Take Note! _____

What Hiring Managers Want

By Kathy Alejandro, Federal Manager and Supervisor

Throughout my career, I have helped hire and promote many federal employees. What do federal hiring managers, like me, usually look for in job applicants?

The three qualities that impress me most in job applications and interviews are experience, experience, and more experience. That's because if I have a staffing need, I want to fill it NOW. So I want to hire someone who can hit the ground running with minimal supervision and training. And applicants who are experienced in the same types of projects demanded by the job opening are most likely to be able to quickly and independently deliver. I also want to hire professionals who:

- Are hard-working and conscientious.

- Really want the job, and go the extra mile to prove it.

- Are professionally reliable. (Yes, when you are screening strangers, the possibility of hiring an axe murderer is, shall we say, less than appealing.)

How can you, as a job applicant, show hiring managers that you have these winning qualities? First and foremost, by loading your application and answers to interview questions with specific examples of successes that relate to the opening. You will thereby prove that you would produce similar successes if you were hired for the job.

But if, on the other hand, you submit an application that omits any required KSAs, you are virtually guaranteed to be rejected. Likewise, if you pump up your application with generic or irrelevant information that lacks specifics, you will probably strike out. After all, you can't expect hiring managers to fill in the gaps and make sense out of your past. That is your job.

Among my pet peeves are applications and answers to interview questions that are filled with conclusions about how qualified the applicant is and what the applicant can do, without providing any examples of accomplishments that support these statements. As someone who has completed many job applications myself, I sympathize with applicants who would rather not take the time and trouble to target their applications to their target job and prepare for interviews. I understand why most applicants opt to simply submit a generic résumé that is filled with descriptions of jobs, projects, and training that do not necessarily relate to the target job.

But by the same token, as a hiring manager, I must evaluate applicants by their applications. And when applications do not provide me with thorough (but concise) descriptions of relevant qualifications, it gives me no reason to consider the applicant qualified for the opening. What's more, when applicants squander opportunities to sell themselves by neglecting to submit cover letters or by leaving some application answers blank, I usually assume that they would not work very hard, if hired. (No fire in the belly.)

Here are some other pointers for preparing winning federal job applications:

- **Write for nonspecialists.** Let me give you an example of why this is important. By training, I am an attorney. But I have served as the selecting official for jobs such as a contract specialist and safety/health specialist—fields in which I have no background. So it is hard for me to understand, let alone be impressed by, applications for such positions that are filled with abbreviations, acronyms, and technical or agency-specific jargon. But I am likely to be bowled over by applications for such positions that cite success stories and other credentials that are free of such impenetrable obstacles.

- **Research your target agency.** Surf your target agency's Web site, read recent articles about the agency in newspapers and magazines, and research your target agency through the online resources provided in Chapters 2 and 13 of this book. Reflect your resulting knowledge in your application. In interviews, mention how you have researched the agency, and then mention specific, relevant news items about the agency to prove it.

- **Proofread and edit.** Typos, grammatical errors, missing words, and misspellings on job applications are absolute no-nos. One of my favorite bloopers involved an applicant who mentioned that he had brought a project "to fruitarian" (instead of "to fruition"). On first blush, I thought the applicant had brought the project to someone who studied fruit or was a vegan! Other applications have included sentences such as "I have letters of accommodation" (instead of "commendation") and, ironically, "I am an excellent roofreader" (instead of "proofreader"). Though such mistakes provide comic relief to hiring panels, they reflect poorly on the applicant's communication skills. But even worse, an error-filled or incomplete application that incorporates a sloppy, half-hearted approach bodes poorly for an applicant's future performance.

    Here is a tip that will be the gift that will keep on giving: Run each of your applications by at least one critical, articulate editor. Your editor will help you eliminate bloopers and sharpen the organization and clarity of your descriptions of your experience.

- **Use inside contacts.** Do you have inside contacts who will vouch for your professional reputation and reliability? An inside contact may be an employee of the hiring agency or a personal or professional associate of a hiring manager. If so, encourage your inside contact to sing your praises to the powers-that-be as soon as you submit your application.

- **Infuse your application and interview with LIFE!** Unfortunately, many job seekers wrongly believe that just because they are applying for a federal job, their application should read as dryly as the *Federal Register*. NO! An application or interview that reflects a high-energy individual who enjoys his or her job, whose personality fits the chosen profession, and who considers the job important and respects the mission of the agency will almost always stand out from the pack.

CHAPTER

Your Bragging Writes

"You can't sit around and wait for inspiration. You have to go after it with a club."
—JACK LONDON, AUTHOR OF THE CALL OF THE WILD

Many job seekers sell themselves short: they omit from their applications many potentially pivotal credentials. Then when they do describe their credentials, they use forgettable, ho-hum terms instead of words that convey the importance of their contributions. Other job seekers fill their applications with vague, self-serving puffery unsupported by specifics.

These kinds of problems are caused by common tendencies. For example, most of us:

➤ Forget some of our important achievements. No matter how devoted we were to previous projects, we forget key aspects of them once they are eclipsed by new projects.

➤ Cannot be objective about ourselves. We have been applying our skills for so long and so intensely that we don't even know which ones are extraordinary anymore. And we have trouble distinguishing which accomplishments would be most important to hiring managers versus which ones are most important to us because of sentimental or other reasons.

➤ Were never taught how to express achievements in terms that capture their true value.

➤ Fear that inventorying our successes will make us sound like conceited blowhards.

This chapter will help you avoid these tendencies and teach you how to craft applications and answers to interview questions that will prove to hiring managers that you are qualified for your target job. It will do so by walking you through a step-by-step process for mining your qualifications for golden selling points and describing them in winning, memorable terms without sounding egocentric.

You will be able to incorporate your selling points developed through this chapter into your cover letters, résumés, application essays, and interviews. In other words, this chapter will help you create a reservoir of selling points that will help you impress hiring managers during every step of the application process.

Selling Yourself

Guess what? If you are looking for a job, you are in sales—even if you have never in your life asked a shopper, "Would you like that in paper or plastic?" Huh? Yes, if you are a job seeker, you are a salesperson. The big-ticket product that you are selling is *you*, and your potential buyers are your target employers.

As a salesperson, you would be wise to consider some basic sales principles:

1. A winning sales pitch addresses the buyer's needs, not the seller's needs. After all, you wouldn't buy a car from a seller whose sales pitch focused on his potential profits from the sale rather than on how the car would fit your needs. Likewise, an employer is unlikely to hire you if you harp on how getting hired would improve your life and how the target opening represents the perfect next step for you, instead of how you would improve the employer's operations. Put another way, on your job application and in your interview, you should ask not what your hiring manager can do for you but what you can do for your hiring manager.

2. Just as a sensible shopper wouldn't buy any big-ticket item, such as a car, without understanding its virtues, an employer won't hire you without understanding your

qualifications. And the only way to make an employer understand your qualifications is by describing them in your applications and interviews. After all, if you don't persuasively sell the product (the product being *you*), no one else will, and so you will probably be passed over for another product (i.e., one of your competitors who gives a more
persuasive sales pitch). You must unabashedly advocate for yourself.

3. A subtle sales pitch is a losing sales pitch. Unfortunately, you can't expect hiring managers to read between the lines, or sleuth-out hidden messages in applications, or interpret the hints of reticent interviewees. In most cases, it takes nothing less than a verbal two-by-four to get and keep the attention of harried, time-pressured hiring managers as they whip through piles and piles of applications. In other words, if you don't explain your credentials loud and clear to hiring managers, they won't notice or be persuaded by them.

But do not mistake an aggressive sales pitch for an egocentric sales pitch; you can toot your own horn without sounding brassy, self-serving, or cocky. To do so, you must describe what you have accomplished and why it was important and how it improved your employer's operations—without asserting how wonderful or valuable you are, predicting how impressed hiring managers will be by you, or describing yourself in unqualified grandiose statements. Remember: Bombast usually bombs.

> **Hot Tip**
> **What Does Your Online Identity Say About You?** Google yourself through the eyes of a cold-hearted, humorless, and judgmental employer. Will your online identity increase or dash your chances for landing your target job?

Instead, support descriptions of your results with concrete examples, hard data, and objective validation of your results. In short, present yourself in factual, specific terms. By doing so, you will provide evidence of your high value that will compel employers to conclude that you are a keeper. That is a more persuasive strategy than directly proclaiming yourself as such or promising what others will think of you.

Put another way, which of the statements below is more impressive?

Fizzle	Sizzle
I know that I would be perfect for this job; this job would be the ideal next step for me.	Evidence that I am highly qualified for this job includes my record of consistently earning excellent annual evaluations. I would be happy to provide copies of them on request.
I manage my agency's X program.	I was specially selected by my Office Director to manage my agency's troubled but high-profile X program.

The "sizzle" statements above are more impressive than the "fizzle" statements because they offer objective evidence or validation of success (excellent evaluations and an endorsement from an office director).

Here is a step-by-step approach for developing factual, validated descriptions of achievements for professionals at all career levels, from entry-level professionals to senior executives.

Step 1: Do the Paper Chase

Collect all documents that can help you identify your golden selling points, including:

> ➤ The vacancy announcement for your target job.

> ➤ A recent résumé. If you don't have one, list your jobs from the last 15 years, describe your main successes at each one, and list your promotions and what you did to earn them. Include special assignments, detail assignments, task forces, workgroups, and committees on which you served.

> ➤ List of your academic degrees.

> ➤ List of professional training courses that you have taken.

> ➤ Copies of your performance evaluations from the last 10 to 15 years.

> ➤ Any academic/professional awards, professional honors, or letters of commendation you have received. For current feds, this includes the write-ups accompanying performance awards and Quality Step Increases (QSIs). If you have won any fellowships or awards from professional societies, cite statistics or descriptive info that conveys their selectivity.

> ➤ Favorable annual evaluations and accompanying comments.

> ➤ Complimentary letters or e-mails from superiors, stakeholders, clients, customers, trainees, contractors, or conference participants. (Don't restrict yourself to positive feedback that you received from your supervisor.) And don't restrict yourself to written positive feedback. Any positive feedback that you receive orally or in writing is available to you to quote as you please, including in your application or interviews.

> ➤ Positive evaluations from attendees of training classes or events that you organized.

> ➤ Work products from your projects, such as documents or Web sites, and positive feedback that you received from people who used them.

> ➤ List of teams or other work groups that you were specially selected for.

> ➤ List of your presentations, speeches, and other public-speaking engagements, including conference presentations and poster presentations.

> ➤ List of your publications.

> ➤ List of Web sites that you contributed to.

> ➤ List of awards, honors, or positive press pieces that you helped your organization earn.

> ➤ Clips in your organization's newsletters, popular press, or trade publications that you wrote or that covered your projects.

> ➤ Record of military service.

> ➤ List of computer hardware and software systems that you can use.

> ➤ Languages in which you are proficient or fluent.

Students and recent graduates should collect these documents:

> ➤ Your academic transcripts. Compute your overall GPA and your GPA in your major, and use whichever makes you look better.

➤ List of your major papers, class projects, independent study projects, your grades on these projects, and any positive verbal praise that they earned.

➤ List of merit-based scholarships, fellowships, and grants. Cite statistics or descriptive info that conveys their selectivity.

➤ List of your honors and awards. Of course, if you were valedictorian and/or gave a commencement speech, note this stellar achievement.

➤ List of your class and conference presentations, major speeches, public speaking engagements, and any associated positive feedback that you received.

➤ Copies of your articles or articles that covered your activities in school papers, academic publications, or the popular press.

➤ List of your student jobs, teaching assistantships, tutoring jobs, summer jobs, internships, and positive feedback that you received in these positions, such as praising evaluations, promotions, and invitations to return to summer jobs.

➤ Extracurricular activities, including clubs, newspapers, athletic activities, artistic and theater activities, and volunteer jobs. Emphasize your leadership positions, such as positions in student government and any study groups, organizations, or events you organized.

➤ Document demands on your time that reflect your multitasking ability (i.e., number of hours per week spent on classes, lab assignments, sports, jobs, and other scheduled activities).

Step 2: Brainstorm Your Achievements

It may be helpful to you to jog your memory about your work history and coax your creative juices before inventorying your credentials. To do so, review the documents that you collected in Step 1, as well as the Idea Generator on page 94 and in Table 9-1. Then experiment with the following seven brainstorming methods for identifying your achievements.

One caveat: Avoid incorporating into your descriptions of your achievements vague statements from job descriptions that begin with phrases like "My responsibilities include . . ." or "My duties include . . . " Why? Because such stale, actionless assertions will bore hiring managers; reading or listening to them is about as exciting as reviewing someone else's "to do" list. Moreover, job descriptions only define general areas of responsibility that you did not necessarily fulfill. And most importantly, they do not capture your most important selling points—your specific successes, achievements, and results.

Method A: Ask Yourself What Makes You ... You

We each have our own professional bents, biases, and personalities that are reflected in almost everything we do. A case in point: If two professionals of equal stature were assigned the same project, they would probably produce two totally different results. Both results might be good, but they would certainly be different. For example, suppose two different

TABLE 9-1	Using the Idea Generator: Achievements Go from Fizzle to Sizzle
Before	**After**
1. My project went well.	1. Created agency's new Web site on deadline and under budget; Web site received special praise from Chief Financial Officer.
2. Write reports.	2. I am an expert in translating technical information into easy-to-read language. Played pivotal role in agency's release of annual report in record time.
3. I am interested in International Relations.	3. Took six courses on the Middle East crisis and earned a GPA of 3.7 in them.
4. Develop contracts.	4. Developed company's first incentives-based supply contracts that give contractors financial incentives for beating deadlines.
5. Manage the books.	5. Closed company's books within three days of end of month for first time in company's history, and earned more than seven unqualified opinions in a row.
6. Deal with customer complaints.	6. Used tact, diplomacy, and programmatic knowledge to transform dissatisfied customers—whose hard-to-resolve complaints were not solved by junior staffers—into satisfied, repeat customers.
7. File documents.	7. Developed company's first electronic filing system, giving company's 200 employees quick access to commonly used forms.
8. Created information security program.	8. Created from scratch the agency's first information security program, which protects the personal data of agency's 5,000 employees and top secret information on the production and transportation of 11 billion coins per year.
9. Run Alternative Dispute Resolution Program.	9. Created company's Alternative Dispute Resolution Program that now saves my agency $2 million annually in legal costs.
10. Manage internship program.	10. Developed internship program employing 50 high school students per year. Program has significantly reduced dropout rates of participants and improved company's image in the community.

Web designers each produced a site showcasing the same government project. One designer might design a site full of multimedia features and lots of color. Another designer might produce a classic site in striking black and white that did not feature any moving graphics. Both sites might be eye-catching, informative, and impressive, but they would certainly convey different looks.

Our uniqueness is reflected right down to the way we complete simple, everyday tasks. Even two receptionists handle calls differently. One might answer calls with a more cheerful, friendly greeting; the other might be more likely to connect callers to the correct contact. Apply the uniqueness principle to yourself by defining what makes you the person you are. What do you do better than your peers and junior colleagues? How does your work reflect your special stamp? In what ways would your employer's operations be different if you had never been born?

Method B: Get Interviewed

Ask colleagues, friends, or relatives to interview you about your professional achievements. Include among your interviewers those who are familiar with your job history as well as those who are not. Encourage your interviewers to ask you probing questions. If you feel comfortable doing so, show the documents that you collected in Step 1 to your interviewers.

> **Hot Tip**
>
> Interpret the description of your target job as a question that asks, "Do you have this experience?" The more ways you can answer this question with, "Yes, I have this experience," and the more proof you can provide of your success in gaining this experience, the higher you'll score in the selection process.

This brainstorming method may sound like a "Mickey Mouse" kind of exercise. But it works. Why? For one thing, the dynamic give-and-take of conversation may fire your brain and revive memories of important achievements better than will the solitary experience of sitting in front of an intimidating blank piece of paper. In addition, colleagues, friends, and relatives who are familiar with your work may remind you of achievements and associated positive feedback that you may have forgotten. And those who are unfamiliar with your work will help you recognize extraordinary aspects of your achievements that you take for granted.

Method C: Do You Deserve a Promotion?

When I lead "how-to-land-a-government-job" seminars, I frequently ask attendees whether they deserve promotions in their current jobs. Almost all of them invariably answer yes. Then, I ask attendees to explain why. In response, long lists of stellar achievements invariably roll off their tongues; they usually cite achievements such as their:

> ➤ High productivity levels and recent increases in their responsibilities.

> ➤ Creation of important programs from scratch with little supervision.

> ➤ Experience in simultaneously managing multiple projects that had tough deadlines.

> ➤ Record of improving audits, investigations, publications, regulations, or other work products.

Several minutes after asking my attendees why they deserve promotions, I ask them to name their most important achievements. They invariably respond to my request with tongue-tied silence and heads bowed in "please-don't-call-on-me" postures—not realizing that they had already answered that question when it had been phrased differently.

My classroom observations suggest that the easiest way for you to identify your best credentials may be to simply ask yourself why you deserve a promotion. Then, write down all of your skills and achievements that pour forth.

Method D: Pretend You're Someone Else

Are you one of those professionals who freely praises everyone but yourself? If so, it may be helpful to try to see yourself through someone else's eyes instead of through your own modest eyes. You can do so by pretending, for a few minutes, that you are the president of the Official [your name goes here] Fan Club. Then, through this alternative identity, review your documents from Step 1 and explain to an employer why they should hire you. This kind of detached, out-of-body experience may free you to abandon your inhibitions, and give yourself the glowing sales pitch that you deserve.

Method E: Take Someone Else's Lead

Ask a colleague, friend, or relative to describe his or her achievements to you. Listening to these descriptions will help psyche you into describing your own achievements.

Method F: Use the Cheat Sheets on This Book's CD

Use the "Application and Interview Cheat Sheets" on this book's CD to help jog your memory and stimulate your creative juices.

Method G: Seek a Second Opinion

No matter what initial brainstorming method you use, show your list of accomplishments to colleagues, relatives, or friends. Likewise, always solicit feedback on your applications and practice interviewing with your trusted advisers. Remember: The only way to really gauge how your descriptions of your achievements come across to other people is to ask other people how they come across. The more advisers you consult, the better; each of them will give you different and usually valid advice on when, where, and how you can deliver your messages more clearly and persuasively and modulate your tone for maximum impact.

Step 3: Quantify Your Achievements

Statements supported by statistics, measurements, counts, and other metrics sound scientific, indisputable, and objective (whether or not they really are). So by supporting descriptions of your activities with statistics, measurements, counts, and other metrics, you will make them sound scientific, indisputable, and objective (whether or not they really are) and thereby avoid sounding like a self-serving braggart. In addition, by quantifying your activities and results you will underscore the massiveness of your achievements; numbers give your achievements weight and heft.

When you consider how to quantify your activities and results, think in terms of time, the number of people/organizations impacted by your work, money, productivity, geography, and any other types of metrics that apply. The Number Generator on page 93 and in Table 9-2 can give you some ideas on how to do so.

A few more tips on quantifying:

> ➤ You may get more ideas for metrics that can help you quantify your achievements by reviewing your current office's annual report, strategic plan, or newsletter/Intranet articles.

(text continues on page 95)

TABLE 9-2	Using the Number Generator: Achievements Go From Fizzle to Sizzle
Before	**After**
Received a graduate fellowship.	Was one of 50 nationwide students out of 1,500 applicants awarded the Homeland Security Graduate Fellowship.
Manage graphic artists.	Supervise 10 graphic artists and manage office's $4 million annual budget.
Solve IT problems.	Solve hundreds of technical support calls per month about problems on network used by 500 staffers. Specialize in troubleshooting "impossible to solve" problems.
Reorganized office.	Saved agency millions of dollars per year by managing the transfer of hundreds of jobs to a shared service provider.
Helped with office moves.	Managed office consolidation involving 700 employees and their office equipment that reduced space needs by 20 percent and saves $5 million in office rent per year.
Answer the telephone and word process.	Screen calls for five department chiefs, and format and finalize 15 controlled letters per week.
Directed the transportation of equipment during Gulf War.	Directed transportation of 500,000 pounds of explosive weapons, 1,000,000 troops, and 50,000 pounds of perishable food from Kentucky to Kuwait during Gulf War.
Manage important accounts.	Manage five bulk corporate accounts that are worth more than $25 million per year.
Serve as time-keeper.	Manage all payroll and time-keeping records of 200 employees. Accurately perform bi-weekly updates. Answer dozens of time and attendance questions from managers monthly.
Help produce Website.	Research and write content of agency's Internet site, which is accessible to all of the agency's 3,000 employees, and receives 100,000 hits per week. Typically write three 800-word articles per month under tight deadlines.
Implemented IT system.	Managed the purchase and implementation of agency's $10 million online hiring system that tripled the number of applications to agency jobs, increased the quality of the applicant pool, and helped the agency meet its diversity goals.
Run trainings.	Deliver anti–sexual harassment trainings to 500 employees per year. Over 95 percent of attendees rated trainings as excellent.

Take Note!

The Idea Generator

Identify Your Achievements

- Which of my academic or professional achievements mirror those demanded by my target job, and/or address the issues and stakeholders addressed by my target job?

- What would I like to be asked about in a job interview?

- Which achievements am I most proud of and/or have I worked mightily to accomplish?

- Which of my achievements have drawn recognition, such as high grades, awards, promotions, bonuses, or verbal praise?

- How do I do my work better/differently from peers or more junior professionals? What do I offer that no one else does?

- How would my employer's services, employee resources, morale, or any other aspect of my organization be different if I had never worked for it?

- What did I do to earn an excellent reputation among my professors or employers and how can I prove that I have done so?

- How have I shown initiative, gone the extra mile, and taken on more than the minimum?

- Did you recognize and seize any opportunities to "save the day" by, for example, helping your organization to conquer crises or setbacks.

- How have I made other peoples' work easier or improved their productivity?

- When have I wisely used my judgment, discretion, or creativity?

- In what contexts have I communicated my knowledge to other students, professors, colleagues, supervisors, and trainees?

- How have my projects become more advanced/increased in responsibility in recent years?

- What special knowledge/skills do I have? What is unique about my education, training, or experience?

- What am I an expert or fanatical about?

- What makes my job or field interesting or important?

- When have I contributed to high-pressure, high-profile, high-dollar, or high-priority projects?

- Which of my achievements helped or impacted the most people?

- Which of my achievements benefited or involved high-ranking executives?

- Have I managed sensitive situations or confidential or top secret information?

- How have I helped save time or money for my organization or streamlined a process?

- Do any of my accomplishments warrant superlatives like the first, the only, the best, the fastest, the highest-rated, the most, the strongest, or in the top tier? You don't have to be the first climber up Mt. Everest to have an important superlative under your belt. You should, for example, brandish your role in automating a process, creating a new Web site, developing new trainings, creating a first-of-its kind, trail-blazing document, or completing a report in record time

- Have I helped pioneer a new approach?

- Am I the only employee, or one of the only employees, qualified/entrusted to conduct an important activity?

- How have I demonstrated my multitasking abilities and ability to meet tight deadlines?

➤ When you can't cite an exact number, estimate figures and use phrases, such as "dozens of . . . ," "a significant increase in . . . ," or "more than 100 . . ."

➤ Use creative (but honest) accounting. For example, a federal attorney was recently asked about her supervisory experience in her application for a managerial position. But because she had only been supervising three professionals at the time, she did not cite that relatively small figure. Instead, she stated that during her 15 years as a supervisor, she had supervised dozens of professionals. Plus, she also quoted some of the praise she had received from her staffers in their thank-you cards to her. Her strategy worked: She got the job.

➤ Also, even if you supervised, led, or trained employees only on an informal basis, count it as supervisory experience (but don't volunteer that your interaction was informal).

➤ If you missed a target, quota, or deadline, don't mention it, but cite whatever stats reflect how much you did accomplish in a short time.

➤ Managers: See "Metrics for Managers" in the "Application and Interview Warm-Up Tip Sheets" folder in this book's CD.

Step 4: Name-Drop and Title-Drop

Applicants who are perched on the highest rungs of the career ladder usually impress hiring managers the most. How can you prove to hiring managers that you occupy a lofty position in your current organization's hierarchy? By mentioning in your résumé, application essays, and interviews the titles of the highest-level managers who have blessed or benefited from your work, the organizations you have interacted with, and the most important projects that you worked on. The common name for this practice is name-dropping. See Table 9-3.

Although name-dropping is generally a faux pas in social situations, professional name-dropping—or, better yet, title-dropping—is an invaluable tool for job seekers. How does citing your high-level associations help your case? By helping you prove that you can operate successfully in high-pressure environments, and that you are adept at the care and feeding of high-level professionals—important skills in government.

By showing that you have earned the trust of senior officials, you will assure potential employers that it is also safe for them to trust you. By the same principle, you will win the trust of your hiring managers by citing in your applications and interviews any staffers in your target organizations who will vouch for you as references.

When you cite your high-level associations, don't restrict yourself to title-dropping your immediate supervisor(s). Go as high up the food chain as you can by mentioning the titles of senior staffers who reviewed, approved, or used your work products, praised you orally or in writing, attended events that you organized, interacted with you, belonged to the target audience of your documents or other work products, or in any way benefited from your toil. Whether your highest-level contact is an assistant or the president of the United States, it doesn't matter: drop their title. Also, mention the names of high-profile documents or other work products that you contributed to.

In addition, format and phrase your résumé and KSAs to brandish your own job titles as well as the names of your employers—particularly if they are large companies, influential think tanks, congressional committees, and important nonprofits.

TABLE 9-3   Title-Dropping Makeovers: Achievements Go From Fizzle to Sizzle

Before	After
1. Gave presentation.	1. Delivered presentation on my summer research project to dozens of graduate students and six professors. Department Chair described project as a "tour-de-force."
2. Arrange travel.	2. Arrange international and domestic travel for five senior attorneys and director of sales and marketing. In a typical month, arrange 10 trips.
3. Serve as Chief Financial Officer for No-Name Inc.	3. Serve as Chief Financial Officer of No-Name Inc.— a start-up fiber-optics company that doubled its revenues in the last two years to $15 million annually.
4. Work as paralegal.	4. Serve as sole paralegal for eight senior attorneys in high-pressure, deadline-driven environment.
5. Led trainings.	5. Designed and delivered trainings on communication skills that were attended by hundreds of senior scientists.
6. Create presentations.	6. Design PowerPoint presentations delivered by Chief Financial Officer at department's monthly "all hands meetings," which are typically attended by dozens of employees and executives.
7. Helped plan conferences.	7. Served as co-organizer of two international conferences that drew more than 300 attendees, including members of Congress, and received glowing reviews in national trade publications.
8. Wrote reports.	8. Wrote 15 quarterly reports to Congress that were scrutinized by agency Director and approved with few edits.
9. Arranged stakeholder meetings.	9. Arranged annual meetings of the Laboratory Directors Conference attended by 75 directors of national research facilities, including the director of Lawrence Livermore National Laboratory.
10. Pitched stories to the press.	10. Successfully pitched stories to dozens of national publications, including X, Y, and Z.

If you are reluctant to name-drop because it feels forced, remember that in the job-searching realm, the squeaky-wheel principle applies; the more you tell your potential employers about your high-level successes, the more likely they will be to hire you.

Moreover, you've worked hard to help make your bosses look good: you've hauled and carried, you've endured the boring meetings, you've knocked yourself out to meet the impossible deadlines, you've trouble-shot the last-minute emergencies—now it's payback time. It is time for your higher-ups to help make you look good. Go ahead, bask in their reflected glow by dropping their titles.

Take Note!

The Number Generator (#$%)

Time

- Number of years of experience you have.

- Number of hours of training you took on a subject (or number of classes or papers you wrote on a subject).

- Tight deadlines you met.

- Your productivity in a specified time period (i.e., number of a certain type of work product you produce per year, or number of articles, reports, or other documents you produced or published within a specified period of time).

- Time-savings in producing a work product with streamlining procedures.

Number of People/Groups Impacted by Your Work

- Number of employees or contractors you supervised, led, recruited, or trained in formal or informal trainings.

- Number of people attending your presentations, conferences, or other events that you manage.

- Circulation of publication or Web site that you work on or increase in circulation that you helped bring about.

- Number of people or organizations that must comply with a regulation you produced or enforce.

- Reductions in the number or rate of deaths, injuries, accidents, or illnesses within a specified time.

- Number of customers/clients/calls that you serve within a specified time period.

- Number of managers you support.

- Number of people using a network or other system you manage.

- Number of people using a product that you designed, produced, or marketed.

- Number of stakeholder groups you interacted with.

Money

- Size of budget you manage and/or budget increases you helped generate.

- Annual revenue of company that you manage.

- Dollar value of contracts that you approve or manage.

- Dollar value of cost savings you produced by streamlining or automating processes or by negotiating contracts.

- Dollar value of accounts, legal cases, property, or equipment you manage or protect.

- Dollar value of merchandise you sell per day, week, or month.

- Increase in production or sales (dollar value or percentage) you produced.

- Sales of product that you helped design or sales generated by catalogue or advertising campaign you helped produce.

- Size of bonuses or number of bonuses you received.

(continues)

Geography

- Number of square feet of building space or number of acres of land that you manage.

- Number of facilities, states, or countries in your jurisdiction.

Other

- Number of your suggestions or regulations you implemented.

- Size of database you manage.

- Number of cases you manage/have won.

- Improvements in product quality or survey results you helped bring about.

- Stats that reflect the selectivity of a scholarship, grant, or another honor that you received.

- Stats proving that you reduced the error rate or improved the efficiency of a process or software program.

Step 5: Validate Your Success

How many times have you done this? You receive positive feedback, such as verbal compliments, exemplary performance evaluations, praising e-mails, awards, or excellent evaluations on events or trainings you ran. You tell only a few select members of your inner circle about your positive feedback, if anyone, and perhaps enjoy a few fleeting hours of glee that ends as soon as your next personal or professional crisis du jour arises.

The next time you clean up your desk, you throw away your praising document, or bury it in a cramped, out-of-the-way drawer instead of storing it an organized, easily accessible file; it is about as likely to ever be dug out again as your second-grade report card. It never even occurs to you to write down whatever verbal praise you received. The result: Your verbal praise is gone with the wind and you quickly forget about your written praise. In other words, you've needlessly wasted your ammunition for advancement!

And so the decision makers who hold the keys to your future—your hiring managers—will never learn about your successes. (Unfortunately, your friends and relatives who may know about your success probably can't promote or hire you.)

The pity of it all! Why work like a harnessed beast to earn accolades without using them to help catapult your career to the next level? Remember: The praise and recognition that you receive from your toil is part of the pay you receive for your work. You shouldn't carelessly throw it away any more than you should throw away your paycheck!

Record Your Success

Whether or not you are job searching now, create an easy-to-find file for documents that validate your success—your success file. Store in this file the following:

> ➤ A running list of your projects that describes how they improved your organization's effectiveness, efficiency, budget, public image, morale, or any other aspect of its management. Title-drop and quantify in your achievement descriptions.

➤ Copies of your work products. These may include printouts from PowerPoint presentations you gave; your academic papers; copies of press releases, articles, or reports you wrote, articles that quote you or cover your projects; explanatory photos, maps, or charts; your artwork; results of surveys, investigations, or audits you contributed to; agendas from events you organized or gave presentations at; printouts of Web sites you helped create; and consumer products or catalogues you helped design.

➤ Transcribed versions of positive feedback you have earned and copies of any written or e-mailed positive feedback from your managers, colleagues, clients, trainees, stakeholder groups, professors, or other associates. These may include annual evaluations, thank-you e-mails, evaluations from trainings you gave or events you organized, and awards you earned or helped your organization earn.

➤ Other evidence of success is cited in The Validation Generator on the next page.

For more guidance on creating a success portfolio and using it to impress interviewers, see my *Washington Post* article, "Make Every Interview a Show and Tell," which is included in this book's CD—and also online on the book's Web site.

Cite Your Success

Use objective feedback from your success portfolio to crown descriptions of your achievements in your cover letters, résumés, KSAs, and interviews. By doing so, you will go a long way toward proving that you are an action-oriented producer by objective standards—not a self-promoting talker.

One way to cite your praise in your application is to copy a technique used by movie ads that string together excerpts of reviews with phrases like, "Feel-Good Movie Of The Year, "White-Knuckle Thriller!" "An Oscar Contender."

You can similarly brandish your good reviews by excerpting quotes from your oral and written praise and including them in your application documents. For example, here are excerpts of written and oral praise featured in a résumé that generated four interviews for senior-level jobs:

➤ He's a vital asset.

➤ His contributions are multi-faceted.

➤ He has gone the extra mile time and time again.

➤ She always provides clients with expert advice and guidance.

➤ He provides exceptional writing/editing services.

➤ She's an excellent team member.

➤ He works independent of supervision.

➤ She is one of the most pleasant, if not the most pleasant, persons to work with at this agency.

Use the Validation Generator on the next page to help you identify positive feedback you have received and that you can quote to validate your success.

Take Note! _____

The Validation Generator: Proving That You Are a Producer

Formal Recognition of Your Performance/Trustworthiness

- Superior performance evaluations. For example: consistently receive very positive annual reviews.
- Your record serving effectively in high-level "acting" positions.
- Performance bonuses and awards, including team awards.
- Security clearances.
- Letters of commendation.
- Patents.
- Grants and fellowships.
- Your publications.

Advancement

- Superior performance evaluations. For example: consistently receive very positive annual reviews.
- Hired from contract or temporary position into permanent position.
- Rapid advancement. For example: Accepted into senior executive service after only 2 years as a federal employee.
- Advanced from a Clerk to Program Manager in 6 years.
- Received two merit-based promotions in 4 years.

Oral and Written Praise

- Oral comments or praising e-mails from a supervisor, senior official, stakeholder, client, contractor, customer, or your staff members.
- Favorable comments on performance evaluations. For example: Please note these comments from my supervisor on my annual evaluation: "Whenever there is a problem here, John comes up with a fool-proof solution. He is an expert problem-solver."

Feedback from Training, Conference, or Other Event

- Drawing a large crowd to event or organizing events that receive standing ovations.
- Favorable evaluations, or oral or written praise from attendees or favorable coverage by the press.

Special Requests for Your Contributions

- Requests by customers, clients, or stakeholders groups from your participation in projects.
- Specially selected to serve on detail assignments, workgroups, committees, or task forces. For example, recruited to serve on EPA's Communication Task Force due to my problem-solving and writing skills.
- Personally selected by CFO to write annual report.

Your Enviable Reputation

- How your work products or advice are incorporated into organization-wide programs or procedures.
- How your projects have served as a model or template or set the standard for subsequent projects.
- Your ability to gain approval of your work from managers without requiring significant revisions.

- Your record of completing projects under budget and on time—or even beating budgets or deadlines.

- Your record for accuracy, which eliminates the need for redundant efforts.

- Your record of completion of increasingly responsible, complicated, or specialized projects.

- Your record of being consulted by other professionals as an expert.

- The numbers and types of publications that have quoted you or covered your projects.

- Your experience providing training.

- Your organization-wide reputation. For example: Because of my expertise in using Excel, I serve as my organization's spreadsheet troubleshooter.

Evidence of Your Trustworthiness

- Authority to award contracts or allocate grants.

- Authority to manage, disburse cash or checks.

- Your management of confidential information.

Students and Recent Grads

- Overall GPA, GPA in your major, or grades in relevant classes on assignments.

- Honors, awards, merit-based scholarships, fellowships, and grants.

- Written and oral praise from professors in response to a thesis defense, exams, papers, independent projects, oral presentations, and other projects.

- Ability to simultaneously multitask school, student jobs, sports, or other commitments.

- Leadership role in student government, teams, contributions to teams or events, experience advising or teaching other students, and associated positive feedback.

- Your selection for particularly competitive summer jobs or internships.

Step 6: Add Power Words and Phrases

These power phrases and words may help you convey your work's importance and value:

➤ I am an award-winning…

➤ I am an expert in…

➤ I played a pivotal role in… (instead of the mealier I helped…)

➤ I was specially selected for a highly competitive X because of my X years of experience in…

➤ Multimillion-dollar

➤ High-dollar

➤ High-pressure

➤ High-priority

➤ High-energy

➤ High-volume

➤ High-profile

➤ High-visibility

➤ High-traffic, fast-paced, or fast-track

➤ Precedent-setting or trailblazing

➤ Record-breaking

➤ Front-line

➤ Deadline-driven

➤ Played a pivotal role in…

➤ I single-handedly…

➤ I produced glitch-free…

➤ I created from scratch…

➤ On time and within budget

Step 7: Match Your Skills and Achievements to the Opening

Once you've created a list of your credentials, tailor them to your target job. How? Don't indiscriminately include in your draft all of your credentials. Instead, winnow down your list of credentials to those that parallel the demands of your target job; help prove you have previously successfully met those demands; reflect your substantive knowledge of the issues addressed by your target organization. You can do so by analyzing the skills demanded by the opening, and then matching your experience to them as explained below.

Analyze the Opening

The skills demanded by each opening are defined in its application questions and job description. Granted, the job descriptions are frequently dense, rambling, and repetitive. But you can extract their essence by:

1. Underlining each important phrase/task only once, not every time it appears.

2. Grouping similar skills under categories.

3. Consolidating similar skills and eliminating redundancies.

4. Listing remaining categories and skills.

Provided below is a typical federal job description followed by a skills analysis of the job.

Policy Analyst

The incumbent will be policy analyst in the Department of Transportation's Office of External Communications. This involves a broad spectrum of specialized and complex analytic, communications, and project management duties related to the mission of the Office of Communications. Develops strategies and plans for a communications program to respond

---

(continues)

to public and Congressional inquiries. Researches, identifies, and establishes viable communications methods and tools to inform the public and internal department organizations of the Office's policies, programs, services, and activities. Independently writes, edits, creates, and updates materials intended to be definitive descriptions of the Office's programs, accomplishments, and policies. Serves as a liaison with stakeholder groups and regional offices, advises them of communications strategies, and solicits updates on program progress from them. Updates HQ officials on regional progress. Ensures communications comply with Agency policies, standards, and formats and content is accurate. Synthesizes, summarizes, and translates complex legislative materials into easy-to-understand documents for varied audiences. Analyzes, synthesizes, and integrates a variety of inputs to produce an optimum written communication approach for designated audiences. Interfaces with headquarters offices to analyze, recommend, and create Agency written materials, products, and Web page designs. Resolves conflicts with internal experts creating and maintaining standard reply information. Helps organize stakeholder meetings and conferences. There will be time periods when priority deadlines must be met and overtime required. Must distribute information and report on legislative tracking to senior officials.

Skills Required by Job

Strategic Planning

- Develops communication strategies and plans for informing Congress, the public, and other internal and external audiences, and for responding to their information requests.

Research

- Collects, synthesizes, and summarizes technical information from varied sources.
- Tracks legislation.
- Collects progress reports on program implementation from regional offices.

Analysis and Writing

- Writes, edits, and updates documents and ensures their compliance with agency standards.
- Describes programs, accomplishments, and procedures.
- Integrates information from various sources.
- Translates complex information into easy-to-understand language for varied audiences.
- Creates hardcopy and Web documents.

Oral Communication/Project Management

- Interfaces with various HQ offices to resolve conflicts in development of standards.
- Advises regional offices; serves as a liaison with stakeholder groups.
- Reports to senior officials on legislation, regional progress on program implementation, and other developments.
- Helps organize meetings and conferences.
- Works independently and works extra hours to meet tight deadlines on document production.

Match Your Skills to the Job Description

To match your skills to those demanded by the opening, review your credentials that you identified through this chapter. Then, select those that fit the demands of your target job, and eliminate irrelevant ones.

➤ *Repeat the keywords.* Your application documents should repeat keywords included in the opening's job description, the "Qualifications and Evaluations" section of its vacancy announcement, and application questions. Why? Because by doing so, your application will highlight the parallels between the requirements of your target job and your credentials, and it will reduce potential opportunities for hiring managers to misinterpret or miss aspects of your relevant credentials.

Suppose, for example, that you were applying for the opening discussed above, which involves "Develop[ing] communication strategies for responding to information requests from Congress, the public, and other internal and external audiences." If you have previously demonstrated this skill, you would be wise to say something like this in your résumé and essays, such as: "Developed communication strategies for responding to information requests from Congress, the public, and other internal and external audiences."

Some applicants wrongly believe that such parroting is perceived by hiring managers as contrived or cheating in some way. *Au contraire!* Rather, by repeating keywords in your descriptions of your achievements, you will help affirm, in no uncertain terms, that your experience exactly matches the job's demands. In other words, the best way to prove to hiring managers that you would do an excellent job on your target job is to show that you have already done it and done it well.

If your credentials don't exactly match the job description of your target job, just include as many keywords as you can in your application. Also, cite your relevant academic experiences. For example, here is an excerpt from a KSA about communication skills that could be submitted by a new grad applying for the above opening with keywords from the job description underlined:

> I <u>wrote</u> and <u>edited</u> a paper on transportation policy for an urban planning class. For this paper, I researched transportation policies, <u>tracked</u> transportation legislation throughout 2007, <u>synthesized</u>, <u>summarized</u>, and <u>translated</u> legislation into <u>easy-to-understand language</u>, and <u>communicated</u> results orally to my class. I received a B+ on the paper and an A- in the class.

➤ *Strengthen your descriptions:* Don't just mechanically regurgitate keywords without adapting them to your background; remember to strengthen your descriptions by quantifying, title-dropping, and providing objective evidence of your success. For example, here is an excerpt from an application for the writer/editor position that embeds keywords within strengthened descriptions:

> I developed communication strategies for responding to five Congressional requests for information about multimillion-dollar federal transportation grants to the states. Such projects involved meeting with representatives of Ways and Means Committee every month for five months and meeting tight deadlines by working many weekends.

CHAPTER 10

Mastering Online Applications

"There have been times when I encountered so many maddening problems on online application systems that by the time I could finally submit my application, I was so wigged out that I bore a scary resemblance to Nick Nolte in his infamous mug shot."
—A FRUSTRATED (BUT ULTIMATELY SUCCESSFUL) FEDERAL JOB APPLICANT

"On the Internet, nobody knows you're a dog."

Like private-sector organizations, many federal organizations are automating their hiring processes through USAJOBS and other systems. But the bad news is that there is no such thing as a glitch-free online application system. Virtually all online application systems (including private-sector ones) have annoying constraints, snags, and potentially fatal traps that can thwart the unwary. This chapter is a must-read for anyone using online application systems because it explains how to easily defeat exasperating, application-busting problems.

Inputting Your Application

Problem 1: Kinds of Vacancy Announcements

Some federal jobs are announced via two vacancy announcements, with different announcement numbers. Unfortunately, it's easy to confuse multiple announcements for the same job. Here is how they differ:

➤ One type of vacancy announcement is open to all applicants, including current and former feds and nonfeds. Applicants who apply to this type of announcement can count their veterans' preference. If hired, they must serve a one-year probationary period. This probationary requirement applies even to experienced feds who have previously completed probation.

   If you are a nonfed, you should always apply only to this type of announcement. If you are a current or former fed, you should apply to this type of announcement only if you want your veterans' preference to count and if you're willing to complete a probationary period. Be aware that if you are a current or former fed without veterans' preference and you apply to this type of announcement, you may be outscored by an applicant with veterans' preference.

➤ Another type of vacancy announcement is open only to current and former feds (applicants with "status"). Applicants who apply to this type of announcement cannot count their veterans' preference but, if hired, will skip probation.

If you are a current or former fed, you should always apply to this type of announcement when it is an option in order to avoid competing against veterans' preference applicants and to skip probation. But if you want to count your veterans' preference and are willing to serve probation, you should also apply to announcements that are open to the public. (For more info on this topic, see the definition of "Merit Promotion Procedures" in Appendix 4, "Glossary.")

Solution: When you start your application, double-check all of its identifying information—particularly its "who may apply" section—to ensure that you are working on the correct announcement. Then, if you receive an electronic acknowledgment of your application after submitting it, carefully check the announcement number cited in your acknowledgment to confirm that you applied to the correct announcement.

Problem 2: Limited Access to Application Questions

Many online applications won't let you view each application question until you have answered all previous questions. This constraint may prevent you from quickly previewing all of an application's questions when you are deciding whether to apply for the job, and when you are strategizing your answers to essay questions.

Solution: In most online applications, you can provide dummy answers to questions (including essay questions) so that the system will let you advance to the end of the application. Then—at any time before the job closes—you can replace your dummy answers with genuine ones.

Problem 3: Electronic Glitches

Like all online systems, online application systems can inexplicably develop vexing, perplexing electronic glitches— the kind that make you want to grab a sledgehammer, smash your computer, ditch your professional career altogether, and join a traveling road show.

Solution: The "human" hasn't been totally removed from "human resources" yet; most online application systems still employ tech support specialists to help applicants troubleshoot technical glitches. So before grabbing your sledgehammer, contact them. See the Mayday box on this page.

Problem 4: Critical Short-Answer Questions

Most online applications ask applicants to rate their professional experience via a series of short-answer questions. Though these applications never say so, in most cases, an applicant must give him- or herself the highest rating on most questions in order to be seriously considered for the job.

Solution: Scrutinize the answers to each short-answer question on your online application to identify the one that represents the most senior experience level; that is the answer that is worth the most points. Then, comb your credentials and interpret them liberally, and give yourself the highest rating you honestly can for each question. Also, make sure that your high self-ratings are corroborated by the descriptions of your achievements in your résumé and any required essays.

Warning: If you can't give yourself the highest rating for most questions on an application, redirect your efforts to another application. (See Chapter 8 for more on short-answer questions.)

Caution

Meet Deadlines! The window of opportunity for applying for each federal job usually slams shut on midnight EST of its closing date. Online application systems can present time-consuming technical glitches at any time. So the only way you can be sure to make your deadline is to finish your application way ahead of time.

Contrary to popular belief, it is not enough to merely start working on your application before the deadline passes; you must hit the "submit" button on your application before the deadline passes.)

Mayday! Mayday! If you need help trouble-shooting technical snags on an online application, contact the application system's technical support staff. Some systems only provide e-mail support; some also have phone support.

The contact info for tech support is probably on your online application or on the main log-in page of the online application system. I have personally issued Maydays on many online systems, and technical support usually responded in 24 hours.

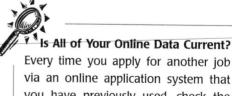

Is All of Your Online Data Current? Every time you apply for another job via an online application system that you have previously used, check the currency of all information stored in the system about you—particularly your contact info and your description of your current job.

Problem 5: Applications That Crash

An online application system can crash or go down for maintenance at any time without warning. If it does so while you're inputting your application, all of your unsaved work will probably be wiped out. Gulp!

Solution: Create and save each application in a word processing file before cutting and pasting it into the online system. Also, as you enter or change text in your online application, save your changes frequently. One more thing: Beware that the "save" buttons in online résumés and after essay questions in many online application systems are easy to miss, so look out for them and use them with wild abandon.

Formatting the Text

Problem 6: Formatting

Online application systems can make you look bad without even trying. Why? For several reasons:

> Modern formatting text features—such as boldface type, bullets, decorative fonts in various sizes, and shading—are not recognized by most online application systems and so do not transfer to these systems. Therefore, résumés and application essays print out from these systems as dense, featureless slabs of text. So if you're not careful when using these online application systems, your best credentials, instead of leaping off the page, may get buried by textural overburden and fail to attract the attention of harried hiring managers.

> Many online application systems either don't have spellcheckers or have defective ones. Therefore, many applications are studded with typos and other errors that, by themselves, can, and frequently do, doom applications.

Solution: Don't write your application directly into an online system. Instead, create, edit, and spell-check your application in a word processing program, then print it out and repeatedly proofread it before copying and pasting it into its online application system. Such quality controls are essential because typos and grammatical errors are among the most common causes for rejections of federal applications. And write in short sentences and short paragraphs and use white space liberally.

Also, as you write your application, restrict yourself to basic formatting features from the ASCII format; that way, all of your formatting will be accepted by the online system. To do so:

> Use capital letters to create headings and emphasize important information, such as job titles in résumés.

> Emphasize headings by skipping lines and creating horizontal lines before and after headings. Create horizontal lines by repeating a keyboard character, such as a tilde (~), plus sign (+), minus sign (-), equal sign (=), or period (.).

> Instead of a bullet, use an asterisk followed by a space (not a tab), or a number followed by a right parenthesis and a space (not a tab).

> Don't use centered or right-justified text tabs, quotation marks, or hyphens because these features change the text or format of your application in odd ways that you would probably not anticipate. (See the next problem for more on this topic.)

JANE WHOEVER
1234 Anywhere Lane
Any Town, Any State   12345
Evening Phone: 101-123-4567
Day Phone: 101-123-1234
Email: JaneWhoever@email.com

Country of citizenship:	United States of America
Veterans' Preference:	No
Highest Grade:	GS-1083-14, 01/1996-Present
Contact Current Employer:	Yes

AVAILABILITY

Job Type:	Permanent
Work Schedule:	Full Time

WORK EXPERIENCE US MINT
Washington, DC US

1/2001 - Present
Grade Level: GS-14
Salary: $115,781 USD Per Year
Hours per week: 40

WRITER/EDITOR/COMMUNICATIONS TRAINER , 1083

* Advise the Mint's Assistant Director for Strategic Planning and other Mint executives on methods for improving internal and external information programs.

* Promote awareness of agency accomplishments by managing, writing, and editing high-priority, reader-friendly documents. These documents—which are scrutinized by the agency's Assistant Deputy Director, distributed to Congress and stakeholders, and posted on the agency's high-traffic web site—include annual and quarterly reports to Congress, articles and fact sheets.

* Supervise five writers. Lead teams of writers, policy experts, graphic designers, and IT professionals that produce hard-copy and online documents. Establish standards for documents; supervise and set deadlines for team members; edit documents for accuracy, logic, and style; and report progress to Assistant Director for Strategic Planning and other executives.

* Serve as one of the agency's main "go to" writers for researching complex, sensitive issues and conveying technical information in easy-to-understand language.

* Help oversee content of the agency's high-traffic Intranet site.

* Always meet or beat tight deadlines. Streamlined production of the agency's recent annual reports so that they are now, without fail, released on time. (Before I managed these quarterly reports, they were routinely released late.) In addition, the Mint's 2005 annual report, which I managed, received a special commendation from the Treasury Secretary for its informative, reader-friendly style. I also managed production of more than 15 of the agency's quarterly reports—all of which were released early or on time.

* Developed and deliver Mint-wide training program—which includes seminars/workshops and one-on-coaching—on how to communicate technical information in reader-friendly language and on career advancement skills. Typically deliver two trainings per month that are each attended by about 30 professionals. Trainings consistently receive top ratings from attendees.

* Evaluate employee training needs: Selected contractor to provide project management training.

Figure 10-1 Sample first page of a well-formatted résumé for USAJOBS.

A longer version of this USAJOBS résumé featured in Figure 10-1 appears in the "Résumé Prep" section on this book's CD.

Problem 7: What You See Isn't What They Get

The application that you send hiring managers may be different in some significant ways from the one they will receive. In other words, what you see isn't what they get. Why? Because online application systems change the text and layout of applications in odd ways that you would probably not anticipate. For example, before delivering applications to hiring managers, some online systems automatically—believe it or not—convert all quotation marks into upside question marks, or move around text that has invalid characters. Unfortunately, hiring managers may not know that such problems may be caused by the application system itself—and not the carelessness of the applicant.

"I've seen online applications that were peppered with upside-down question marks or chunks of misplaced text because the applicant had inadvertently used invalid characters," laments one hiring manager. "It's a shame, because those applications might have been from qualified applicants, and they will never know why they were rejected." What's more, these types of quirks vary from system to system in unpredictable ways.

Solution: Here's how to view and edit exactly the same version of your applications that hiring managers will view:

> ➤ Start your application with plenty of time to spare before your deadline. When you reach the very end of your application, put a check in the box (if there is one) that asks whether you want to receive an e-mailed copy of your application.

> ➤ Submit your application. Immediately thereafter, a copy of your completed application should either be e-mailed to you or posted on your password-protected space on the online application system. These submitted versions of your applications should be identical to the ones delivered to your target organization. So double-check their formatting and proofread them well.

> ➤ Print and carefully review your application. If you identify problems in your application, reenter your application. (In some systems, you must go to the page that lists your previous submissions to reenter, change, or delete your previous applications.)

> ➤ If there are problems, revise your application as necessary. Then, submit your application again. In most systems, your latest submission will override your previous one, until the job closes. Repeat these steps as many times as necessary until your target job closes.

Hot Tip

Less Is More. Harried, time-pressured hiring managers appreciate brevity and conciseness. So don't feel obliged to max out the generous character limits on most online résumés and application essays. Only use as much space as you need to prove you're qualified for the job. Omit any irrelevant or dated information that—no matter how personally important it may be to you—would not be important enough to help convince a hiring manager to hire you.

Problem 8: Essays That Are Too Long

After you hit the "save" button for an essay or résumé on an online application system, it may, without warning, automatically delete any characters that exceed the essay's character limit.

Solution: Create and save your résumé and essays in a word processing file. Always do a character count before you cut-and-paste these documents into your online application and check that they will not exceed the system's character limits.

Making Deadlines

Problem 9: Missed Deadlines

Unfortunately, many applicants believe that as long as they log onto the application system and start working on their online application before their deadlines, they'll be able to slip their application in under the wire and make their deadlines. But under most circumstances, only applications that are submitted—not just started—by their deadlines are accepted. As a result, many late-starters miss their deadlines and so are rejected.

Solution: Hit the "submit" button of each online application before its deadline.

Problem 10: Unexpected Problems

Some online applications require applicants to fax, e-mail, or upload to the application various documents, such as transcripts and performance reviews. But if you are unexpectedly stumped by last-minute fax busy signals, uploading glitches, or difficulties accessing necessary computers, faxes, or scanners, you may miss your deadline.

Solution: Long before your target job's due date, identify everything you must submit to apply to the job and how you will access all necessary hardware to do so. Also, label all documents so that the hiring agency will correctly match them to your main application. After you submit these documents, confirm with your target job's agency contact person that he or she received them.

> ### Hot Tip
>
> **Oh, That Sinking Feeling!** What should you do if you realize that your online application contains a mistake or should be revised in some way after you've already hit the "submit" button? *In most systems, your latest online application will override your previous one as long as the job is still open.*
>
> So just reenter your application, and then correct and resubmit it. Alternatively, if you discover the problem after your target job has closed, call the agency contact person for your target job to ask how or whether your problem can be fixed.

Problem 11: Skipping the Last Step

Many applicants unfortunately assume that all they have to do to submit an online application is input their résumé and answer all application questions. Unfortunately, they either don't understand or forget that in order to submit their application, they must hit its "submit" button.

Solution: When you're ready to submit your online application, hit its "submit" button. After you do so, the system should almost immediately e-mail you or post a confirmation of your submission on a password-protected Web site. If the system does not provide such confirmation, you probably haven't applied to your target job.

Problem 12: Application Lost

Believe it or not, confirmation that your application has been electronically sent does not guarantee that your target agency has received it. After you hit your application's "submit" button, your application can mysteriously disappear into the electronic ether before reaching the hiring agency, even if you have received an e-mail confirming its delivery. I know a number of applicants who missed out on federal jobs because they only learned after their target job's closing date that their application had never reached the hiring agency—even though they had received e-mails confirming their submissions.

"He isn't feeling well today and won't be able to make it to his keyboard."

Solution: After you submit your online (or paper) application, call the hiring agency to confirm its delivery. Also keep a copy of the application system's electronic confirmation of your submission as well as confirmation of any faxes you sent to your hiring agency so that you will be able to prove that you made the deadline, if necessary.

Checking Your Application Status

Problem 13: Uncertain Updates

Although some agencies update applicants on the status of their applications via e-mail or updates on a password-protected Web site, others do not. What's more, online status updates may contain mistakes or outdated information.

Solution: If more than 45 days have elapsed since your target job closed, find the contact info for the agency contact person for your target job, call that person, and ask whether the job has been filled and/or when the agency expects to make a decision.

Retrieving Online Applications

Problem 14: Multiple Accounts

Many applicants create more than one account on the same online application system, but then only remember creating one account. Therefore they lose résumés and other information stored on forgotten accounts.

Solution: Limit yourself to just one account on each online application system, and record your password information in an easily accessible place.

Problem 15: No Contact Information

When each job closes, its vacancy announcement is removed from USAJOBS and the hiring agency's Web site. Nevertheless, after your target job closes, you may need its vacancy announcement to, for example, find the phone number of its agency contact person or to review its job description as part of your interview preparation.

Solution: Print out and keep a copy of the vacancy announcement of any job you apply for.

Problem 16: Loss of Data

You may want to access one of your previously submitted online applications in order to: (1) prepare for an interview or (2) recycle passages of it into applications for similar jobs. But online application systems do not provide reliable data storage. What's more, in recent years, tens of thousands of stored online applications have been accidentally lost.

Solution: Save printed and electronic versions of all of your applications and associated vacancy announcements.

11

Crafting Irresistible Résumés

"I'll read a concise, neat, deftly formatted résumé immediately. Long, difficult-to-read clunkers or résumés that have mistakes immediately get buried in the bottom of the résumé pile—perhaps never to be exhumed again."
—A FEDERAL HIRING MANAGER

On the CD...

This book's CD features templates for online and hard-copy résumés that you can quickly customize to your own background.

"*I see you've flown around the world in a plane, and settled revolutions in Spain. Around a golf course you're under par. Metro-Goldwyn has asked you to star. Very impressive, I must admit, but we're looking for someone with marketing experience.*"

When I recently asked a hiring manager how long he spends reading the typical résumé, he answered, "twenty seconds at most." I chuckled in response. So he emphasized, "No, really; I'm busy and impatient, so that is all the time I can give. Plus, I can tell almost instantly whether or not a person has what I am looking for."

My interviews with dozens and dozens of hiring managers about their job-screening techniques indicate that—believe it or not—the pace of "the 20-second hiring manager" is, if anything, leisurely. This means that, to be effective, your résumé—your personal marketing document—must serve as a verbal two-by-four that instantly knocks out hiring managers.

To score an instant knockout, your résumé must be: (1) formatted to be eye-catching, skimmable, and error-free; and (2) phrased to immediately peg you as the zero-risk applicant who would solve the hiring agency's problems, not create new ones. Your résumé should meet these two requirements whether it is a hard-copy or an online document, and whether it is targeting a specific opening or submitted as part of your networking campaign.

This chapter, along with the CD accompanying this book, provides guidance and templates to help you craft résumés that meet these requirements and meet the special information required of federal résumés.

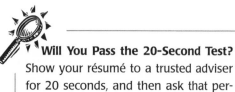

Will You Pass the 20-Second Test?
Show your résumé to a trusted adviser for 20 seconds, and then ask that person to describe your best credentials. If the adviser can't do so, keep working on your résumé.

The Test of Time

Compare the two résumés shown in Figures 11-1 and 11-2. Which one would pass the 20-second test?

(*text continues on page 117*)

Sam Eastman

1234 Yellow Brick Road
Any Town, Any City 12345

Objective

To achieve my personal and professional goals by working on a management team where my education and experience in the graphic arts can be best utilized. Specifically, I can contribute in the areas of planning and achieving short and long range goals, team building, staff planning and development process improvement and profitability. My education, dedication, focus and diverse business experience provide the foundation for achieving these goals.

Education

M.A.S. Business - 1985
Johns Hopkins University, Baltimore, MD
B.S., A.S. Printing Management & Technology - 1975

Rochester Institute of
Technology, Rochester, NY
A.A.S. Liberal Arts - 1973
Mitchell College, New London, CT

Experience

1999-Present
Desktop Operator-Jones Integrated Graphics, Silver Spring, MD
I joined Wallace while in the process of ceasing operations at the pre-press business I owned and operated until Dec. 1999. I provide Macintosh, PC and Scitex-based electronic pre-press services including scanning preflight file preparation, RIPing, trapping, imposition, film output and digital proofing. Additional duties include conventional proofing and platemaking. I have continued to build my knowledge of electronic pre-press, network and digital asset management, which I feel are the key areas for me to stay abreast of in order to return to a formal management position.

1995-1999
Founder/Owner-Incredible Designs, Inc., Jessup, MD
Founded a pre-press service bureau based on my cumulative experience and education in the Baltimore/Washington graphic arts market. The business was targeted at providing more sophisticated Scitex-based pre-press services to the smaller design, publishing and printing buyers in the market, which was being contested by newly formed conglomerates and low-end service bureaus. Built the sales up to $250,000 with only several part-time employees and myself. I was responsible for all business operations.

1993-1995
Vice President Sales-Eagle Color, Forestville, MD
I joined the firm to try to revitalize falling sales, and have the opportunity to purchase an interest in the firm, which was privately owned. Developed and serviced new accounts, provided strategic planning and equipment upgrading plans. The owner's unexpected death forced the closing of operations and the return of leased equipment. My efforts to purchase the name and assets of the firm broke off when a closer inspection of the firm's financial and contract labor (union) obligations made it more logical to start with new equipment at a different location.

1980-1993
Vice President/Director-Harry W. King Co., Baltimore, MD
Originally joined the firm as a CSR/Planner. Promoted to Production Manager in four years; a shareholder and Vice-President of Production Operations in another two years, and elected to the Board of Directors in 1990. I reported directly to the President and the Board of Directors. Responsible for all printing operations including estimating, customer service, production planning, inventory control and contract labor relations.

Personal

Married 25 years, three children age 8, 17 and 20. My spouse owns and operates a successful music studio in Columbia, MD. My primary interests include motor sports and outdoor activities, although much of my spare time is devoted to assisting in the operation of the music studio and supporting our children's activities.

Figure 11-1 Can you identify Sam Eastman's profession in 5 seconds? If not, hiring managers won't be able to do so, either. And a résumé that doesn't serve up even that basic information instantly will not pass the 20-second test, and is destined for the circular file. (Any errors in the figure appeared in the original document.)

The most important principle of formatting is that what stands out on the page is what stands out in the reader's mind. But because nothing—not even Sam Eastman's job titles—is formatted to stand out, nothing stands out to the reader. Notice, for example, that Eastman's job titles are no more prominent than his zip code! Moreover, Eastman's job summaries are lackluster because they are wordy and not achievement-oriented. What's more, this résumé, which is based upon a real-life résumé that was submitted for a public affairs job, provides no qualifications that fit the target job. No wonder the federal government rejected this résumé's real-life counterpart.

JOE TINMAN
Expert in Federal Contract Management

1111 Yellow Brick Road ♦ Anywhere, Kansas 01234
Work: (111) 123-4567   ♦   Home: (111) 234-1234   ♦   E-Mail:JT@E-mail.com

---

Social Security Number: 012-34-5678 | U.S. Citizen

OBJECTIVE

SENIOR CONTRACT SPECIALIST | Position Number: 123456

SUMMARY OF QUALIFICATIONS

- Ten years of experience managing all phases of multimillion dollar contracts.

- Warrant: Award contracts worth up to $10 million without additional approvals.

- First-Rate Reputation: Consistently earn very positive annual evaluations.

- B.A. in Economics from Georgetown University.

FEDERAL EXPERIENCE

US MINT
801 9th Street; Washington DC 20220

CONTRACT SPECIALIST (1102 Series) | April 2004 to Present
Office of the Chief Financial Officer
Supervisor: John Doe (You may contact at 202-234-4467)
Salary: $107,770 (GS-14/Step 3): 40 hours per week

Management Achievements:

- Currently manage 15 contracts for IT services worth a total of $100 million.

- Designed the Mint's first multi-million dollar performance-based contract for IT services. My techniques have served as a model for all performance-based contracts that followed.

- Supervise all work of five contract managers.

Figure 11-2 Can you identify Joe Tinman's profession from the first page of his résumé within 5 seconds? It is easy because this résumé heeds the principle that "what stands out on the page is what stands out in the reader's mind." It emphasizes important information and is uncluttered even though it includes extra info required for federal résumés. Its other virtues include its "Summary of Qualifications" and concise, achievement-oriented bullets. A template for this résumé, which I have provided to countless numbers of successful job seekers, is featured on this book's CD and Web site.

Requirements for Federal Résumés

Federal agencies require résumés to include some persnickety details that are not required by other employers. Wonder if you really have to include all of these details in your résumé? The truth is that many federal hiring managers wouldn't ding you for submitting a standard, non-government résumé instead of a federal résumé.

But, on the other hand, some federal hiring managers automatically reject all applications that omit required information. And because you can't predict whether your résumé will be judged by a tolerant or a nit-picking hiring manager, the safest strategy is to meet all federal requirements. (But keep in mind that most Capitol Hill offices prefer regular nonfederal résumés.)

Every federal job application identifies all of the information that applicants are required to provide. Listed here are the types of information that applicants are usually required to provide:

Information About the Opening

➤ Announcement number, title, and grade

Your Personal Information

➤ Name, address, and day and evening phone numbers

➤ Country of citizenship

➤ Social Security number

➤ Veterans' preference, if you have it

➤ Reinstatement eligibility, if you are using it

➤ Highest federal civilian grade held, including job series

Education

➤ Names of each college or university you currently or previously attended.

➤ Address of each college or university

➤ Degree and date; if no degree, state total number of credits and expected date of completion.

➤ Name of high school

➤ Address of high school

➤ Date of diploma or GED

Work Experience

For each paying or volunteer job you worked during the last 10 years and for relevant earlier jobs, state the following:

➤ Job title

➤ Employer's name and address

> Supervisor's name and phone number: say whether current supervisor may be contacted

> Starting and ending dates (month and year)

> Number of hours worked per week

> Salary

> Accomplishments

Other Qualifications

> Current job-related certificates and licenses

> Job-related training courses, including the title and year

> Job-related skills, including languages, computer software/hardware, and special equipment

> Honors, awards, and special accomplishments, including publications, public speaking credentials, individual and team performance awards (including dates), leadership activities, and memberships in professional or honor societies

---

Hot Tip

How to Craft a Winning Résumé for USAJOBS.GOV. For more instruction on how to format online résumés for USAJOBS that will stand out from the pack, see Chapter 10.

Your Cache of Résumés

Depending on your job-search strategy and your target organizations' requirements, you may create some or all of the following types of résumés during your job search:

> Federal résumés for various online application systems. For tips on formatting online résumés, see Chapter 10, as well as the sample well-formatted online résumé for USAJOBS featured in the "Résumé Prep" section of the CD accompanying this book.

> Hard-copy federal résumés for agencies that still accept paper applications.

> A nonfederal hard-copy résumé that omits the extra federal information. You will need this type of résumé to: (1) submit your résumé to networking contacts, either by hand delivery, snail mail, or e-mail; and (2) bring your résumé with you to interviews.

Options for Creating Résumés

Here are options for designing eye-catching, reader-friendly formats for online and hard-copy résumés:

> Create résumés for online application systems using the formatting and editing tips provided in Chapter 10.

 **On the CD...**

Customize to your own background the hard-copy federal and nonfederal résumé templates that are contained in this book's CD..

➤ Create résumés using résumé templates that come with Microsoft Word. To find them, open a Word document, then click "New" under the "Office Button" on the upper left corner of your toolbar. Under "Templates" on the left side of the screen, click "Résumés and CVs." Select additional options, as appropriate.

➤ Design your own format for federal or nonfederal résumés. See the formatting tips provided in Appendix 3.

Formatting the Résumé

Your résumé should stand out—but not for the wrong reasons. A résumé that is longer than a wedding train, has tiny margins, is handwritten in calligraphy, is printed on paper bright enough to cause snow-blindness, and is packaged in a big binder will generate attention without drawing an invitation for an interview.

What *will* impress hiring managers is an inviting, neat, organized document that has wide margins; clean, conservative, good-sized type; prominently formatted headings, job titles, and employer names; and bulleted lists that send a hiring manager's eyes flying down the page.

You will also impress hiring managers by doing the following:

➤ Heeding the most important formatting principle: What stands out on the page is what will stand out in the reader's mind. To make important information stand out on the page, use capital letters, various type sizes, various font styles, indents, and boldface type. Check, for example, that your job title stands out more than your zip code.

➤ Following instructions for formatting online résumés (including creating online bulleted lists) that are provided in Chapter 10, and instructions for formatting hard-copy résumés (including creating bulleted lists) that are provided in Appendix 3.

➤ Expressing subordination through formatting. That is, headings should be bolder than regular type and positioned to stand out; information that follows the headings should be formatted to reflect its subordinate status.

➤ Using white space to break up large blocks of text and enhance its readability.

➤ Creating a balanced layout that sensibly distributes information on the page(s). Remember that your résumé, and particularly the first page of your résumé, represents valuable acreage. Don't sell yourself short by wasting this prized real estate on empty space or unimportant information.

➤ Formatting your résumé consistently. This means that once you pick a format, stick to it throughout your résumé. For example, the margin size, alignments of text, size of the spaces between the bullets in a list and the accompanying text, and amount of space following headings should be consistent. In addition, headings of comparable weight should be formatted identically.

➤ Printing out your résumé, repeatedly proofreading its text, and eyeballing its format for eye-appeal and consistency. Also, subject your résumés to the editing techniques recommended in the CD chapter entitled "Writing Killer Application Essays (KSAs and ECQs)," which accompanies this book. When you're satisfied with your résumé's content and format, check it again, and then show it to an objective adviser.

How to Hit the Bull's Eye. Interpret the job description of your target job and its accompanying "Qualifications and Evaluations" as a question that asks, "Could you do this job?"

Prove that you could indeed do the job by filling your application with descriptions of your professional and academic credentials and achievements that parallel the demands of your target job. Prove that you would excel while doing your target job by crowning descriptions of those credentials and achievements with descriptions of the positive feedback and objective validation they drew. (See Chapter 9 for instruction on crafting winning descriptions of your achievements and credentials.)

Target Practice

No matter which résumé format you use, target your résumé (as well as the rest of your application) to the skills sought by your hiring agency by:

➤ Phrasing your job summaries to reflect the demands of the opening; use keywords from your target job's vacancy announcement when possible. Also, use Chapter 10 and the Application and Interview Cheat Sheets on this book's CD to identify your best, most relevant selling points.

➤ Using the principles of primacy and "recency" to emphasize your best credentials. In other words, position your most important credentials as early in each section of your résumé as possible and format them to leap off the page when possible.

➤ Tailoring your objective to match the opening.

➤ Using a "Summary of Qualifications" or "Career Highlights" section to hit hiring managers with your best shot(s) up top. (But unfortunately, most online systems do not provide space for this feature.) These types of introductory sections may be particularly helpful if your most relevant experience preceded your current job. Why? Because you may use an introductory section to lift your old but essential experience/ credentials to the top of your résumé so that they will immediately grab the attention of hiring managers (instead of languishing at the end of your résumé where they may be easily overlooked).

➤ Eliminating irrelevant information.

Want to see examples of the résumés of professionals who are in the same field as you? Do so by viewing the job-specific résumés that come with Microsoft Word. Find these résumés by opening a Word document and then clicking "New" under the "Office Button" located on the upper left corner of your toolbar. Click "Résumés and CVs" under "Templates" on the left side of the screen, Then select "Job-specific Résumés."

The Components of a Résumé

Provided below are some additional tips on crafting each section of your résumé. Many of the tips are incorporated into the résumés in this book's CD.

The Header

Create a header that has a balanced design and does not create holes in the center of the page. Your header should lead off with your name formatted in large, bold letters. (You're the star of your show, so highlight your name as if it were posted on a movie marquee.) If you have advanced degrees or certifications, position the abbreviations for them after your name.

Quickly tell hiring managers what you do by positioning a title right after your name on the top of the page. If your current job title is not flattering, or if you're currently unemployed, use an alternative job title such as "Expert in . . ." or "Specialist in . . ." "Advanced Expertise in…" instead of a title. Alternatively, if you have won prestigious awards, give yourself the title of "Award-Winning. . . ."

Your header should also include your street address, phone numbers, and e-mail address.

Also, consider "fluffing and buffing" your LinkedIn and Facebook profiles and including them in your header. Likewise, if you maintain a professional Web site that would strengthen your case, include its address in your header. See Appendix 3 for guidance on how to insert a horizontal black line below your header and how to insert special characters into your contact info.

The Objective

An "Objective" is not required for federal résumés. However, you may include an objective in your federal résumés unless your formatting is constrained by an online application system that does not accommodate this feature. To be effective, your objective—like all other résumé features—should brandish what you offer rather than what you want from your target job.

This principle is violated by many résumé objectives, which itemize everything that the applicant would need from a job to reach a state of professional Nirvana. (Such objectives might as well be relabeled as "the gimme section.") Other objectives pile on meaningless info. For example, the objective in Figure 11-1 describes Eastman's desire to achieve his personal goals. Whaaat?!?!? (Is Eastman looking for a job or a date?) And when Eastman's objective finally does get around (at last!) to identifying what he offers, he cites—ironically, after promising to get specific—everything but the kitchen sink. Sorry pal, the credibility meter just hit zero.

By contrast, Tinman's objective in Figure 11-2 cites his target job. Wow—What a concept! Tinman's objective is specific, succinct, informative, and has the added advantage of being true!

Another way to craft an objective is to concisely define how you would add value to the agency. Here are some examples:

An administrative position using my 6 years of experience organizing meetings and arranging travel for senior executives.

A position on an IT Help Desk where my knowledge of large networks and trouble-shooting expertise will improve network efficiency.

Are you aiming to switch into the federal sector from the private sector or the nonprofit sector? If so, consider incorporating into your objective your reason for wanting to switch—which should emphasize your desire to advance your target agency's mission or to help the public good—rather than me-o-centric reasons, such as your pursuit of job stability (even if that is why you want to make the switch). For example, your objective might state something like this:

A federal position that would enable me to apply my 20 years of specialized private-sector experience in cyber-security to national security issues.

Summary of Qualifications

Federal résumés are not required to include a "Summary of Qualifications." But if you're an experienced professional, consider positioning several quick-read summary bullets near the beginning of your résumé (as does Joe Tinman's résumé, Figure 11-2) to:

➤ Broadcast your best-selling points to hiring managers who will only skim your résumé or neglect to read the entire document. These selling points may, for example, include your degrees, current or previous security clearances, licenses, and certifications—particularly a certification by the Qualifications Review Board for the senior executive service.

➤ Summarize your most relevant credentials. For example, if you were applying for a job requiring communication skills, you could emphasize your communication skills by including a bullet about your communication skills in your summary of qualifications. For example:

Polished Communicator: Delivered five presentations to executives and represented my organization at four national industry meetings in two years.

➤ Emphasize older, but relevant and important, qualifications from earlier jobs that would probably otherwise be overlooked because of their positioning deep in the document.

➤ If you participated in a selective detail assignment, fellowship, or other program, consider saying so in your Summary of Qualifications. For example:

Currently serving in an AAAS Fellowship—a highly selective program that places Ph.D. scientists in policy positions in federal agencies.

Work Experience

Position your "Work Experience" section before your "Education" section—unless you're currently a student or a recent grad, or your degree(s) relate more to your target job than does your work experience.

What you offer today is more important than what you offered yesteryear. So sequence your jobs in reverse chronological order (most recent to earliest job), and devote more space to recent than to earlier jobs, unless your earlier jobs are more relevant to your target job. (Because federal agencies don't accept functional résumés, they are not an option for applicants for agency jobs.)

Either omit information about jobs that ended more than 10 or 15 years ago or list them under an "Early Experience" or "Other Experience" heading unless they are directly relevant to your target job. Include only very brief descriptions of early irrelevant jobs, or list only the titles of such jobs without providing any descriptions of them at all.

If you have worked more than one job for the same employer, identify the name of that employer only once—by citing it as a bolded heading in the center of the page. Then list

each title underneath that employer's heading; position these
titles flush with the left margin, bold them, and cite the starting
and ending date of each job and other required information.
Under each job title, cite your achievements in a bulleted list.
By doing so, you will avoid wasting space by repeatedly citing your
employer, and you will emphasize your ascent up the career ladder.

Hot Tip

Run Google searches on terms like *sample résumés* and *example résumés* together with your job title to find résumés that will help you craft your own résumé.

Do not craft your job summaries as job descriptions that itemize
your assigned duties and responsibilities. (After all, reading a series
of job descriptions is just about as interesting as reading someone else's "to-do" list"…snooze!)
What's more, when you describe your duties or responsibilities, you only reveal what you were
supposed to do (who cares?), rather than what you actually achieved (wow!).

So instead, craft each job summary on your résumé as a set of snappy, fast-read, achievement-
oriented bullets that inventory your relevant successes. When you do so, follow these guidelines:

➤ Don't waste space by starting bullets with the pronoun "I"; hiring managers already
know that your résumé describes your work without your telling them so. And omit
job-description-like phrases such as, "I was responsible for . . ." or "My duties
included . . .".

Instead, build each bullet to convey a specific achievement, home-run triumph,
credential, award, or honor that parallels the demands of your target job. Do so by
following each bullet with a different action verb, such as id*entified, managed, organized, streamlined, designed, presented, earned,* and so on. (To find lists of action verbs,
Google *action verbs for résumés.*) Note that each action verb following a
bullet should be in the first person. Note also that "first person" is the verb form
that accompanies the pronoun *I* if *I* were present. You can test for the first person by
silently inserting the pronoun *I* in front of each verb (see Table 11-1).

TABLE 11-1 Action Verbs	
Wrong Verb Form for Bullet	**Correct Verb Form for Bullet**
Manages Web site.	Manage Web site.
Tracks corrrespondence.	Track correspondence.

➤ Remember that the order in which your résumé presents information is almost as
important as what information it presents. Hiring managers are most likely to read
and remember what they read first. So sequence bullets for each job summary according to their relevance to your target job—not according to how much time you spent
on the activities they describe; your most relevant bullets should precede your less
relevant bullets, even if you spent little time on them.

For example, suppose you currently spend 20 percent of your time on project
management and 80 percent of your time running trainings, and you're applying
for a project management job. Then your project-management bullets should
precede your training bullets.

➤ Break up long lists of job-summary bullets into categories, such as "Management
Achievements," "Communication Achievements," and "Strategic Planning
Achievements." Some of the résumés included in this book's CD use this method.

Show and Tell. If you're a writer/editor, graphic artist, photographer, video producer, or Web designer, or if you manage the production of other types of tangible work products, consider creating a Web site, online portfolio, or LinkedIn profile that showcases your work; be sure to provide relevant Web site addresses to hiring managers in your cover letter or résumé.

If you don't want your online portfolio to be accessible to the public, store it in a password-protected Web site, and only provide the site's password and address to selected hiring managers.

Other options: If your work is featured on other organizations' Web sites, include relevant Web addresses in your cover letter or résumé.

Alternatively, if possible, upload to your application a neat, eye-catching list of relevant Web sites or upload relevant documents themselves, such as PDF copies of your published articles, reports you have managed, press coverage for your employer that you have generated, brochures for conferences that you have organized, or other work products.

➤ Write for lay people who are unfamiliar with your field and current organization, and the projects, computer systems, databases, regulations, and programs you manage. Eliminate acronyms and avoid or explain technical terms. This is important because your résumé may be passed on to hiring managers and other executives who are not familiar with the specifics of your current and previous jobs or even with your field at all.

➤ Briefly explain any significant gaps between employment dates, such as when you returned to school or became a caregiver for a seriously ill family member. If you added to your professional credentials in any way during this period through volunteer work or by serving on a board, giving lectures, participating in a public service campaign, organizing alumni events or community activities, taking courses, doing freelance/consulting work or self-study, say so.

➤ Briefly describe the mission or operations of any obscure employers you name.

➤ Craft your job summaries to corroborate your answers to your application's short-answer questions. This is important because if your application rates a top-contender, human resources officials will cross-check your answers to short-answer questions against your résumé; as explained in Chapter 8, if such cross-checking reveals that your résumé doesn't support your answers to short-answer questions, your application may be eliminated from the competition.

Note that some online applications contain a window that requests the name and contact information of your current boss, and asks you via a yes/no question whether you permit hiring managers to contact your current boss. If you don't want your current boss to know about your job search, or you suspect that your current boss would not give you an enthusiastic reference, feel free to answer the question with a no.

In such cases, if appropriate, consider including in the description of your current job a statement saying that you don't want your current boss to know about your job search until you have a firm offer, but that you would be happy for the hiring manager to contact an alternative manager or colleague; if you follow this strategy, provide the name and contact info for your alternative reference.

Education

List your academic credentials in reverse chronological order. If you're currently a student, identify your target degree, the university, and expected graduation date. If you're working toward a degree while also working a job, prove your multitasking mettle by saying so. For example:

> Concurrent with full-time employment: working toward JD, Howard University Law School, Washington, DC (degree expected in 2016).

If you're a student or a recent grad and your grade point average is B-plus or better, say so. Also, if you took, or are currently taking, any classes that parallel the demands of your target job, list them under the heading "Sample of Courses."

Other Headings

Include in your résumé a heading titled "Leadership Experience," if possible. Why? Because every employer values leadership experience. Even if you never led the cavalry into battle, organized a mutiny against a Captain Bligh–like rogue, or negotiated a billion-dollar deal on Wall Street, you probably still have sought-after leadership credentials. These credentials may, for example, include experience orienting freshmen at your college, serving in student government, tutoring, or organizing campus events. So scour your record for your experience in supervising, orienting, advising, coaching, organizing, training, negotiating, and mentoring—and then brandish it in your leadership section.

Other potential headings include the following:

➤ Awards and Honors

➤ Licenses and Certificates

➤ Public Speaking

➤ Consulting Experience

➤ Publications

➤ Systems and Software

➤ Training Courses

➤ Professional Associations

➤ Foreign Languages

➤ Military Experience

➤ Volunteer Experience

➤ Community Service

Excluded Information

Your résumé should not mention anything about your marital status, children, religion, or irrelevant hobbies because such information should not influence hiring decisions, and may compel hiring managers to (illegally) discriminate against you. Also, don't waste space by stating that your references are available upon request; that is assumed.

Résumé Length

I recently heard a résumé expert being interviewed on a radio show. During the interview, the résumé expert was asked about résumé lengths. In response, the expert listed expected résumé lengths for various types of professionals. Four pages for this type of professional . . . five pages for that type of professional . . . and so on.

Less Is More

To me, that kind of advice is just crazy talk! It makes no sense. The real deal is that all federal and nonfederal hiring managers are very busy; they have neither the time nor the desire to hack through dense biographies. In fact, they want to read long-winded tomes about as much as you want to do a line-by-line reading of the phone book. So, no matter where you are in your career or what your target job is, the correct length of your résumé is the minimum length you need to prove that you're qualified for your target job.

So, rather than aiming for a specific résumé length, aim to: (1) format your best credentials prominently and position them as close to the top of the document as possible; (2) keep your résumé as short as possible; and (3) ruthlessly edit redundancies, dated information, and credentials that don't relate to your target job.

When you are deciding whether to include a certain credential, ask yourself if a description of that credential could realistically help you get the job, and if you were reviewing your own résumé as a hiring manager, would that credential really matter to you? If not, purge it.

If you cannot fit all of your important credentials/achievements into the body of an online résumé because of space limitations, consider presenting them in an "Additional Information" section that may be included in the application.

Break the One-Page Rule

Don't eliminate important information or create a cluttered résumé in order to cater to the "one-page" myth. It's much wiser to create an attractively formatted multiple-page résumé with good-size headings and copious white space than it is to jam your relevant experience onto a cramped one-pager that will alienate hiring managers. The one-page rule simply does not apply to anyone who has been working for any significant amount of time.

> **Hot Tip**
> Whenever e-mailing your résumé, send it as a PDF attachment. That way, its formatting won't be fouled up during its electronic journey.

The one-page rule is particularly irrelevant to applicants to federal agencies. How come? Because the extra informational requirements of federal agencies inevitably add length to résumés. Moreover, hiring managers always cross-check answers to short-answer questions and essay questions against résumés, and they penalize applicants for discrepancies. So craft your résumé to validate all achievements described in the body of your application, even if doing so extends your résumé.

Quality Controls

Don't send off your résumé impulsively. Instead, let it go cold, then look at it again through the eyes of a stranger; ask yourself what you would think of the person described in the résumé. Would you understand whom they work for and what they do, and be impressed by their accomplishments if you had no prior knowledge about them? When you hold up the description of your target job together with your résumé, is the fit obvious? Is your résumé clear and straightforward? Does it include all of your relevant accomplishments?

Also, check that your previous jobs are described in the past tense. Confirm that each bullet conveys a unique, distinct accomplishment without covering overlapping info. Proofread for typos.

Once your résumé passes muster, show it to your trusted advisers and encourage them to be critical. This is important because the only way you can really find out how you come across in your résumé to other people is to ask other people, "How do I come across in my résumé?"

Whatever problems your advisers find with your résumé (however disheartening it may be to have your advisers point them out to you) would also ultimately be found by hiring managers, who are, after all, ordinary people, not organically different from anyone else. Remember: It is much smarter to face constructive criticism that can help you find and fix résumé flaws than to save your feelings now but let your résumé flaws eventually silently sink your prospects.

Résumé Padders and Liars Need Not Apply

If you lie on your application or in an interview for a federal job, you will likely end up having some 'splainin' to do, as Ricky Ricardo would say.

Consider the cautionary tale of Laura Callahan.* In April 2003, she landed a coveted position as the Deputy Chief Information Officer in the Department of Homeland Security. But when Callahan—who often used the title "Dr."—was screened for a Top Secret security clearance, investigators discovered in May 2003 that the B.A., master's degree, and Ph.D. in computers listed on her résumé were from a diploma mill that was located in a refurbished motel. Ouch!

Callahan's troubles only snowballed when—in the wake of the brouhaha over the bogus degrees—many of her colleagues unleashed a torrent of allegations against her for other whopping ethical and managerial blunders made during her previous high-level stints at the White House and Department of Labor. After being suspended from her federal job, Callahan resigned in March 2004. How the mighty have fallen.

---

*See Wikipedia's article on Laura Callahan and the article's references.

Hot Tip

How to Get Your Résumé Read. If your online application allows you to upload hard-copy documents to your application, don't just submit the required online version of your résumé. Consider also uploading a well-formatted, easy-to-read PDF version of your résumé. Why?

Because it is an axiom of life that the easier a document is to read, the more likely it will be to actually get read. Therefore, hiring managers will be more likely to read your uploaded, easy-to-read hard-copy résumé than the difficult-to-read online résumés of your competitors.

As a result, your uploaded résumé will probably help you stand out from the pack. (Remember: The best way to stand out from the pack is to do more than the pack and to do better than the pack.) Find Web sites that convert documents into PDFs for free via Google searches.

More Tips to Get to the Top.

Review the chapter entitled, "Writing Killer Application Essays (KSAs and ECQs)" on the CD accompanying this book, whether or not the application for your target job includes application essays. Why?

Because that online chapter provides dozens and dozens of winning tips, available nowhere else, about how to describe your achievements in clear, compelling, attention-grabbing, and memorable terms and thereby convey the true depth, breadth, and importance of your contributions and impress hiring managers with your top reputation.

Take Note! _____

Perseverance Success Story: I Got the Job!

By Andrew McDonald, Engineer

After working at the same federal agency for seven years as a mechanical engineer, I decided that it was time to move on and find other challenges. I started looking for a new job. Now, I am working for another federal agency, learning new things and earning a significantly higher salary.

I landed my promotion strictly through my own efforts; I had no contacts helping me. I did it by:

1. ***Searching USAJOBS at least once a week.*** I was diligent about regularly searching USAJOBS, because each job listed on the site has its own rolling window of opportunity. If I had not regularly checked the site, I might have missed out on applying for some great jobs.

   If I am going to submit a package, I want it to reflect my best effort. So I spent about 1 week on each opening that really interested me. I never used the shotgun approach because I believe that it only produces more rejections. Who needs that?

2. ***Using keywords.*** I incorporated keywords from job descriptions in vacancy announcements into my résumé and cover letters. For example, because the responsibilities for the job description for my current job included "blueprint reading" as an important responsibility, I included it in my résumé. Although I ordinarily wouldn't have mentioned such an obvious duty, I knew that doing so might improve my chances. Anything for a higher score! Also, I noticed that some vacancy announcements even list keywords that are desirable in applications. If you find such keywords listed in a vacancy announcement for a job that is similar to your target job, mention them throughout your application.

3. ***Researching the agency.*** I read through the Web site of each agency that I applied to. Based upon this research, I was able to specify in my cover letter how I would be able to contribute to the agency's goals.

4. ***Telling success stories.*** My applications included specific examples of my projects that showed that I was qualified for the target job.

5. ***Designing graphically pleasing layouts.*** When I was on a selection panel for hiring another engineer, I learned what torture it is for hiring managers to trudge through the long, densely worded paragraphs. The experience made me appreciate easy-to-read, graphically pleasing layouts. So my goal was to design application documents that presented my credentials to hiring managers in an easy and efficient manner. I did this by:

   • "Bulletizing" my résumés and cover letters as much as possible.

   • Repeatedly examining the hard-copy versions of my documents. Because the layout on a computer screen is subtly different from that of a hard copy, you have a greater chance of missing typos and column misalignments on the computer.

   • Checking that headings stood out, information was distributed on the page in a balanced way, font sizes were easy to read, and that I had used enough white space to break up the text without wasting space. I made sure that my layout was consistent (fonts, margins, etc.) throughout all of my documents.

   • Using as few words as possible in order to make the best use of the precious seconds that the hiring manager spent on my application.

6. ***Working on my applications in multiple, short sessions.*** I found it much easier to attack these very difficult-to-write documents a little bit at a time, and not to even try to finish them in a single session. This multi-session approach enabled me to improve my application by repeatedly reviewing and editing my answers.

When ideas about which credentials I should include and emphasize on my application occurred to me when I was doing other things, I quickly jotted them down and then incorporated them during my next writing session. Because of such improvements, my answers were more thoughtful than they would have been if I whipped out my application in a single sitting.

7. ***Recruiting a colleague to provide feedback.*** I recruited a colleague to provide me with objective feedback on my applications. This person helped me simplify passages that were too technical for nonengineers, edit unnecessary information, and add background information where needed. Seeking and using my colleague's feedback took extra time. But this time was well spent because, from my experience serving on a selection panel, I know that the quality of applicants' applications determines who gets the job.

8. ***Preparing for the interview for my current job.*** I reviewed Internet sites that provided "how-to" advice on interviewing and listed standard interview questions. Sure enough, many of those standard interview questions did pop up in my interview. But because I was prepared to answer these questions, I handled them with more confidence and speed and with less fumbling than I otherwise would have.

For example, when my interviewer asked me to discuss an on-the-job mistake that I had made, I could—because of my preparation—quickly cite a nonserious scheduling snag that had developed on one of the construction projects I was managing. I was careful not to say that I had messed up the project irreversibly. Instead, I emphasized how I quickly resolved the scheduling problem, reworked the schedule to prevent delays in the completion of the project, and learned from the experience how to avoid similar snags in the future.

During the interview, I also mentioned some specific information about the hiring agency's recent construction projects that I had read about on its Web site. I thereby showed my interviewers that I gone to the trouble to research its activities.

Shortly after the interview for my current job, I was offered and accepted the job. My new agency operates under a pay scale called pay banding, which gives managers more flexibility in setting salaries than does the General Schedule system under which my previous job operated. Because of this difference and because my current boss was impressed with my qualifications, my new agency significantly beat my old salary. I didn't even have to negotiate for a promotion. Moreover, as I had hoped, I am now managing very different types of projects than I had managed at my previous job, and I am broadening my experience.

During my job search, which lasted over a year, I was rejected for a number of jobs. With some applications, I did not even get a response. But I didn't let the disappointments stop me. I expected this and persevered. I also found it helpful to keep reminding myself that if you put in the extra effort to create a concise, eye-catching, and verbally pleasing application, I would eventually be rewarded because, as writer Silvana Clark said, "There is so little traffic on the extra mile."

Sour Toppings

Although Callahan was evidently not qualified for her job, many professionals who do have enviable qualifications top them off with false degrees or phony experience. Too bad. The principle ignored by such embellishers is that, even ethics aside, it is usually more effective to trumpet genuine achievements through the methods discussed in this book than to trump-up false achievements.

In other words, spend your energy finessing descriptions of your finest qualifications rather than creating phony toppings that can end up biting you back.

"*Oops! The padding just fell out of your résumé.*"

What This Means for You

Federal job applications that include false or inflated credentials are more likely than ever to be discovered. Why? Because after the Callahan scandal, many human resource staffers were trained on how to spot fabrications. Applicants who are busted for lying may be barred from reapplying to the federal government. And applicants who do manage to get hired under false claims may be fired, fined, or even jailed.

Which does not mean that you must spotlight your weaknesses under klieg lights. But it does mean that you shouldn't invent degrees, titles, or experience that you simply don't have, or cover gaps in your résumé with whole cloth. Here's a litmus test: If you can't imagine a credential holding up under a background check, don't use it.

CHAPTER

12

Application Essays (KSAs and ECQs)

Who Needs 'em?

"Good writing is clear thinking made visible."
—BILL WHEELER, WRITER

"It's plotted out. I just have to write it."

Much to the relief of federal job applicants, federal agencies were directed by the president in 2011 to eliminate essay questions (usually called KSAs or ECQs) from job applications that are used in initial screens of applications. Therefore, most federal job applications no longer include these types of much reviled questions.

Nevertheless, federal agencies are still allowed to use essay questions in follow-up screens of applications and on applications for jobs in the senior executive service. Therefore, at some point in your hunt for a federal job, you may discover a juicy opening that is attached to an application that has essay questions.

If this happens to you, don't panic or impulsively reject the opening. Instead, consider whether throwing your hat in the ring would be—like many other good things in life—worth a few extra hours of thought and toil.

After all, most people don't forgo the chance to obtain a driver's license just because taking a driving test is a giant hassle, or sacrifice the opportunity to go to college just because they would have to complete lengthy college applications to do so. Indeed, when blocked by obstacles, most successful people refuse to back down and—much to their ultimate joy—stubbornly persist.

So, if you find a juicy opening that includes essay questions, don't succumb to the understandable temptation to reject it merely because its application includes essay questions that demand extra effort; instead, muster your moxie and give the application your best shot!

Comprehensive instruction on writing killer KSAs and ECQs is provided on the CD of this book in a chapter called "Writing Killer Application Essays (KSAs and ECQs), and KSA & Interview Prep Cheat Sheets."

Note that, in rare cases, applications ask people to support their answers to short-answer questions with "mini essays" about their relevant experience/credentials. (See Chapter 8 for guidance on answering short-answer questions.) If your application requests such mini essays, use the worksheets in the "KSA/ECQ Prep" section of the CD accompanying this book to help you generate impressive descriptions.

13

Cover Letters
That Open Doors

"You will automatically beat out 95 percent of your competition if you submit an error-free cover letter that concisely describes how you meet the requirements of the opening."
—A FEDERAL HIRING MANAGER

Hot Tip

Hot Tip

Whenever e-mailing your résumé, send it as a PDF attachment. That way, its formatting won't be fouled up during its electronic journey.

. . . And the Last Shall Be First. Even though an effective cover letter is key to making a good first impression with potential employers, most job seekers thoughtlessly dash off their cover letter in the last minute. Whether your cover letter is the first or last step of your application preparation, devote enough time to it to create a first-rate document.

Your cover letter will probably be the first part of your application that hiring managers will read. What's more, your cover letter may be the only part of your application that hiring managers will really read. Why? Because while many hiring managers only skim job applications, virtually all of them read one-page cover letters from top to bottom.

A skillfully crafted cover letter may get your potential employers panting with anticipation for the next page of your application and thereby kick-start opportunities. Conversely, a flawed cover letter will probably get your application kicked out of the competition before it really has even begun.

But despite the potentially make-or-break importance of effective cover letters, many applicants completely omit them from their applications. This type of naked, uncovered application may as well announce the words, "I don't care enough about getting this damned job to write a cover letter." Other applicants submit typo-tarnished, long-winded cover letters that are the written equivalents of *A&E Biographies*, or terse cover letters that reveal only about as much information as a captured soldier may disclose to the enemy: name, rank, and serial number. Neither of these strategies makes for a compelling sales pitch.

But remember that you have only a precious few (and fast) opportunities to impress hiring managers, and you should milk each of them to the max. If you don't, hiring managers won't learn about, let alone be impressed by, your credentials and enthusiasm. So be sure to introduce each of your job applications with a concise, well-written, target cover letter. (Note that if your online job application doesn't include a window that is specifically for a cover letter, upload a PDF of your cover letter to your application, if possible.)

In addition to writing cover letters to introduce your formal applications, you may also write cover letters as part of your networking campaign. That is, as you meet key contacts and potential employers, they will invariably ask you to send them your résumé, which of course, should be introduced with a cover letter or cover e-mail.

In this chapter, you will learn about the multifaceted powers of cover letters, review samples of effective cover letters, and learn how to write first-rate cover letters that will help you make a great first impression.

Cover Me: I'm Going In

Use your cover letter to:

➤ Introduce yourself: identify your current title and target job.

➤ Concisely summarize your most relevant educational and professional credentials: use bullets to encourage a fast read.

➤ Showcase your knowledge of your target organization: explain why your target agency provides particular appeal and complement your target agent's recent achievements, if possible.

➤ Serve as an impressive writing sample: a skillfully formatted, well-written cover letter will provide tangible evidence of your communication skills.

➤ Convey enthusiasm and zest.

➤ Explain any special circumstances about your background or application.

➤ Name a contact in your target organization who can vouch for you, if possible. Such name-dropping will help confirm your credentials as the zero-risk applicant.

➤ One more thing: state that you're applying for a noncompetitive appointment, if you're doing so.

Scoping Out Your Target Agency

Your target agency probably fills its openings with applicants who are passionate about the agency and the issues it addresses. Why? Because hiring managers believe that employees work hardest and put their hearts and souls into what they are passionate about. In other words, they believe that applicants who show fire in the belly for their organization will turn out to be loyal, self-motivated go-getters.

How can you prove that you are passionate about your target agency and its mission? By demonstrating your knowledge of your target agency in your application and interviews.

The Importance of Crafting Targeted Cover Letters. A generic, untargeted cover letter is about as likely to capture the attention of its intended hiring manager as junk mail is to capture your attention. By contrast, a tailored cover letter is virtually guaranteed to capture the attention of its intended hiring manager—just as mail that specifically and personally addresses you is virtually guaranteed to capture your attention.

Remember that government organizations are as different from one another as are private companies. So, in order to convey knowledge of your target organization's programs, goals, hot-button issues, achievements, and culture, you must research your target organization. Start your research by debriefing any of your target agency's employees who may lurk within your network. Also, use the following free online resources to become an expert on your target agency:

1. Your target organization's Web site, Facebook page, and Twitter feeds. This is absolutely required reading for applying and interviewing for any job in a federal agency or Congress. Pay particular attention to your target organization's press releases, annual reports, and strategic plan.

2. The Web sites of national newspapers, particularly the *Washington Post*. Also, do keyword searches of your target organization on the Web sites of *Federal Times*, *Government Executive*, *The Hill*, *Roll Call*, *Federal Computer Week*, *Government Computer News*, and FedSmith.com. Such media research is important because, unlike private-sector organizations, most federal agencies are frequently covered in the news.

3. Descriptions of agency performance on various key government-wide initiatives at http://www.performance.gov. Also, if you are seeking an IT-related job, research your target agency's IT performance at ITdashboard.gov.

4. The annual survey and agency profiles at http://bestplacestowork.org/BPTW/about.

5. The literature search function of your public library's Web site, which allows you to retrieve articles from magazines and newspapers from any computer for free. To conduct such searches, you need only provide a valid library card number.

6. *Washingtonian* magazine's "Best Places to Work" issues, which appear every other year in the fall.

The Tone of Your Cover Letter

Your cover letter should convey a friendly, energetic, and efficient tone. And like all of your other application documents, it should prove that you care about your target organization by addressing its needs. Remember: hiring managers are only concerned about what you can offer them and how you would solve their problems, not about what you want from them or their target opening.

Show that you care about your target agency by citing your knowledge of its recent accomplishments and by using terms like "offer" and "contribute" rather than phrases like "this would be a fantastic opportunity for me."

Also, craft your cover letter with a human voice. Eliminate acronyms and any other terms and expressions that may stump hiring managers who are not familiar with the lingo and practices of your field or previous employers.

The Structure of an Effective Cover Letter

These are the elements that should appear in your cover letter:

➤ Your Address

➤ City, State Zip code

➤ Date

➤ Name of Contact Person

➤ Contact Person's Title

➤ Name of Agency

➤ Address

➤ City, State Zip code

➤ RE: Name and number of job opening

➤ Dear Name of Contact Person:

➤ *Opener:* An energetic, concise introduction of who you are and how you would advance your target organization's mission. Cite one of your target organization's recent achievements, if possible.

➤ *Middle:* Several concise listings of employer-centered information that summarizes your achievements/skills, and explanations of any special circumstances associated with your application or special connections who would vouch for you.

➤ *Conclusion:* Thanks and look forward to hearing from you.

➤ Sincerely,

➤ Your Name

➤ Enclosures: Résumé and KSAs (if applicable)

The Anatomy of Your Cover Letter

Let's take a closer look at the critical parts of a cover letter.

> Notice how concise and to the point this format is. Also notice how space is saved by the "RE" and "Enclosures" lines that eliminate the need to provide this information in full sentences.

The Salutation

Address your cover letter to the contact name on the vacancy announcement for the opening. Be sure to spell the name correctly. If the contact person's first name is gender neutral (such as Terry or Sandy), call the contact to determine whether to address the person as Mr. or Ms. If a contact person is not listed on the vacancy announcement, call the human resources office of the hiring agency to identify the proper recipient of your application. Alternatively, open your cover letter with "Dear Hiring Manager" or "Good Morning" rather than the impersonal "To Whom It May Concern" or the sexist "Dear Sirs."

> Purge your cover letter of presumptuous statements, such as, "I know you will find that I am a perfect match for the position." Instead, describe how your credentials match the requirements of the opening, and let hiring managers decide for themselves that you're a perfect match for the position.

The Opener

Purge the clichéd phrases from your application. For example, avoid these hackneyed expressions:

➤ Enclosed please find my application. (*snooze . . .*)

➤ Please accept the enclosed application. (*yawn . . .*)

➤ I am contacting you in order to . . . (*snore . . .*)

➤ I am interested in . . . (*someone get the defibrillator paddles to resuscitate this application!*)

➤ I am forwarding the enclosed résumé for your consideration . . . (*wake me up when you say something different from your dozens of competitors!*)

Instead of relying on these overused openers, use an energetic opener that demonstrates your knowledge of your target employer, explains why you want to work for that agency, and defines how you would contribute to its success. Also, be sure to immediately orient hiring managers by identifying your current title. For example:

➤ Congratulations to the General Services Administration (GSA) for excelling in the "teamwork" category on GSA's annual employee satisfaction survey. As a logistics expert and a veteran of several award-winning workgroups, I share GSA's team-friendly work ethic. Please consider me for the logistics specialist opening.

- As a contract manager with an MBA and 5 years of experience in innovative contract management, I am qualified to contribute to EPA's efforts to streamline procurement procedures, which were recently covered in *Fast Company*.
- I couldn't be more excited about the recent announcement that NASA will return to the Moon. I would welcome the opportunity to support NASA's many dynamic programs with my top-notch skills as an Administrative Assistant.

Alternatively, if you cannot cite any relevant information about the hiring agency, simply state your credentials:

- My qualifications match the qualifications that you seek for senior attorney. I am currently a senior attorney with Smith & Westlock, the largest firm in South Dakota.
- As an information technology analyst, I specialize in improving the efficiency of large networks used by federal agencies like yours.
- Does XYZ agency want to get more for less on its contracts? If so, I can help because I saved ABC agency $500,000 on its supply contracts last year as a procurement specialist at ABC. My credentials also include . . .

One avant-garde method of revving-up a cover letter is to begin with a memorable quote, either about success, problem solving, efficiency, or another topic relevant to the situation. You can obtain relevant quotes by Googling keywords like quotations, together with words like goals, business, and success.

Hot Tip

If You Have Your Own Web Site . . . . If you have your own Web site that showcases skills relevant to your target opening, consider directing hiring managers to it in your cover letter.

Middle Paragraphs

Do not repeat your entire résumé. Instead, review only your most relevant qualifications based on the job description and the "Qualifications and Evaluations" identified for the job in its vacancy announcement. For example, suppose you were writing a cover letter for a target job that had four "Qualifications and Evaluations." Your cover letter could quickly prove to hiring managers that you met all of their requirements by featuring four bulleted items—each of which (in one or two sentences) covers your credentials for one qualification and evaluation. Use the techniques discussed in Chapter 10 to help you write achievement-oriented statements.

For this section of the cover letter, here are some tips:

- Craft your cover letter to provide a page-turning bird's-eye view of your best credentials that will compel them to read the rest of your application. This means that your cover letter should not provide job descriptions that itemize your duties and responsibilities. Remember: When you describe your duties or responsibilities, you reveal only what you were supposed to do, rather than what you actually achieved.
- Only summarize your relevant credentials in your cover letter, and reserve associated details for your résumé. For example, suppose you were applying for a job that would require you, if hired, to write various types of documents. You would be wise to provide a sweeping statement in your cover letter about your vast writing experience,

such as, "My credentials include five years of experience producing reader-friendly written communications, such as X, Y, and Z, for political appointees—with the particulars of such experience described in the job summaries in your accompanying résumé.

➤ Prominently state whether you have a security clearance even if your target job doesn't require one. You will thereby provide objective evidence of your trust-worthiness.

➤ State whether you have veterans' preference or whether you want to be considered for a noncompetitive appointment.

➤ Explain any special situations presented by your application, such as your willingness to relocate or the five-year gap in your work experience, which you spent caring for a sick relative. (Federal applications don't require coverage of credentials that are older than 10 years, so ignore gaps that are older than that.)

➤ Use active and conversational words rather than stilted, pompous, and bureaucratic words.

➤ Mention any of your relevant connections and state that they would enthusiastically vouch for you.

➤ If you are aiming to switch from the private sector or from the nonprofit sector to the federal sector, explain in one sentence your reason(s) for wanting to do so. Your explanation should emphasize your desire and unique qualifications for contributing to the mission of your target agency or to the public good—rather than your me-o-centric motivations for wanting to switch sectors, such as your need for greater stability (even if that is why you want to make the switch).

The Last Paragraph: Au Revoir

Conclude your cover letter with the appropriate information.

➤ Identify the best way for you to be contacted. If your phone numbers and e-mail address are not on your letterhead, provide them in your closing.

➤ Express thanks for being considered.

Cover Letter Formatting and Length

First, about length. Craft each cover letter to be a fast read. Your cover letters should never exceed one page, no matter how experienced you may be. Remember that the point of a cover letter is to compel the hiring manager to read the rest of your application, which will, in turn, compel the hiring manager to invite you to an interview. Contrary to popular belief, the purpose of a cover letter is not to reiterate your entire biography and to throw in everything else that may possibly interest the hiring manager.

The bottom line is that if you bury your best credentials in verbal dross, you will dig your own grave. In other words, give hiring managers just the needle—without the haystack.

Caution

Don't Use Your Current Employer's Stationary. If you're a current fed, don't use the stationary or envelopes of your current employer to communicate with target employers. Doing so is a flagrant violation of federal regulations and will almost certainly trigger a rejection. Also, conduct your job search from your home e-mail account rather than from your employer's account.

Caution

Know Thy Reader. An application that was churned out on an assembly line without being tailored to the hiring agency usually gives itself away sooner rather than later.

For example, I have seen many cover letters submitted to federal agencies that—believe it or not—profess the applicant's desire to "work for a company like yours," or work for a nonprofit company.

As one hiring manager explained, "If an applicant is that careless on a job application—something that he or she really cares about, that is in his or her direct interest, when they are supposed to be putting their best foot forward—I wouldn't trust them to work on projects that are not directly tied to their self-interest."

Caution: Since essay questions were recently removed from the overwhelming majority of federal job applications, some applicants resort to filling their cover letters with long essays addressing the "Qualifications and Evaluations" element of the job posting. I advise against this approach because, according to my own hiring experience and my interviews with hundreds of other hiring managers, the overwhelming majority of hiring managers are more impressed with a cover letter that hits the right notes concisely and directly than with a long-winded tome.

As explained here, a better approach is to use your cover letter to address each of your target job's "Qualifications and Evaluation" listings with a one- or two-sentence overview that is supported by the details provided in your résumé.

With regard to formatting, consider your objectives in preparing the cover letter. You want to:

➤ Create a layout that is visually appealing and open. Therefore, margins should be 1.25 inches wide.

➤ Draw attention to your skills by using boldface type, bulleted lists, indented lists, and columns.

Tips to Save Time and Space

Use your time and the space in a cover letter wisely:

➤ Identify your target opening in a "RE:" line of a paper application or in the subject line of an e-mailed application.

➤ Identify the enclosures in an "Enclosures" line of a paper application.

➤ Add a "P.S." to emphasize an important fact, observation, or credential. Studies show that a P.S. is the most read part of a letter. That's why so many fundraising letters include part of their pitches in a P.S.

Proofread Your Cover Letter

Proofread your cover letter fastidiously. Indeed, most hiring managers say that typos in an application can instantly kill an applicant's chances. And a typo that appears in a cover letter will invariably look as big as a barn! Proofread your cover letter by:

➤ Spell-checking it. But don't rely solely on spellcheckers, which cannot recognize all mistakes. For example, spellcheckers won't flag words that should be capitalized or tell you if you used the word "their" instead of "there."

➤ Print out your letter. You will find awkward passages and errors in paper copies of documents that you would miss on the screen. It is particularly important to print out e-mails. Never send an e-mail to a potential employer without first proofreading a paper copy of it.

➤ Reading your letter out loud.

➤ Ask yourself why your sentences are sequenced in their current order. If you don't have a good reason, your document is probably not logically organized, so rethink it.

➤ Get distance from your letter, and then read it again. If you are tight on time, let your letter go cold by doing something else—such as watering your plants—for a few minutes and then return to your letter. Even a few minutes away from your letter will increase your objectivity and help you find mistakes in it.

➤ Soliciting objective, honest feedback on your letter from trusted advisers.

Figures 13-1 through 13-5 are examples of cover letters.

1234 Yellow Brick Road
City, State, Zip Code
January 31, 2008

Mr. Frank Howard
Personnel Analyst
US Mint
801 9th Street NW
Washington DC 20220

Dear Mr. Howard:

Subject: Marketing Manager Position (#08-65-59)

As a Marketing Manager at Wal-mart since 2002, I have been tracking the Mint's record-breaking sales successes. I would like to work to help the Mint increase its sales even further.

A synopsis of my credentials:

YOUR NEEDS	MY CREDENTIALS
Knowledge of business principles	Five years of experience as Marketing Manager at Wal-mart, and a B.A. in Business Administration from University of Maryland.
Computer proficiency	Expert in using PC Lotus, Ledger, Excel, PeopleSoft, PowerPoint, Word, and various web creation programs.
Negotiating skills	Saved Walmart $500,000 since 2000 by negotiating pricing of advertising. Completed training courses in negotiating.
Communication skills	Experienced in creating PowerPoint presentations summarizing monthly marketing trends for senior managers.

I am eager to speak with you about the Marketing Manager position. My telephone numbers are (123) 123-4567(w) and (012) 123-4567(h), and my e-mail address is Jones@e-mail.com. I sincerely appreciate your time and consideration.

Sincerely,

Trudy Jones

Enclosure: Resume and KSAs

Figure 13-1 This cover letter format is—hands down—the premier cover letter format in the job-hunting world. For one thing, the opener reflects the applicant's impressive knowledge of her target organization. But most important, the letter's tabular format broadcasts the applicant's suitability for the opening—even to hiring managers who would only skim the letter. Hey! A harried, time-pressed hiring manager wouldn't even have to read the letter—just quickly scan it—to become immediately convinced that the applicant is a perfect match for the opening . . . a keeper.

Based on my client's success with this memorable format, I virtually guarantee that it would help you stand out from the pack. Each of my many clients who have used this cover letter format has landed interviews with it—and many of those have gone on to land their associated targeted jobs. What's more, many of my clients' interviewers have specifically told my clients that it was this cover letter format that specifically vaulted them to the top of the applicant list.

Directions for creating tables are provided in Appendix 3. When using this format craft the "Your Needs" column to reflect the opening requirements. If you don't fulfill some of its requirements, omit them from the letter.

An alternative, but similar cover letter approach, would be to build your cover letter around a list (customized to your target opening) of "The Top Five Reasons Why I Would Succeed on This Job."

1234 Yellow Brick Road
City, State ZIP Code
August 1, 2008

Ms. Jackie Harper
Personnel Officer
Office of Human Resources
National Science Foundation
4201 Wilson Boulevard
Arlington, Virginia 22230

RE: Project Management Position (111-PM-45)

Dear Ms. Jackie Harper:

Congratulations to the Office of Management and Budget (OMB) for winning the 2008 Presidential Award for Management Excellence! As a recent college graduate who is knowledgeable about the latest performance-based management techniques, I would like to join NSF's staff as a project manager.

My qualifications include:

- **A BA in Business Administration from Northwestern University.**

- **Polished communication skills:** All of my classes in my major required papers or oral presentations. My GPA in my major was 3.50, and I graduated with Departmental Honors in my major.

- **A proven record as a self-starter and team-player:** As an undergraduate, I juggled a heavy academic course-load along with a 15 hour-per-week campus job and my responsibilities as co-captain of the lacrosse team.

I would be happy to provide any additional information about my background that might be helpful. I will be moving to the Washington DC area within the next two months. I can be reached on my cell phone at (012) 123-4567 before or after I move to Washington DC. My e-mail address is Linda.Watson@e-mail.com. Many thanks for your consideration, and I hope to hear from you soon.

Sincerely,

Linda Watson

Enclosures: Resume and KSAs

Figure 13-2 An exemplary letter from a recent graduate. Notice how the applicant demonstrates knowledge of the National Science Foundation by referring to its recent management award, which was posted on results.gov. The applicant also cites her own grades as objective validation of her skills and mentions her extracurricular activities as evidence of her work ethic and team-friendly credentials.

LINDA WATSON
1234 Yellow Brick Road
City, State ZIP Code
Phone: (123) 123-4567 (w); (012) 123-4567 (h)
E-Mail: Linda.Watson@e-mail.com

January 31, 2007

Ms. Jackie Harper
Personnel Officer
Office of Human Resources
U.S. Fish and Wildlife Service
3345 Wilson
Blvd.
Arlington, VA
20456

Dear Ms. Harper:

Perhaps I am the "multi-talented Webmaster" that you seek (Position 123-WM-789). My credentials include:

- Seven years of experience as a Webmaster at EPA designing and updating high-traffic websites that broadcast scientific information in engaging screen formats.

- A solid record of earning superior performance evaluations throughout my career.

- An M.S. in Systems Administration from the University of Colorado.

- A B.A. in Graphic Arts from the University of Colorado.

I would also bring to the position my lifelong passion for conservation, which is reflected in all of my work experience, and my hobbies, which include bird watching, and reading publications, such as *Wildlife Conservation* and *National Geographic*.

Attached is my resume and KSAs. I would appreciate the opportunity to discuss the position with you further and show you my portfolio of web pages. Thank you for your time and consideration.

Sincerely,

Linda Watson

P.S.   Congratulations on the favorable write-up of the Fish and Wildlife Service in last month's issue of *Government Executive*!

Figure 13-3 This letter is enlivened by the applicant's mention of her lifelong passions, which relate to the writer's target job, and the clever use of an attention-grabbing P.S.

SALLY BAKER
1234 Yellow Brick Road   •   City, State ZIP Code   •   123-123-4567

Mr. John McCarthy   December 15, 2008
Personnel Analyst
Small Business Administration
Two Gateway Center
Newark, NJ 07102

                                        RE: Administrative Assistant (XX-AA-123)

Dear Mr. McCarthy:

PROBLEMS CANNOT BE SOLVED AT THE SAME LEVEL OF AWARENESS THAT CREATED THEM.
                    — ALBERT EINSTEIN

As an Administrative Assistant at Verizon, I continually strive — in the spirit of Albert Einstein's philosophy — to master new software and people skills that improve office organization. At Verizon, I am known as "the office fixer" and "the event fixer." I could similarly smooth the operations of your office.

I am an expert in:

• Organizing large events attended by dozens of high-level officials, including CEOs of telecommunications companies.

• Managing the busy schedules of executives using the latest e-mail, electronic calendar, and palm pilot software.

• Arranging conference calls and virtual meetings.

• Shepherding high-profile documents through the approval process.

• Establishing and maintaining electronic filing systems for easy retrieval. For example, during a pivotal point in my supervisor's recent contract negotiations with a contractor, I quickly retrieved an urgently needed legal document that compelled the contractor to agree to contract terms that saved Verizon $50,000.

I am methodical enough to comprehensively plan events and projects, and flexible enough to calmly confront the unexpected.

I would be happy to meet with you to discuss your needs and my skills further. Please call me at the phone number on my letterhead, or e-mail me at Sally.Baker@e-mail.com. I do appreciate your consideration.

Sincerely,

Sally Baker

Figure 13-4 Effective use of the quote method. Notice how this applicant has skillfully tied the quote into her own on-the-job approach. Also notice how this applicant's credentials are crafted to sound impressive even without mention of awards or performance evaluations.

1234 Yellowbrick Road
Anywhere, USA
E-Mail: SSuccess@e-mail.com
December 1, 2007

Mr. Jayson MucketyMuck
Director of the Office of Executives
US Department of Energy
1000 BigWig Avenue
Washington DC 20008

Hello Mr. Jayson:

Thank you for requesting more information about my background. As we recently discussed,
I am eager to contribute my communication skills and environmental background to Federal
Energy Regulatory Commission's important work securing the US's energy security.

As a federal communications expert and freelance writer, I offer special expertise in
conveying technical information in easy-to-understand language, pitching stories to the
press, advising political appointees on sensitive issues, producing high-impact documents,
and leading trainings on communication skills.

My credentials include:

☐ **A life-long passion for environmental and public health issues.** I have a Master of
   Public Health and a Master of Environmental Management from Yale University. Also,
   dozens of my articles have appeared in popular publications, such as *Audubon*,
   National Parks, and three environmental law reviews.

☐ **Fifteen years of experience promoting the achievements of high-profile agencies,**
   including the Labor Department and EPA. I offer a solid track record of earning
   positive press coverage for my employers in national media outlets; defending agency
   positions; and writing Congressional testimony, annual reports, speeches, talking
   points, and easy-to-read fact sheets and web documents.

☐ **Skill in working with editors in high-pressure, deadline-driven environments.** I
   have contributed to *The Washington Post*, WashingtonPost.com, flight magazines and
   law reviews.

☐ **Experience as a communications trainer/mentor.** I have delivered seminars on
   communication skills to The Council of Editors, The National Institutes of Health, and
   other organizations.

I would, of course, be happy to follow-up in any way that you might suggest. I will call you
soon to discuss any leads you might have.

Thanks very much for your time and consideration.

Sincerely,

Susan Success

Attachments: Resume and list of publications.

Figure 13-5 This cover letter was successfully used to pursue a networking contact—not to apply for a specific
opening. It quickly hits the applicant's high notes, effectively uses bullets, and warns the recipient of the sender's
impending follow up. When your networking contacts ask you to send your résumé and/or a concise summary
of your credentials, do so immediately. Your speed and efficiency will testify to your efficiency and encourage
your networking contact to similarly act quickly on your behalf. Also, if appropriate, accompany your networking
letters with several relevant work products that showcase your skills, as covered in "Prepare to Give the Portfolio
Treatment" in Chapter 15.

Waiting for a Response to Your Application

"Between the wish and the thing lies waiting."
—ANONYMOUS

How long will the wait last? Granted, the federal hiring system is generally not known for its need for speed. Nevertheless, it has—in recent years—greatly accelerated its selection processes. I know from my own experiences and those of my clients that more and more agencies are meeting or beating new guidelines to complete each selection within 80 days of its closing date.

Here's an example of federal efficiency: I recently received an e-mail confirming that I ranked among the "best-qualified applicants" for a Labor Department opening the very same day that it closed, and then was invited to interview for the job two weeks after that. Nevertheless, some agencies still miss the 80-day deadline, and so selection times vary from agency to agency.

Getting Status Updates

Once you have thrown your hat into the ring and submitted your application for a federal job, how can you track your application through the selection process?

Many agencies provide applicants with updates (either by e-mail or on password-protected Web sites) confirming submission of their applications, informing them whether they have been chosen as a best-qualified applicant, and then telling them after a final selection has been made—whether or not they were selected. Check such confirmations carefully and immediately contact your target job's contact person if you identify a problem.

Communicating with the Silent Type

Unfortunately, some agencies are not very conscientious about communicating with applicants during the selection process. Grrrr!! It's so frustrating to twist in the wind, without updates on your application status! So, here's how to get around the computers and impenetrable automatic phone recordings that may stand between you and a real agency representative.

If more than three weeks have passed since your target job's closing date, call the agency contact person identified on your target job's announcement, and ask him or her if your application rated among the best-qualified applicants or, in government lingo, "made the cert." If not, ask how high you scored. The resulting feedback you receive may help you determine whether your application strategy is on the right track or warrants an overhaul. You may also ask whether you will be interviewed, how many applicants are competing for the job, and who the selecting official is.

Don't be shy about calling agency contacts. I have personally contacted many of them, and I assure you that these staffers are generally very obliging and helpful. Keep in mind that it is their job to answer applicants' questions. You're well within your rights to consult them, and you won't alienate the hiring agency or damage your application in any way by inquiring about its status.

If more than 10 days to two weeks have elapsed since your interview, or the date your interviewer promised to make a decision has passed, call your interviewer, reaffirm your interest in the job, and politely ask when he or she expects to make a decision.

But it is probably best not to leave phone messages for interviews. Why not? Because if you do, you will be rendered powerless while waiting (perhaps futilely) for a return call. Instead, keep calling without leaving messages until you reach your target hiring manager.

Even if such contact yields no helpful information, you may further your case by staying in touch with your interviewer. I know, for example, of one busy hiring manager who had totally forgotten about an opening he was filling until he received a polite request for an update from an applicant whom he had interviewed some weeks before. The result: He hired the applicant.

If the selection process drags out, occasionally call or e-mail your interviewer, but not too often. As one hiring manager observes, "There is a fine line between getting credit for being persistent and for getting a reputation for being a persistent pest."

Solicit Feedback

If you're notified that you've been rejected for your target job, call your interviewer and express thanks for having been considered, mention your interest in future openings, and ask for some honest feedback on your interviewing skills. After all, you've got nothing to lose by doing so. And for your bravery you may be rewarded with some suggestions that could help you nail your next interview.

Alternatively, you may be heartened to learn that the hiring decision turned on factors, such as veterans' preference, that were unrelated to your credentials. And it is even possible that your hiring manager may still help you land employment pay dirt; I have heard of a number of instances where an interviewer was so impressed by a runner-up that she or he immediately helped that applicant land another current opening.

Establish a Rolodex Contact

If you've established a positive rapport with the selecting official (particularly if you sent a postinterview thank-you letter), even if you weren't selected, you may occasionally touch base with the selecting official; the individual may provide you with future leads.

PART III

THE TALKING STAGE

Welcome to the home stretch of your job campaign: the talking stage, which includes interviewing, negotiating your salary, and responding to agency decisions. To get here, you skillfully created a written application that proved that you are a top-tier professional, the cream of the crop, a potential keeper. Now, at last, your paper chase is, for the most part, over.

Instead of depending entirely on what you write, your ability to beat out your final few competitors and then convince hiring managers to give you a top salary will largely hinge on what you say and how you say it during, at most, a few short meetings. Do you feel the pressure build?

But no worries, as the Aussies say. This chapter and the cheat sheets on this book's CD will tell you everything you need to know to confidently, coolly, and compellingly talk yourself into your target job and target salary.

Like the preceding parts of this book, Part III features pivotal advice, available nowhere else, straight from federal hiring managers—the gatekeepers to federal jobs. I know that this advice can vault you ahead of the competition and raise your salary offer because it has done so for hundreds of my clients.

15

Acing Your Interviews

"Forget gimmicks like echoing the body language of your interviewer. Any intelligent interviewer sees right through that. What I look for is evidence that the applicant understands my agency and its goals, and is going to work like the dickens."
—HOWARD HYMAN, FEDERAL HIRING MANAGER

Congratulations! The powers that be were so impressed by your written sales pitch that they have summoned you for an interview. This means that you probably beat out dozens, or even hundreds, of competitors to rank among the best and the brightest.

So, go ahead, savor your victory, crank up the sound track of *Rocky*, and do some victory laps around your cube. But once the music stops, it's time to start preparing for your interview.

What Interviewers Want

What does your interviewer expect from you during your interview? Your interviewer wants to check that you look as good and as qualified in person as you did on paper. Your interviewer wants to confirm that you're the zero-risk employee who:

➤ Will solve the organization's problem, not create more problems.

➤ Can do the target job well.

➤ Really wants to work there, cares about the organization, and is positive and upbeat.

➤ Is mentally stable, reliable, team-friendly, and will fit with the organization's culture.

"O.K., which cup is your job under now?"

Remember that during the interview phase of the selection, you're competing against the cream of the crop; you and your competitors probably constitute the top 5 percent of the applicant pool. And because each of you is highly qualified and could probably do the target job well if given the chance, the petty differences among you that would not matter one bit in other contexts may assume heightened importance during interviews.

Unfortunately, you have only one or maybe two relatively brief interviews to pull ahead of your highly qualified competitors and prove that you're the zero-risk applicant who deserves to be hired. To do so, aim to:

1   Do everything better than your competitors during your interview(s).

2.   Milk every interview minute for all it's worth.

3.   Devote all your interview time to proving that you're the zero-risk applicant. (Don't waste any time on irrelevant aspects of your background, such as what city you were born in or topics like religion, which could alienate interviewers.)

The best way to achieve these goals and beat your competition is to prepare for your interview more than your competition will. I promise you that most of your competition won't prepare for their interviews at all; they will wing them and therefore risk crashing and burning. By contrast, if you prepare for your interview by using the techniques explained in this chapter, you will significantly improve your interview performance—and thereby significantly increase your chances of beating out your competition.

Research the Hiring Agency

I'll bet that you would rather form a personal relationship with someone who recognizes and appreciates your uniqueness than with someone who is obviously desperate to start a relationship with someone—anyone. Likewise, employers would rather form a professional relationship with an applicant who recognizes and appreciates their organization's uniqueness than one who is obviously desperate to land a job—any job.

In other words, if you saunter into your interview with the attitude of, "If it's Tuesday, it must be the Transportation Department," you will turn off the interviewer. Instead, seize the interview questions—such as "Why do you want to work here?"—as invitations to describe your long-term passion for the issues addressed by your target organization and to show your understanding of how the organization works. (Remember: Passion is "in" these days.) Prepare to do so by following the tips on researching federal agencies covered in Chapters 2 and 13.

Also, the more you know about your interviewers before interviews, the more comfortable you will feel when you meet them and the more you will be able to tailor your answers to their interests, as well as avoid potentially thorny subjects. So Google your interviewer(s) and check their profiles on LinkedIn, Facebook, and other social networking sites.

Also, consider downloading an up-to-date profile of your interviewer (for a very reasonable fee) from http://www.leadershipdirectories.com, a site that features profiles of most federal managers. But if your research reveals that the hiring agency is mired in scandal, or that your interviewer has been tainted by "youthful indiscretions," well . . . um . . . the less said about such awkwardness, the better.

During a *Good Morning America* segment about job hunting, Diane Sawyer said: "I'm so surprised by the way a lot of kids come in to see me to talk about getting jobs. . . . And I'm amazed how few of them have watched the shows they want to work on."

If you neglect to research your target organization before your interview, you will come across as apathetic and unprepared as those hapless applicants to *Good Morning America.* But if, by contrast, you show your interviewers that you're knowledgeable about your target agency, you will prove that you care about it (whether or not you really do), and you will thereby win over your interviewers in a BIG way.

Hot Tip

Know Thy Interviewer(s). When you are invited to an interview, ask your agency contact for the name and title of each staffer who will interview you.

Craft Answers to Common Questions

"It usually takes more than three weeks to prepare a good impromptu speech."
—MARK TWAIN

Ironically, the more you prepare for the interviews, the more spontaneous and articulate you will sound during those interviews. You can craft winning answers to interview questions by:

1   Rereading the description of your target job and your application. (You may be asked your KSA or ECQ questions again during the interview. Also, you may be asked to expand upon short-answer questions that were included on your application.)

2. Researching your target agency.

3. Listing your relevant credentials and success stories so that you can incorporate them into your answers. Review Chapter 9 for tips on how to convey your successes in impressive terms, and use the Figure 15-1 worksheet to develop your "success stories."

Worksheet for Telling Impressive Success Stories

My goal and why it was important to my organization: _____

_____

_____

My actions to achieve my goal: _____

_____

_____

Special obstacles I conquered, if any: _____

_____

_____

My results: _____

_____

_____

Positive feedback, if any:

_____

_____

Figure 15-1 Worksheet for telling success stories. A worksheet similar to this one, as well as instruction on effective storytelling, is included in the "Writing Killer Application Essays (KSAs and ECQs)" section of the CD accompanying this book. Also, use Chapter 9 to craft compelling stories that include objective validation of your success.

4. Reviewing the rest of this chapter, as well as the interview and application prep cheat sheets included on this book's CD.

5. Preparing concise answers to the list of common interview questions provided on this book's CD. Federal hiring managers rely heavily on these common questions. Therefore, if you prepare for them, you will be prepared for most of your interview questions. A case in point: I recently rehearsed common interview questions with a college senior before she interviewed for a job as a policy analyst at EPA. After the interview, she said we had nailed over 80 percent of the interview questions. And she got the job.

6. Remembering that you will probably have only a few brief minutes, at most, to answer each question during interviews, and time zooms by when you are under pressure. So time your answers during practice sessions and limit each answer to a maximum of about 1½ minutes. Also, keep in mind that your interviewer may

cut you off and interrupt you at any time while you are
answering questions.

So begin each of your answers with your best material
(i.e., descriptions of your most important, most relevant,
and most recent credentials and experiences), and work
backwards from there. If, while answering questions
during interviews, you're not sure whether or not to keep
talking, ask your interviewer, "Would you like more
information on this?"

7. Anticipating other likely questions by asking your colleagues what questions they think you will be asked.
Also, inventory the types of challenges that your target
job will probably present and practice discussing specific
examples of how you've already successfully tackled such challenges. For example,
will your target job require you to meet tight deadlines or mediate conflicts or
develop new training programs?

8. Conducting mock interviews with your trusted advisers. The more people you
role-play with, the better for you. Each person you practice with will give you
different and complementary advice—most of which will help you on your day of
reckoning. When you role-play, encourage your advisers to provide you with honest
feedback. After all, there is only one way to find out how you are coming across
(both on paper or in person)—that is, by asking others, "How am I coming across?"

> **Hot Tip**
>
> Consider yourself Mirandized from the moment you arrive at your interview: No matter how chummy or casual your interviewer may be with you, remember that anything you say during an interview can and will be held against you. So, don't say anything in your interview that will implicate you as anything but the zero-risk applicant.

The Two Main Types of Interview Questions

The real question behind most interview questions is, "Why should we hire you?" Common
Why-should-we-hire-you? questions include:

➤ Tell me about yourself.

➤ What do you do on your current job?

➤ Why do you want to work here?

When I ask hiring managers why they selected a particular applicant, they invariably
answer that their pick had the most experience in the areas required by the opening. They
consider past experience important because they operate on the "past is prologue" ethic.
They assume that if an applicant did the target job well before, she or he will do so again
in the future.

So use Why-should-we-hire-you? questions as invitations to show hiring managers that
you could do the job because you have already done it in the past, and have done it well.
Prove that by citing your successes that parallel the demands of the opening and the
positive feedback they drew.

The real question behind many other common interview questions is, "Why shouldn't
we hire you?" Common Why-shouldn't-we-hire-you? questions include:

➤ What are your weaknesses?

➤ What don't you like about your job?

➤ What is your five-year-plan?

By hiding the Why-shouldn't-we-hire-you? question behind other questions, your interviewer hopes to trick you into revealing why you would be a problem, not a problem solver. If you fall for this trick, you will probably be rejected.

Don't do your interviewer's work for him. It's his job to identify your foibles and your job to conceal them. Does this sound to you like a game of hide-and-seek? In a way, it is. Although you shouldn't lie in interviews, you also shouldn't volunteer self-incriminating information; unfortunately, if you do, you will lose points for your deficiencies, not gain points for your candor.

Table 15-1 provides possible answers for many common interview questions.

But here are some more interview tips:

➤ Whenever discussing mistakes, focus on something that happened a long time ago, was relatively trivial, and is irrelevant to the opening's demands. Emphasize how you learned from your mistakes and how you would act differently now.

➤ Never criticize a previous boss, colleagues, or job. Why? Because whenever you trash anything or anyone, you invariably raise doubts about whether the problem was caused by you or the trashee, no matter how blameless you actually were, and you thereby stop being a zero-risk applicant.

➤ By the same token, don't criticize yourself or even imply that you have personality defects, judgment problems, family challenges that could interfere with your job, or any other characteristics not possessed by the zero-risk employee.

Some Other Question Types

You may be asked some "What would you do in this situation?" types of questions. You may answer some of these types of questions by explaining how you would research your options and weigh alternatives. But if you're asked a hypothetical question that tests your willingness to break laws, pass the test by stating that you would refuse to break them. You may also answer hypothetical questions by relating the cited hypothetical situation to a similar challenge that you have previously conquered successfully.

Prepare to explain why you would like to leave your current job for your target job. Your reason should enthusiastically emphasize your desire to contribute in some way to the mission of your target agency and your unique qualifications for doing so; your answer should not address any negative situations that are driving you away from your current job. Reassure the employer that you're a goal-oriented professional, not a job-hopping flake. You may also mention additional education that you might want to eventually pursue.

If you aim to switch into the federal sector from the private sector or a nonprofit, explain why. Your explanation should emphasize your desire to contribute to the mission of your target agency or the public good, rather than me-centric reasons, such as your pursuit of job stability (even if that is why you want to make the switch). For example, consider saying something like:

The opening appeals to me because it would provide one-of-a-kind opportunities to write federal regulations addressing national security issues that have been my lifelong passion; there is simply no way to write federal regulations from the private sector.

(text continues on page 161)

TABLE 15-1	Answers to Common Interview Questions	
Question	**Avoid Unimpressive Answer**	**Give Impressive Answer**
Tell me about yourself.	Save your biographical filibuster for your retirement party. Don't give a long review of your entire career, and don't provide personal background info that is irrelevant to your target job and may alienate hiring managers.	Provide a quick, concise, logically organized summary of your most relevant academic and professional credentials—even if they're included on your résumé. Emphasize your recent achievements over ancient ones. Only cite personal background info that is relevant to your target job. See template for answering this question on this book's CD.
What is your weakness?	Consider yourself Mirandaized from the minute you arrive at your interview: everything you say can and will be held against you. So don't say anything that will confirm your unworthiness for the job. Also avoid clichés like: "I don't have any weaknesses," "I'm a perfectionist," or "I work too hard."	Craft your answer to demonstrate your self-awareness, humility, or committment to self-improvement. Here are some techniques that have helped professionals land jobs in various government organizations, including the White House: 1. Describe how you stay current in your field, and identify training that you would like to take. 2. Describe a non-deal-breaking gap that you've fixed. For example: "I previously underestimated the importance of X. So now, I emphasize that more." Or "I used to shy from public speaking. So I joined Toastmasters, and I now enjoy it." 3. Acknowledge that as a new employee you would have a lot to learn about your target organization; explain how you would quickly get up to speed and have previously done so. 4. Say: "I inventory lessons learned after each project, and so I try never to repeat mistakes. I also incorporate lessons learned into instruction to others."

(continues)

T A B L E 15-1 *(continued)*		

Question	Avoid Unimpressive Answer	Give Impressive Answer
What are you most proud of?	Before consulting me, one of my clients answered this question by referrring to his role as husband and father. In response, 'My interviewer's face fell,' he recalls. P.S. He didn't get the job.	Describe a high-impact project that parallels the demands of your target job, how your results improved your organization's operations, and positive feedback you received. That's what my client —the proud parent and husband—did when asked that question again in the next interview. P.S. He got the job.
Why should we hire you rather than another applicant?	If you say, "I don't know the other applicants so I can't compare myself to them," your interviewers will hit the eject button. Don't be meek, overly humble, or apologetic.	Identify your unique, desirable skills, strong work ethic, and team-friendly approaches. Also cite your reputation, as reflected in your record of excellent performance reviews and awards. Express confidence without cockiness.
Can we call your current boss?	Don't say, "We don't get along. Please don't call him."	If you don't want your interviewer to call you current boss, say, "I would prefer if my current boss didn't know about my job search. Here's a list of my references, including several previous bosses."
What would your boss and colleagues say about you?	Don't spread negative gossip about yourself.	Cite positive feedback you have received and your team-friendly approaches: For example, "If the comments I have received on my performance evaluations are any indication, my boss would praise my contributions. Moreover, my ability to work well with others is reflected in my record of earning team awards and the fact that I share a spirit of camaraderie with my colleagues."
How do you deal with conflict?	Don't say, "I won't compromise when I know I am right."	Say something like, "I look for common ground and ways to compromise. For example. . . . Also, I believe that disagreements don't have to become conflicts. Colleagues should be able to discuss disagreements amicably. When I get overruled or overrule someone else, I just do it graciously, and move on."

Question	Avoid Unimpressive Answer	Give Impressive Answer
What is your management style?	Don't just pound your chest and say you're the boss. Explain your decision-making style, how you maximize productivity.	Say something like, "I am a decisive, effective, and fair manager who creates a collegial office. I believe that a manager's job is to get the work done. To do that, s/he must understand the work and relevant obstacles, understand the people who do the work, and make sure they have the guidance and resources they need to do it."
What would you do during your first week on a management job?	Don't pledge to buffalo through the office and immediately overhaul it.	During my early days, I would hold off on making any big decisions, even though I know a lot of people would probably immediately suggest changes to me. Instead, I would initially talk to as many people as possible and read whatever I could to really understand the organization and its constraints.
What would you do if you were overloaded, with more work than you could possibly complete on time?	"I would try to get someone else to do some of the work."	Say something like, "I would logically prioritize my projects and discuss those priorities with my supervisor."

Whether or not you are applying for a supervisory job, you may be asked to describe what qualities are important for supervisors to demonstrate. When you prepare your answer (before your interview), consider what qualities your previous supervisors demonstrated that were most beneficial to you, your colleagues, and your office's overall productivity and morale. (Remember to stay positive: No griping about previous bosses!)

Also mention that you are ready, willing, and able to quickly adopt whatever new approaches and techniques that would be required by your sector switch. Provide an example or two of how you have previously hit the ground running in a new environment.

Interviews for senior-level positions are particularly likely to cover leadership/supervisory skills. So, be prepared to cite examples of your successes in rewarding and disciplining employees, conducting strategic planning, managing change, motivating staffers, and promoting diversity.

Hot Tip

If you must travel a long distance to get to an interview or to start your job, ask your hiring manager if the agency would be willing to cover your travel expenses. Federal agencies do have discretion to cover such costs. Alternatively, a federal agency can opt to interview you by phone.

Hot Tip

Interviews—What Works, What Doesn't Work. According to a survey of 300 recruiters by Korn/Ferry International, "The strongest candidates effectively correlate their experience in a concise and compelling manner." Survey results also indicate that about 33 percent of interviewees are unprepared; 24 percent show overinflated egos; and larger percentages strike out because they talk too much, show bad hygiene, or are poorly dressed.

Questions to Ask Your Interviewer

Your opportunity to ask questions is another opportunity to impress your interviewer, so don't waste it with silence. Even if you already know more than you ever wanted to know about your target job, prepare insightful questions to ask your interviewer. See the list of possible questions on this book's CD.

Save your questions about salaries and benefits until after you receive an offer, however. The goal of your interview is to reel in an offer. Questions about salary and benefits probably won't help you achieve that goal because they are about what *you* want rather than about what your hiring manager cares about or what your target agency wants.

Therefore, questions about salary and benefits are unlikely to help you win over hiring managers. What's more, such questions may even provide grist for rejections. So, wait until you have received an offer before you ask about salary and benefits.

The Portfolio Treatment

One important way to stand out from the pack is to use my patented "portfolio treatment" on your interviewers. That is, bring to your interview a sample of your work products and positive feedback generated by them. I know this technique can help you wow hiring managers because it has helped scores of my clients do so.

Why the Portfolio Treatment Works

The portfolio treatment works so well because:

➤ Actions speak louder than words. Sales pitches that incorporate tangible work products are more impressive and convincing than uncorroborated promises of future productivity.

➤ By giving a copy of your portfolio to your interviewer to keep, you will leave an impression with your interviewer(s) that will linger long after you have left the interview.

➤ Tangible, eye-catching work products appeal to multiple senses and so are more vivid and memorable than oral pitches alone.

Rest assured: Your competition probably won't give the portfolio treatment to interviewers. Therefore, by giving the portfolio treatment, you will help prove that you are the most organized and forward-thinking applicant in the competition. A case in point: I recently coached a federal IT specialist at the U.S. Mint, who was applying for a job in another agency. During his interview, he submitted to his interviewers a neatly packaged portfolio of printouts of eye-catching Web pages he had produced. The result? The IT specialist was told by his interviewers that he was the only applicant who had shown them work products, which bowled them over. The IT specialist got the job.

But beware, too. Keep your portfolio to a reasonable size. A hiring manager recently told me that he rejected an interviewee because he was overwhelmed by her success portfolio, which was "fat enough to choke a rhinoceros."

How to Prepare a Winning Portfolio

To prepare to use the portfolio treatment, bring to your interview a portfolio with pockets that hold several copies of your well-formatted hard-copy résumé, business cards, reference list (see section later in this chapter for guidance in developing the list), and a sample of documents that validate your relevant successes.

These documents may include:

➤ Writing samples such as reports, articles, newsletters, press releases, press clips, or printouts of PowerPoint presentations that you wrote or that cover your projects.

➤ Programs from events you organized or conferences that featured your presentations.

➤ Explanatory maps, charts, and photographs.

➤ Samples of artwork, manufactured products, catalogues, or packaging that you designed.

➤ Praising e-mails from managers, colleagues, or clients; positive performance evaluations; evaluations from conferences or trainings you organized; justifications for major awards; or written recommendations from your references—even if you are not asked for them.

➤ For students and recent grads, copies of your relevant papers (preferably with praising comments from professors) or a list of relevant papers and their high grades.

Label your portfolio to be self-explanatory to the hiring managers who may review it when you are not with them, and identify your contributions to any group projects. Remember: You will stand out from the pack if you do more and better than the pack. Lastly, make sure your labels and your portfolio's contents are typo free!

Rather than presenting your interviewer(s) with a hard-copy success portfolio, you may opt—if appropriate—to present your interviewer(s) with an online success portfolio. For example, I recently coached a social media expert who had bookmarked on her iPad the relevant social media Web sites that she had previously created, and then showed them to her interviewers during her job interview.

"I wrote another five hundred words. Can I have another cookie?"

The result: She got the job. And one of her interviewers (whom I happened to know) later told me that the social media expert's presentation of her Web sites had been pivotal: It was what put her ahead of her (tough) competition for the opening and compelled her interviewers to hire her.

But beware: If you plan to present an online portfolio during a job interview, make sure ahead of time that you will be able to connect to the Internet from your interview location. And even if you are assured that you will have an Internet connection during your interview, come to the interview equipped with a "plan B" (backup plan) in case unexpected technical snags kill your Internet connection.

But whatever format your success portfolio takes, before your interview, practice quickly walking your interviewers through its contents. As you do so, point to relevant sections and look up! During your interview, give a copy of your success portfolio to each interviewer for keeps, if possible. Artfully weave into the conversation mention of your success portfolio and explain that you brought it to show the range of experience you offer your target organization.

The Morning of Your Interview

Get pumped for your interview by listening to energizing music, reciting motivating slogans, and listening to pep talks from friends. Wear to your interview a new, crisp outfit that is in a contemporary, professional style. A pants suit or the equivalent is fine for women. Make sure that your personal hygiene, including your hair and nails, are in tip-top shape.

Arrive at the interview office about 10 minutes early. Build plenty of extra travel time into your schedule for traffic, getting security clearance into the building, finding your interview office in a large labyrinth, primping, and "de-jittering."

During Your Interview

Even if you're regularly tossing back fistfuls of tranquilizers, be cheerful, relaxed, enthusiastic, and friendly—no one wants to hire a sourpuss. Here are some additional day-of-interview tips:

> Smile. I know of cases in which less qualified applicants beat out more qualified applicants for jobs simply because they smiled during their interviews and generally related more positively to the interviewers. Also, maintain eye contact with the interviewers. And exude confidence without acting cocky or superior.

> Congratulate your interviewer for any major awards or recent major accomplishments earned by your target organization, the effectiveness of its Web site, or any other worthy achievements you discovered during your research. When delivered in a sincere manner, your flattery will reinforce your enthusiasm and knowledge for your target job and help ingratiate you to your interviewers.

> Assume no prior knowledge about your credentials from your interviewers. Feel free to incorporate into your interview answers or descriptions of your credentials that are included on your application. Assume that your interviewer will probably either neglect to read your résumé or forget what it says by the time your interview rolls around. And, even if your interviewer does remember your application, she or he wants to hear you describe your selling points.

> Describe your successes to interviewers just as you would describe them to strangers, even if you're interviewing for another job within your current organization and you already know your interviewers. Why? Because it's dangerous to rely on the selective, defective memories of decision makers who hold your fate in their hands.

Moreover, if you don't tell your interviewer what you offer and why she or he should hire you, you will likely be overshadowed by applicants who do tell them so.

This is important because many federal hiring managers have told me that they have rejected inside applicants because they treated their interview too casually, acted entitled to their target job, or neglected to sell themselves during interviews. Instead, these hiring managers hired outsiders who treated the interview with seriousness and deference, and persuasively sold themselves.

What's more, if you are an inside applicant, remember that outside applicants may be free of documentable baggage and offer the type of beguiling mystery that tends to fade away with the day-in and day-out familiarity that you offer. All of this means that you should prepare for insider interviews and take them as seriously as will outsiders.

➤ Furthermore, if you are an inside applicant, exploit any opportunities that may accompany your "home team advantage." For example, if you have potentially influential insider references, ask them to sing your praises to your potential employer before you apply or as early in the application process as possible. After all, your insider references won't do you much good if you are eliminated from consideration before they have gone to bat for you.

➤ Present yourself as a problem solver (not a problem) by proving that you would be able to help your organization solve problems. Do this by presenting potential solutions to problems or obstacles currently facing your target organization, which you may craft during your interview preparation or during your interviews. For example, I know a Web content developer who landed her job, in part, because during her interview she tactfully suggested winning ways that her target organization could use to improve its Web site. Also, see the "Blow Away Your Competition" box on page 168.

➤ Incorporate into your answers plenty of specific examples of your successes that parallel the demands of your target job. This will be easy if you memorize some of your biggest successes before the interview. In addition to citing your on-the-job and academic successes, you could also cite successes from volunteer work or your contributions to professional organizations, jury duty, the PTA, or any other important organizations. If you are a recent grad, emphasize your knowledge of the latest developments in your field.

➤ Exploit any common ground that you share with your interviewer. It may sound hokey, but it's true: people tend to like people with whom they share something in common, whether it's a hometown, a mutual friend, or unbridled passion for Tibetan dance.

➤ Take notes during the interview or check your list of questions. If there's a question you didn't anticipate, think it over before answering. If you need to, say something like," I need just a moment to think that over."

➤ If you're asked about a skill you lack, admit it—don't lie. But after you acknowledge your lack of a credential, quickly mention a similar credential that you do offer and emphasize that you are a fast learner, then give an example of how you have previously demonstrated this skill. As one hiring manager advises: "Don't just say that you haven't done X and leave it at that. Give me something to work with—some reason to think that you will be able and willing to rise to the occasion."

➤ If you face a firing squad —I mean a panel interview—focus on each interviewer as he or she asks a question, then move down the line to other panelists.

Hot Tip

Special Strategies for Phone or Skype Interviews

- **Be serious.** Treat phone and Skype interviews just as seriously as face-to-face interviews.

- **Know thy interviewers.** When you are invited to a phone or Skype interview, ask for the name and title of your interviewer(s). Immediately write down this information and the scheduled time for the interview.

- **Provide your résumé.** A few days before your interview, check that each potential interviewer has received the résumé and other materials, such as your success portfolio, that you sent him/her. Consider including in your materials a photograph of yourself dressed professionally and posed in a professional setting.

- **What's in a name?** If your interviewer will be Skyped, create a Skype user name that sounds professional, if you don't already have one. (Warning: User names like "studmuffin1" probably won't win you any points with your interviewers.)

- **Practice . . . practice . . . practice . . .** A few days before your interview, check that your Skype technology works and that you have all necessary Skype codes to connect with your interviewer(s). Also, collect a telephone number you can use to reach your interviewer(s) and vice versa in case problems arise with your Skype connection.

  Also, tape yourself speaking on Skype and practice Skyping with your trusted advisors in order to: (1) identify how to strategically position your Skype camera; (2) pose yourself so that you will look natural, comfortable, and professional, and give appropriate eye-contact to your interviewers, and be framed correctly by the camera during the interview; (3) arrange the lighting in your room so that you will be illuminated correctly.

  Warning: Any movie camera can flatten the affect of the person being filmed. So use your pre-interview practice to help you determine how to convey yourself on camera with the appropriate level of animation.

- **Neatness matters.** Clean up and organize the work area where you will be photographed by the Skype camera! (No one wants to hire a potential hoarder!)

- **Primp for success.** Dress for Skype sessions just as professionally as you would for in-person interviews.

- **Ditch cell phones.** If your interview will be conducted by phone, use a landline rather than a cell phone that may lose its connection or create static that will make you sound like you are being interviewed from the bottom of the ocean.

- **Hunker down in your bunker.** Shortly before your interview begins, prepare your interview room by suspending call waiting, unplugging all phones besides your interview phone as well as alarm clocks, TVs, radios, and other potentially noisy devises in the room.

  Remove all other people and pets from the room, and hermetically seal yourself inside the room with DO NOT DISTURB signs prominently displayed on all doors to the room. If by chance, your doorbell rings, during the interview, ignore it. (This is no time to visit with the neighborhood welcome wagon or negotiate with the repo man!)

- **Be punctual.** "Arrive" at your interview early, in case your interviewers contact you early or your equipment fails.

- **Prepare for liftoff!** Clear your desk and strategically position on your desk your telephone, résumé, the description of your target job, any terse notes that might be helpful, and a pad and pen for note-taking. It is usually fine to jot down a few notes during job interviews or quickly check reference materials as warranted, but if your interview is Skyped, only turn away from the camera if it is absolutely necessary. (Interviewers do not want to watch the top of your head as you scramble through notes!)

- **Be friendly.** When you introduce yourself to your interviewers, sound friendly, enthusiastic, and smile even if you are only talking on the phone without Skype. This is important because your voice and tone will convey in your smile.

- **No slouching!** Maintain good but natural posture throughout your interview. The more confident your posture is, the more confident and authoritative your voice will sound (and the better you will look on Skype). Write down the name of each interviewer as he or she introduces himself or herself. If possible, try to match each interviewer to their name (particularly the most senior interviewer), so that you will be able to track who you are talking to throughout the interview.

- **Don't blather on.** Because you and your interviewer(s) will be deprived of the telling physical cues evident during face-to-face interactions, pause occasionally to give your interviewer opportunities to change conversational directions, if they so desire. As you answer questions, occasionally ask your interviewers if he or she would like further clarification or more information about particular issues at hand.

- **Fill in the silences.** If your interviewers pause and thereby produce extended silence on the line, offer segue comments if appropriate, such as, "you may be interested to know that . . ." or "I just wanted to mention that the announcement for the opening emphasizes x skills, and my experience in that includes . . ." or "I noticed in today's newspaper a story that relates to what we are discussing . . . ."

- **Check in during silences.** If you must pause to consider a question before answering it, say "Excuse me, but I must think about this question for a moment . . . ." That way, your interviewer won't suspect that you killed your phone connection—either accidentally or intentionally.

- **Give the personal touch.** As you answer questions, occasionally address your interviewer by name, as do guests on radio interviews. For example, "Well Mr. Smith, I think that . . . ."

- **Engage interviewers.** Don't fixate on your own screen image during Skype interviews. Instead, focus on your interviewers when they speak, and look into your webcam when you speak to give your interviewers eye contact.

- **Don't "step on" your interviewers.** Accommodate potential time delays by making sure that your interviewers have stopped talking before you respond to their questions and by speaking slowly.

- **Follow-up.** Immediately after your phone interview is finished, follow up just as you would on an in-person interview by providing any requested references and other materials, and ending thank-you notes to your interviewers.

Your Close

When your interview ends, offer a parting salvo that summarizes your key credentials. Then say, point blank, "I'd like to work here, and if offered the job, I would accept it." That way, you will assure your interviewer of your fire-in-the-belly state for the opening. This is important because I know of some hiring managers who only hire applicants who provide such assurance.

Collect the business cards of everyone who interviewed you. Feel free to ask your interviewers how many other applicants are being considered for the opening. But, most important, ask your interviewers when they expect to make a decision. That way, you will know when you should call to follow up in case you don't hear from them. Also, ask your interviewer whether the agency's snail mail is slowed by security screens. This information will help you decide whether to send your thank-you note by snail mail or e-mail.

Blow Away Your Competition! I know a federal human resources (HR) specialist who was invited to an interview for a very appealing but highly competitive job. During the interview, her interviewer mentioned that the hiring agency was having trouble motivating employees who lacked promotion potential.

Even though the interviewer did not solicit a solution to the problem, the HR specialist developed a creative problem-solving plan after the interview and then presented it during a follow-up interview. By contrast, all of her competitors had either ignored the problem altogether or had proposed pat, obvious solutions.

The HR specialist was offered the job immediately after her interview. She was later told by her interviews that her success was largely due to her problem-solving initiative. To similarly stand out of the pack, ask your interviewer to identify some of the big challenges currently facing the hiring office. If you can provide a thoughtful solution right away, do so. Otherwise, concisely sketch out your approach in your postinterview thank-you letter or your next round of interviews.

Some Interview Don'ts

Some rules should go without needing to be said, but I'll say them anyway because many applicants ignore them.

➤ Don't be late to your interview.

➤ Don't leave your cell phone or BlackBerry on during your interview.

➤ Don't forget to listen to your interviewer(s) and don't talk too much. As one hiring manager put it, "When I interview people, I ask myself whether I would want to spend lots of time with this person." No one wants to be hermetically sealed in meetings with an unstoppable talker.

➤ Don't be negative about anyone or anything.

➤ Don't mention your personal problems.

➤ Don't slam the selection process, no matter how many hoops you were forced to jump through. Don't express doubt about whether you would take the job, if given the choice.

➤ Don't curse and don't use sexist language. One federal applicant recently nixed his chances by referring to his female interviewers as "you gals."

➤ Don't act annoyed if the interviewer is delayed or interrupted, no matter how disgusted you are.

➤ Don't lie or try to fake skills that you don't have. For example, an applicant whose résumé boasted of fluent French recently lost out on an overseas job because she responded with a deer-in-headlights stare to a basic interview question asked in French.

➤ Don't reveal that you are a loose cannon by admitting to breaking rules in previous jobs.

➤ Don't act desperate, no matter how desperate you feel.

➤ Don't challenge the judgment of the interviewer or be argumentative about anything.

➤ Don't answer questions with empty responses such as, "That is a tough one" or with mere yes or no responses. If an answer doesn't occur to you right away, pause for a moment and think about your response. If you need clarification of the question, ask for it.

➤ Don't bring anyone with you to the interview. The blooper-of-the-century award goes to an applicant who brought her mother. When the interviewer asked the applicant to identify her goals, she responded, "To move out of my mother's house." (I suspect that the applicant's mother shared that same goal for the applicant!)

> **Take Note!** _____
>
> *A Job Interview That Changed History*
>
> Know what sunk Senator Edward Kennedy's presidential aspirations? Not Kennedy's fatal car accident in Chappaquiddick, Massachusetts, in 1969. Rather, what doomed Kennedy's presidential bid was an interview that he gave during his campaign for the 1980 Democratic nomination during which he was asked why he wanted to be president—the political equivalent of the "Why should we hire you?" job interview question. In response, Kennedy fumbled, stammered, and then petered out altogether.
>
> Kennedy's unpersuasive answer is widely cited as the last nail in the coffin of his presidential possibilities. If you are ever similarly stricken by hoof-in-mouth disease during a job interview, at least be grateful that your performance will not be replayed over and over again on national television.

➤ No matter how chummy your interviewer may act or how comfortable she or he may make you feel, don't get lulled into a false sense of friendship. Don't spill any information about yourself that you wouldn't print on your résumé.

Guerilla Interviewing Tactics

Most hiring managers who conduct job interviews are not full-time interviewers; they are full-time managers and technical experts. And sadly, in many cases, their lack of interviewing expertise shows.

Many interviewers, for example, will fail to prepare questions or neglect to read your résumé before your interview. Some interviewers will prattle on about their own rise to the top without asking you about your credentials. Others may ask irrelevant questions that recall the Barbara Walters's "What type of tree would you like to be?" school of interviewing.

If you don't seize control of such lousy interviews, your interviewers will—through no fault of your own—be left without a clear, let alone a favorable, impression of you. Here are a couple of ways to rescue such wayward interviewers and score your break-out performance:

➤ If your interviewer is endlessly prattling about the job without asking you any questions, say something like, "If I understand the position correctly, you are looking for X, Y, and Z skills. May I illustrate how my background reflects these requirements?"

➤ When the interviewer asks you whether you have any questions, say: "Yes, I do have several questions. But first, if you don't mind, I would like to tell you a little about some of my important qualifications that we haven't yet had a chance to cover."

➤ At the end of the interview, say, "I just want to mention before I leave that there are three main reasons why my background has prepared me to contribute to this organization. . . . "

The Fear Factor: Sidestepping Employers' Secret Fears

So you think that looking for a job is a scary proposition? Well, here's a shocker: Many hiring managers are just as afraid of the hiring process as you are.

What are hiring managers so terrified of? The possibility of making a bad hiring decision—a bad hiring decision that they will have to live with for a looooooooooong time.

The fear of selecting the wrong job applicant is especially strong in government, where it is particularly hard to fire employees. Federal hiring managers may literally have to live with their bad hires until death do them part. This principle was recently underscored by a federal executive after I asked him whether he had ever made any bad hiring decisions during his 25 years in government. In response, he offered to introduce me to his staffing mistakes, "They all work right over there," he said, pointing to a cubicle farm that encircles his office.

But as pivotal as a hiring manager's fears may be, they are almost never openly acknowledged during the selection process. Indeed, the hiring manager's secret insecurities are like the proverbial elephant in the room—the huge, dominating presence that is carefully avoided without being discussed.

Even though you probably won't be directly asked to address a hiring managers' secret fears, you can head them off before they cause you trouble. Table 15-2 provides profiles of the five most common types of problem employees and strategies for reassuring interviewers that you will not present such problems.

Providing Your References

Offer your interviewer a list of at least three references.

Compile the Selection

Select references that are:

> **Respected.** Your references should be people of professional stature, not your bowling buddies. If you have contacts at your target agency, or if you know anyone in common with your interviewer(s) who would vouch for you, cite that person. You will thereby go a long way toward proving that you're the zero-risk applicant. Interviewers generally trust references from people who they know more than references from strangers.

> **Enthusiastic.** Before you ask a contact to serve as a reference, ask whether the individual can give you an enthusiastic endorsement. If your contact expresses any reluctance or hedging, don't use the person as a reference. After all, if you detect ambivalence, so will the hiring managers. As one hiring manager recalls, "When I call the former employer of a job applicant, I always ask them if they would hire the applicant again. If the reference pauses at all before responding, I know what their true answer is, and I won't hire the applicant."

> **Prepared.** Don't assume that your references will be able to spontaneously describe why he or she thinks highly of you. Prepare the person to do so by giving

him or her your résumé and reviewing your salient qualifications. You may also remind your references of projects you completed for them and the positive feedback they provided you on those projects. To this end, give your references copies of the write-ups for awards or positive performance evaluations that they gave you. Also, describe to your references your target jobs and which aspects of your background you would like them to emphasize. In particular, if you suspect that the hiring manager has any hesitations about your credentials, ask your references—if appropriate—to provide hiring managers with reassurance that will defuse those hesitations.

> **Accessible.** Don't use references who are on vacation, irresponsible about returning calls, or otherwise potentially unreachable when you need them. If, for example, your reference is yak-riding through Nepal, don't list him. Also, confirm your references' contact information before you give it to the hiring managers. I have heard of finalists getting rejected simply because their interviewers reached the references of other worthy applicants before reaching theirs.

Blow Away Your Competition! One of my clients learned through the grapevine that his interviewer suspected he would not be assertive enough to carry out some of the management tasks required for his target job. In response, my client strategically defused his hiring manager's hesitation by asking his references to artfully weave into their reference his ability to get tough when necessary. The result: He got the job.

In compiling the list of references, you may encounter some problems. For example, suppose you don't want to list your current boss as a reference but your interviewer asks you for a reference from your current boss? Respond to such requests by stating that you would prefer not to tell your current boss about your job search until you have a firm offer. Also, you may, if appropriate, cite or provide the positive performance evaluations and/or bonuses that a current or previous boss has given you, and use a current or former colleague or another manager as a reference instead of your current boss.

On the CD...

This book's CD features copies of my *Washington Post* articles on how to answer the "What are your weaknesses?" interview question and how to prepare your success portfolio for interviews. It also features a tip sheet for discussing your weaknesses, a tip sheet for answering the standard "Why do you want to work here?" question, lists of frequently asked interview questions and potential questions for you to ask interviewers, an interview preparation checklist, and other cheat sheets to help you ace your interviews.

Presentation

Present your references in a neat list. One way to do this is to arrange them in a table. (See Figure 15-2 on page 176 for an example.) Your name should be prominently printed at the top of the page, followed by the table. The column headings should be "Name," "Relationship to Me," and "Contact Info." Note that each "Relationship to Me" description should define the reference's connection to you, as well as cite some positive aspects of your credentials that your reference can confirm. And be sure to provide the current contact information for each of your references.

TABLE 15-2   Proving That You are a Problem-Solver, Not a Problem

Profile of Problem Employee	How to Prove That You Are a Problem-Solver
The Wolf in Sheep's Clothing: This type of employee looks great on paper, interviews well, and appears well adjusted. But lurking beneath a presentable veneer is a sociopath who lies, cheats or steals, or behaves otherwise unstably or unreliably. Because of hiring managers' fears of saddling themselves with a wolf in sheep's clothing, objective validation of an applicant's mental stability may even trump professional qualifications. Many hiring managers have told me, "I would rather hire someone who is technically mediocre but who I know is sane and reliable than an off-the-street applicant who is a first-rate technician but whose personality is an unknown quantity."	1. If you have inside contacts, name them in your cover letter, application, and interviews. 2. Arrange for your inside contact to vouch for you as early in the selection process as possible. (I have heard many hiring managers profess regret that an inside contact endorsed a candidate too late—after the candidate's application had already been rejected.) 3. Even if you do not have inside contacts, during your interviews, mention the names and titles of people who will provide you with exemplary references. 4. See "Prepping Your References."
The Team Wrecker: A government employee who doesn't work well with others is usually an employee who doesn't work out at all. In the words of one hiring manager. "When I hire someone, I want to know that they are not going to run out of the office crying because someone looked at them the wrong way and leave me in the lurch right before a critical deadline."	Cite examples of your team and leadership successes, including team awards, contributions to important workgroups, and elected positions in professional organizations. Show your interviewer thank-you letters or e-mails from managers, staffers, customers, or stakeholders. Also mention that you take suggestions/criticism well. Students: Cite your contributions to group projects, team sports, musical groups, theater projects, school papers, volunteer work, or your participation in Outward Bound–type programs. You may also mention how your experience in a large family taught you how to work with varied personalities or how your travels increased your cultural sensitivity.
The Outshiner: Virtually every hiring supervisor wants to hire staffers who will help improve their stature without outshining them. But the Outshiner diminishes the stature of supervisors by hogging the limelight and/or going over their heads.	Mention that you understand that your first loyalty is to your supervisor, and that you would keep him/her informed of important developments that warrant his/her attention. Cite examples of how you have flagged hot-button issues in a timely manner for your previous supervisors, if possible.
The Lazy Bones: This type of employee needs constant nagging, hand-holding, and prodding to get anything done.	Convince hiring managers of your dogged work ethic by: 1. Citing your work ethic if you are asked about your strengths or what you are proud of. Say something like, "I consider myself reasonably smart, though I am not the smartest person in the world. But I won't let anyone outwork me. I am the employee who will be here until 10:00 PM, if necessary. And I have a record for reliability. I am my office's Cal Ripken."

Profile of Problem Employee	How to Prove That You Are a Problem-Solver
	2. Citing projects that you completed with little supervision and instances when you took the initiative, put in long hours, and did what was needed to get the job done. . . no matter what. 3. Citing your record of meeting deadlines and multi-tasking many projects. 4. If you're a student or a recent grad: citing your independent projects, your demanding electives, and your record of simultaneously working toward a degree and managing a grueling work schedule, if appropriate. 5. Asking your hiring manager to consider hiring you as a temporary employee for an initial 90-day trial period, and then at the end of this trial period, converting you into a permanent employee if you measure up. (Agencies can accomplish such conversions relatively easily.) This suggestion will provide employers with a no-risk option for evaluating you. Moreover, because you will probably be the sole candidate to propose a trial period, you will stand out from the pack.
The Pointy-Headed Pontificator: This type of employee might as well wear a sign across their forehead that reads, "I don't do projects." The Pointy-Headed Pontificator has no specialized knowledge, contributes little to tangible work products, and fancies him/herself as decision-making management material: A thinker, not a doer. Though most managers do value critical thinking skills, their main, burning desire is to hire go-getters who get things done.	Don't describe yourself as a "big picture generalist" who is above getting your hands dirty. Instead, bill yourself as the "go-to person," the super charged, indispensable, unflappable professional who managers consult when they need a question answered, a problem solved, a customer satisfied—immediately.

It's Not Over When the Interview Is Over

Question: What is the first thing you should do when you get home from an interview?

Answer: Write a thank-you letter to everyone who interviewed you.

It may seem unfair that you are obliged to thank an interviewer who hasn't really helped you yet. Indeed, if you are like most job applicants, you think that your interviewer should thank you for traipsing down to the office, submitting to a battery of questions, and perhaps even graciously agreeing to itemize some of your weaknesses during your interview. But, like it or not, your fate hinges on the decision of your interviewer. And by thanking the individual or members of the panel, you may win them over. This is because:

➤ Very few applicants bother to write thank-you letters. Therefore, your thank-you letter will help you stand out from the pack.

Take Note!

An Interview Success Story: Heidi McAllister, Environmental Educator

While living in Mexico, Heidi McAllister, a U.S. citizen, nailed a federal job in Washington, DC, solely through her application and a phone interview; she never even had a face-to-face interview with a hiring manager. Heidi explains here how she learned how to give a killer phone interview.

"I had been living in Mexico and working as a consultant in environmental education mostly to the Mexican government for about 13 years when I started applying for jobs back in the United States. Soon after beginning my job search, I had about six phone interviews. All of them seemed to go smoothly, but none led to a job offer. As the rejection letters rolled in, it became obvious that something was wrong with my interviewing skills.

"So I researched interviewing strategies and soon realized that I hadn't been selling myself enough. I know why I had been holding back: I am self-deprecating; I like to poke fun at myself. So tooting my own horn doesn't come naturally to me.

"But my research showed me how I could sell myself without coming off as egocentric. All I had to do was cite concrete examples of my achievements that matched the requirements of my target job. No need to sound pompous, haughty, or conceited; I just had to be factual and specific. I used this technique for the first time during my phone interview for a federal job as an Environment Program and Training Specialist. For example, in response to the question, 'What are the necessary components of an environmental education program?' I ticked off the countries where I had helped design environmental programs and described the sponsoring organizations, target audiences and components of my programs, and the positive feedback they earned.

"I previously would have answered this question by naming the essential components of environmental education programs. But I think the adage 'actions speak louder than words' applies here. By showing that I had taken action—that is, set up successful environmental education programs—I impressed my interviewers more than if I had merely talked about what an environmental education should be.

"Likewise, I incorporated into many of my other interview answers specific examples of my achievements as well as objective evidence of my success. I was able to quickly identify these examples because I had studied my résumé just before the phone interview began and because I could quickly glance at my résumé, which was strategically positioned in front of me throughout the session. I know that my interviewing strategy worked because, within several weeks, I was offered the job, which I enthusiastically accepted."

➤ A thank-you letter will remind the interviewer of your strengths. As one hiring manager put it, "If a letter is right in front of me, it is a tangible nudge that forces me to think about the candidate again." Otherwise, an interviewer who screens many candidates can, soon after the interview, easily forget the credentials of even outstanding candidates.

➤ By thanking your interviewers, you'll prove that you really want the job and that you're polite, conscientious, and demonstrate followthrough—all prized traits.

Hot Tip

Deflecting Your Liabilities. What are your unspoken liabilities—aspects of your application that you suspect may, rightly or wrongly, turn off interviewers? Perhaps, for example, you sense that you're perceived as too young, too old, an outsider, too entrenched, or a job-hopper.

Instead of letting your interviewer's unspoken fears silently sabotage your application, you could address them gingerly or obliquely. For example, suppose you find yourself sitting across from an interviewer who is significantly younger than you. You could say something like, "You may think that, because I have a significant amount of experience . . . that I might be rigid and might not take direction well. But I want to assure you that I understand that you would be my supervisor and that it would be my obligation to support you. I am certainly prepared to accommodate and profit by any approaches that you may suggest. I also want to emphasize that I am energetic and flexible."

Here are some other tips:

- Explain how the combination of your knowledge of the latest techniques in your field and with your extensive experience make you a uniquely well-rounded applicant.

- Stay current in your field. (Sorry, you can't prepare for this one for the last minute.) No matter what your age is, you will go a long way toward increasing your marketability by emphasizing your knowledge of the latest computer applications, management trends, policies, regulations, and overall approaches in your field and the methods you use to stay current. (Remember: you don't want to come across like the IT expert who stopped learning about new software after mastering DOS.)

  Your methods for staying current in your field may, for example, include contributing to professional organizations, providing training, receiving or giving mentoring, taking online or brick-and-mortar classes, publishing articles or books, obtaining certifications, or completing self-study. Also, if possible, provide success stories about how your use of the latest tools or techniques in your field together with your varied and extensive experience helped your current organization operate more efficiently.

- Refrain from including your entire work history in your résumé. Remember: Federal job applications only require applicants to cover their last ten years of experience. Only include much older experience if it directly relates to your target job.

- Most hiring managers care only about applicants' latest experience anyway. So if your résumé waxes endlessly about decades of ancient experience, you will probably only emphasize your age and bore harried hiring managers without advancing your case.

- Ensure that your dress and grooming don't reinforce negative stereotypes about older people. (Sorry, I meant "more experienced" people.) For interviews, dress neatly and wear new clothes and contemporary styles. (Hint: if your interview outfit is the same vintage as John Travolta's *Saturday Night Fever* suit, it is overdue for an update.) Also, before each interview, get a haircut and if you color your hair, do so professionally.

- Reassure hiring managers that you enjoy working, would stay on the job for the long haul, and have no plans to retire any time soon, if you are at or near retirement age.

- Ask your references to describe you to your potential employers as a high-energy, forward-thinking professional who offers a wealth of valuable experience.

- If appropriate, discuss in your interview your experience in shattering gender or racial glass ceilings. But shield yourself from hiring managers' political and religious biases by excluding your standing on either topic.

References for Joe Anyone		
Name and Title	**Relationship to Me**	**Contact Information**
Jane Doe, Deputy Director of EPA's Office of Toxic Sludge	Has been my supervisor at EPA since January 2005. She can verify my technical knowledge of toxic sludge, my ability to write reader-friendly reports on technical topics, my project management skills, and my ability to meet tight deadlines. She awarded me a merit-based promotion in January 2011.	Work: (123) 123-4567 Cell: (111) 123-4567 Email: JaneDoe@email.com Please note that Jane Doe will be unreachable from August 1 to August 7.
Jack Fox, Chief of External Communications at EPA's Office of Toxic Sludge	During 2011, he approved dozens of press releases I wrote about new toxic sludge regulations, and delivered two keynote speeches that I wrote for him on new methods for mitigating toxic sludge to large audiences at annual meetings of toxic sludge associations.	Work: (111) 354-6789 Cell: (101) 123-4567 Email: JackFox@email.com
Harry Smith, Professor of Earth Sciences at Smarty Pants University	Was my professor of two upper-level hydrology courses I took in 2010 toward my master's in geology at Smarty Pants University. I earned an A- in each course.	Work: (000) 123-4567 Cell: (001) 123-4567 Email: HarrySmith@email.com

Figure 15-2 Example format for providing references.

Content and Format

A thank-you letter should be brief and zippy, no more than several paragraphs. It should:

1. Thank the interviewer for his or her time and trouble.

2. Summarize what you discussed in the interview.

3. Reaffirm your interest in the position.

4. Concisely summarize relevant qualifications.

5. Add any important information that you neglected to mention during the interview.

6. Be error free. Spell-check and proofread your letter, and then get a second opinion on it.

A thank-you letter sent by overnight delivery generally makes a stronger and better impression than e-mails that are almost instantly read, deleted, and forgotten. But speed does count—your thank-you should arrive before your interviewers make a decision. So, if your target agency's snail mail is delayed by security screens, consider personally dropping off your thank-you letter the day after your interview.

Alternatively, if you have no other options, e-mail your thank-you letter immediately after your interview. (But as one hiring manager observed, "E-mails are just one step above doing nothing.")

Note that your thank-you may be formatted as a printed business letter or be a handwritten card in neurotically neat penmanship. See Figures 15-3 and 15-4 for samples of thank-you letters.

A Final Checklist for Interview Success

The interview is critical. Be sure you've checked off all the items on this list.

_____   Ask for the name and title of each interviewer when you're invited to the interview.

_____   Research your interviewers via Google, social networking sites and *The Yellow Book*.

_____   Research your target organization: review its Web site, particularly its annual report, strategic plan, and recent press releases. Also, search major publications for recent coverage of your target organization's hot-button issues, as discussed in Chapter 13, and try to identify obstacles and problems that your target organization may be confronting and ways you could help the organization conquer them.

_____   Craft answers to common interview questions. (See list on CD.)

_____   Prepare a few questions to ask your interviewer. (See list on CD.)

_____   Role-play interviews with as many friends and colleagues as possible.

_____   Pack your briefcase with a pad, pen, and success portfolio containing your résumé, business cards, list of references, and documents that validate your ability to succeed on your target job.

_____   Prepare your references to be contacted by your interviewer.

_____   Choose your interview outfit.

_____   Plan to arrive at your interview location early, to leave time for traffic jams, getting cleared into the building, and finding your interview office in a large building.

_____   After the interview, send a thank-you letter or e-mail.

If you're rejected from your target job, ask your interviewer for feedback on how you may improve your interview skills. Also, occasionally contact any interviewers who are encouraging to you, and inquire about any additional upcoming openings they may have.

May 1, 2008

Mr. John Doe
Office of Legislative Affairs
National Science Foundation
4201 Wilson Blvd., Suite 1245
Arlington, VA 22230

Dear John:

Thanks so much for explaining to me the ins-and-outs of working at NSF. I would like to reaffirm my enthusiasm for the Legislative Affairs Specialist opening.

I would be very excited to contribute to the fascinating and important scientific issues addressed by NSF and to work in the agency's uniquely academic environment. Moreover, the creative possibilities and *esprit-de-corps* offered by joining a new "class" of Legislative Affairs Specialists would be extremely appealing.

I greatly appreciate the time you took to explain the challenges of the job. I believe that I am prepared for the task; I am experienced in handling ever-changing priorities and deadlines.

I trust that all my references will confirm that I have the skills you seek. In particular, Jane Smith, the Legislative Director of the Mine Safety and Health Administration, can offer insights into my adaptability, which I understand is an important job requirement. (Jane's work number is 111-012-2345)

Again, I would welcome the opportunity to join your staff, and I very much appreciate your time and consideration.

Sincerely,

Jane Q. Public

Figure 15-3 Sample thank-you letter: business format.

Dear Mr. Harris:

It was a pleasure discussing the opening for a Public Affairs Officer and meeting Jack Gold and Cindy Smith. Your energetic presentation, your office's congenial atmosphere and your office's many new dynamic programs added to my enthusiasm for the opening.

As I mentioned when we met, I have four years of experience producing the same type of employee newsletter that Public Affairs will soon launch. In addition, my editorial experience at ABC News and my writing experience at MSNBC.com would allow me to make immediate contributions to your multimedia outreach campaign.

My cell phone number is (123) 123-4567, and my e-mail is JHarris@e-mail.com. I hope I will have the opportunity to contribute to the Office of Public Affairs. And thanks again for your personal attention.

Sincerely,

Sam Murphy

Figure 15-4 Text of sample hand-written thank-you card.

16

Commanding a Top-Dollar Salary

*"By negotiating the salary of my first federal job, and successfully campaigning
for promotions I received since then, I increased my total take-home pay for the last 15+ years
by more than $250,000, not even counting resulting increases in my pension."*
—LILY MADELEINE WHITEMAN, AUTHOR OF THIS BOOK

So, you've received an offer for a federal job. As Sally Field might say, "They like you! They really like you!"

The mere utterance of an offer from a hiring manager may fill your nervous system with happy hormones and send you into raptures of relief. But don't let the thrill of your victory compel you to accept an unacceptable salary. Remember: Many employers in all sectors—including the federal sector—offer new hires the lowest salaries they can get away with. That's simply how the game is played.

But the federal government has even more leverage over most new recruits than do other types of employers. That's because the typical federal job seeker wrongly believes that federal salaries are nonnegotiable. Such unfortunates usually cave to lowball salaries without so much as asking, "Is this salary negotiable?" They may thereby unwittingly sacrifice hundreds of thousands of dollars in salary over the course of their careers.

"We reward top executives at the agency with a unique incentive program. Money."

Don't Buy into the Myth That Federal Salaries Are Non-Negotiable

The real deal is that salaries for many federal jobs—like those of private-sector jobs—are flexible. But the raw reality is that you are unlikely to ever receive your full worth without asking for it. Even if the meek shall inherit the earth, they shan't earn a decent salary without negotiating for it. In order to help backfill for the ongoing federal retirement wave, many federal organizations have adopted new flexibilities on pay and benefits. This means that the bargaining power of federal selectees is currently particularly high.

This chapter introduces the various pay scales used by federal agencies and then reviews the tried-and-true methods for negotiating top-dollar salaries. I know that these negotiating methods work because I have personally used them many times, as have my clients—much to the benefit of their bank accounts.

CHAPTER 16   Commanding a Top-Dollar Salary

Take Note! _____

Look up the Salaries of Current Feds

Several tantalizing sites reveal the salaries of current feds. For example, you may peek at the salaries of employees of federal agencies by Googling "Asbury Park Press" and "federal salaries" (then scroll down the page to the link to Federal Employees.) And you may check out the salaries of congressional staffers at http://www.legistorm.com.

Show Me the Money: Federal Pay Scales

A variety of pay scales operate in federal agencies. Most of these pay scales incorporate annual cost-of-living increases from 2 to 5 percent. In addition, many feds receive annual bonuses. (But, before you start drooling, be aware that the average federal bonus equals 1.6 percent of annual salary.) Also, some pay scales provide locality pay for feds working in cities where the cost of living is high and offer feds the option of creating flexible spending accounts for their health needs and certain other needs, and commuting feds may receive free metro tickets or free or discounted parking. Additional possible perks include on-site daycare and workout facilities.

Listed here are the most common federal pay scales. To access current salary tables for these and other pay scales, enter the term "salary tables" into the search window at http://www.opm.gov.

General Schedule System

General Schedule (GS) jobs are graded from GS-1 to GS-15. Each GS grade has 10 steps. Salaries rise with each increase in grade and each step. Entry-level jobs are usually graded through GS-9; mid-career jobs are graded GS-11 to GS-13; senior-level jobs are graded GS-14 and GS-15, and also include all jobs in the senior executive service (SES).

Feds working in cities where the cost of living is particularly high receive locality pay, which can boost pay by as much as 12 percent over base pay rates.

Most feds in the GS system receive a grade increase after satisfactorily completing their probationary period or their one-year federal anniversary. Thereafter, they automatically receive a step increase every one, two, or three years, depending on their position on their career ladder. (For more info, type "within-grade increases" into the search window at http://www.opm.gov.)

Feds are also eligible for merit-based promotions consisting of a grade or step increase. The following rules govern such merit-based promotions:

➤ Above the GS-5 grade, feds must remain in each grade and step for at least one year before being promoted to the next grade or step. (But currently, the federal government is considering eliminating this one-year time-in-grade requirement.)

➤ Feds generally cannot skip grades as they advance up the career ladder. (An exception: GS-14s can move directly into SES jobs without first landing GS-15 jobs.)

➤ To rise above the ceiling grade of his or her current job, a fed must convince supervisors to raise his or her ceiling or move into another job with a higher ceiling.

These regulations frequently work like speed bumps on federal careers. Moreover, employees do not necessarily receive merit-based promotions after fulfilling their time-in-grade or step requirements; they frequently wait longer than minimum waiting periods for such promotions.

Although the GS pay system is the most common pay system for federal white-collar employees, more and more federal agencies are abandoning it.

Pay Banding Systems

Most agencies and jobs in the excepted service are on "pay banding" systems that consolidate many pay grades into fewer, more flexible pay bands. (Agencies and jobs in the excepted service are listed at http://www.makingthedifference.org/federaljobs/exceptedservice.shtml.)

Pay banding systems generally pay better than the GS system. But many pay banding systems have replaced automatic raises with raises that reward employees for good performance. In addition, it's generally easier (though still relatively hard) to fire pay banded employees than to fire GSers.

High-Demand Professionals

Special, particularly well-paying salary rates apply to some high-demand professionals, including some IT specialists, financial services executives, doctors and other medical practitioners, scientists, and engineers.

Senior Executive Service (SES)

If you're new to the SES, your hiring agency should top your previous salary. Some agencies always offer new SESers a set percentage increase (usually 10 to 15 percent) over the person's previous salary; other agencies are free of such restrictions.

But SES salaries vary from agency to agency. Agencies that have been certified by the Office of Personnel Management for adopting performance-based appraisal systems for SESers can pay higher SES salaries than can uncertified agencies. The performance-based systems of certified agencies reward high performers with raises but eliminate automatic annual raises. The SESers receive annual bonuses between 5 and 20 percent of basic pay. Also, SESers accrue eight hours of vacation time every two weeks.

Law Enforcers

A patchwork of laws has created differences in salaries and benefits for law enforcers across the government. What's more, the types of jobs that are classified as law enforcers vary inconsistently. Therefore, some security professionals who do law enforcement work are not officially classified as such.

Blue-Collar Workers

These people are covered by the Federal Wage System.

Variations in Salaries Among Agencies

It is important to understand that federal salaries for the same job can vary considerably from agency to agency. And as more and more agencies abandon the GS system for their own pay systems, such variation is increasing.

Here are a few tips. Agencies in the excepted service generally pay better than agencies in the civil service; many of my clients have received large pay increases just by moving from the competitive service to the excepted service. In addition, particularly high salaries tend to be paid by agencies addressing corporate finance because they compete with Wall Street to recruit staffers. These agencies include the Securities and Exchange Commission, the Federal Reserve, the FDIC, the Commodities Futures Trading Commission, and some Treasury Department agencies.

Salaries of Congressional Staffers

Each congressional office and committee establishes its own policies on pay, student loan repayments, and leave. Therefore, salaries and benefits for the same job may vary considerably from office to office.

Most offices only allow staff to take vacations when Congress is not in session. And staffers are frequently expected to remain on the job through late-night sessions. Some positions are eligible for comp time and overtime pay; some are not.

Generally, congressional staff jobs pay much less and offer much less job security than do comparable jobs in federal agencies. Here are a few rules of thumb within those constraints:

1. Jobs on congressional committees usually pay better than jobs on the staffs of congressional members.

2. Jobs on Senate staffs tend to pay better than jobs on House staffs.

3. Most jobs in Congress offer less negotiating leeway than those in federal agencies. But any job may offer wiggle room. It never hurts to diplomatically ask hiring managers if they are willing to negotiate salary or offer tuition reimbursement, parking or metro tickets, or other benefits.

The Basics of Negotiating

Each vacancy announcement for an agency job on USAJOBS identifies a salary range for the opening. But how does a hiring agency determine what salary to offer you? Usually based on your salary history. For example:

> ➤ If you're currently employed, the hiring agency will usually match or best your current salary or a current, reasonable competing offer. Professionals who transfer from nonprofit jobs, congressional staff jobs, or other sectors that pay much less than federal agencies may get considerable salary bumps when moving to federal agencies. But conversely, professionals who transfer from corporations paying extravagant salaries may not fare quite as well.

Hot Tip

Promises. . . Promises. . . . Suppose your boss has promised you an impending promotion. But before fulfilling his promise to you, he announces that he will be leaving his current position—for whatever reason. Be sure to ask your current boss to make good on his promise before departing. This is important because your boss's replacement will be under no obligation to fulfill your current boss's promises, no matter how much you deserve the promotion.

➤ If you're currently unemployed, the hiring agency will, in many cases, match or best your most recent salary or a current and reasonable competing offer. The hiring agency will probably determine your current salary based on your most recent pay stub. But if possible, when the hiring agency requests this document from you, instead try to submit to the agency your most recent W-2 or 1099 tax form. Why? Because unlike your weekly pay stub, your tax forms will include any bonuses or overtime you received, thereby increasing your hiring agency's determination of your current salary.

➤ If you're a new college grad, the hiring agency will probably offer you its standard offer for recent grads, or match or best a current and reasonable competing offer. Here are the guidelines for standard offers for new graduates under the GS pay system:

➤ An applicant with a college degree but without any specialized experience in the field qualifies for a GS-5 position. But an applicant who has at least a B average or other desirable college credentials can expect to start at a GS-7 position.

➤ An applicant with a master's degree qualifies for at least a GS-9 position.

➤ An applicant with a Ph.D. qualifies for a GS-12 position.

If you're a recent high school grad with no work experience, you will qualify for GS-2 jobs. But if you have some work experience, you may start at the GS-3, GS-4, or GS-5 levels.

Here is an additional rule of thumb: The more work experience you have in addition to degrees, the higher grade you will probably land. But keep in mind that the hiring agency will probably offer you the lowest step in your grade level—unless you negotiate for a higher step.

Wiggle Room

Although you probably can't raise the ceiling of your opening's salary range, you probably can negotiate for a higher offer within your opening's salary range. Nevertheless, many job seekers accept a federal salary offer without negotiating—only to regret upon discovering that colleagues with comparable credentials are earning more than them; and grade increases are not necessarily granted frequently, and their pace generally declines as employees move up the federal career ladder.

The brutal truth is that you may be locked into your starting grade, or close to it, for a significant chunk of time. This possibility increases the importance of negotiating the highest starting salary that you can up front.

The Power Play: Preparation

The time between your receipt of an offer and your response to it is the only time during the selection process—and perhaps the only time during your career—when the tables are turned in your direction and you get to call the shots. Yes, until the salary negotiations began, the hiring agency ran the show and the selection process revolved entirely around its demands.

Finally, during salary negotiations, you can assert your salary and benefits needs, and the agency—temporarily rendered powerless—twists in the wind awaiting your next move. But don't get too excited. Once you accept or reject the offer, the tables will turn again. The natural order will return, and the hiring agency will once again wield the upper hand.

Salary-Boosting Research

Before you negotiate, improve your bargaining position by taking these actions:

1. Study the vacancy announcement for the opening and identify how your credentials exceed its requirements. Also, visit the career section of the hiring agency's Web site and the salary table on http://www.opm.gov/ that covers your job.

2. Get a competing salary offer from another employer in writing, if you can swing it. As previously mentioned, a hiring agency will usually match a current and reasonable competing offer from another employer. This is one of the best-kept secrets in government!

> **Hot Tip**
>
> During tough economic times, federal agencies still negotiate salaries. Nevertheless, austerity measures that may be implemented by public-sector employees (as well as by private-sector employees) during tough economic times may slow career climbs. Therefore, during tough economic times, new hires may remain at or near their starting salaries longer than usual. So, during such times, it is particularly important for applicants to optimize negotiating opportunities.

To get a competing offer, you might have to apply for jobs that you don't even want. Granted, this requires work. But, this strategy may boost your federal salary by thousands of dollars per year—not a bad potential payback for your efforts.

3. Get a copy of the classification standards used by the hiring agency to determine the grade level of the position. Access these documents by typing "classification standards" into the search window at http://www.opm.gov/. Alternatively, you can probably obtain a copy of the classification standards that apply to your opening from the agency contact person identified on its vacancy announcement.

4. Discuss your offer with any feds you know. Your federal contacts should be able to help you gauge the reasonableness of your offer. (Probably because federal salaries are part of the public record, they are generally not protected by the kind of "cone of silence" that protects private-sector salaries. So feds are relatively open about their salaries.)

Your Move: Begin the Negotiation

You get that call: you're offered the job. When you're selected for a federal job, the human resources (HR) officer will probably call you with a job offer. In response, express enthusiasm for the offer, but don't commit to it. Ask the HR officer to specify your salary offer, if she or he hasn't done so.

In response, say that you would like to clarify the offer because you would appreciate being considered for a higher salary. Ask, "Is this salary negotiable?" Based on my own negotiating experience and the experiences of countless numbers of my clients, these four words may literally be the most valuable words in your vocabulary. I know of many cases in which all the applicant did was ask whether the salary offer was negotiable, and bingo! The hiring agency significantly raised its salary offer.

You may also ask the HR officer about other benefits, such as student loan repayments and coverage of your moving expenses. (See negotiating checklist.)

Keep in mind that your selecting official probably has much more power to raise your offer than does the HR officer; in most cases, the HR officer's hands are tied. So if the HR officer doesn't respond to your negotiating invitation by referring you to the selecting official, ask the HR officer if you can discuss your offer with the selecting official.

It is always more effective to negotiate in person than over the telephone, where facial cues are unavailable. So if possible, make an appointment to discuss the position in person with the selecting official.

> **Hot Tip**
>
> **Body Language Speaks Volumes.** When you negotiate, convey confidence with your body language and speaking style. Sit in a slouch-free posture, maintain eye contact, keep your hands folded on your lap or the table, smile, suppress nervous/jittery mannerisms, and don't speak too fast no matter how eager you are to conclude your negotiations.

Revving Up for the Negotiations

Few people enjoy negotiating their salaries. It feels uncomfortable, undignified, and even somewhat unseemly—disturbingly similar to haggling over the price of a used car. But, distasteful though the negotiating process is, you owe it to yourself to advocate for what you deserve. Remember: If you don't ask for what you deserve, you probably won't get it.

You have probably worked hard to persuasively sell yourself throughout your hiring process. Now, don't sell yourself short during your salary negotiations. And for a few minutes of uncomfortable assertiveness, you may earn thousands of additional dollars or more per year. Isn't that worth a few minutes of discomfort? In other words, the fact that negotiating is uncomfortable is not a good enough reason to avoid negotiating. See Table 16-1 for some negotiating language.

TABLE 16-1	Negotiate Rather Than Demand
Ultimatum or Demand	**Negotiating Questions**
Thanks for your offer. But I need a much higher salary and reimbursement for my moving expenses to take the job.	I am so excited about the possibility of contributing my skills to this organization. But is there any flexibility or wiggle room in your salary offer and could your office help cover my moving expenses?
I appreciate your offer. But I'm afraid that compensation might be a deal-breaker.	I'm excited about this job. I'd like to work out an agreement that would make both of us feel great. Would it be possible for you to raise your salary offer? I think I deserve consideration on this because. . .

The Face-to-Face Meeting

Open your meeting with your hiring manager by briefly mentioning some of the reasons you were so pleased to receive an offer and how you would add value to the organization. Then go into negotiating mode. If you really do want this job, don't issue any ultimatums or deal-breaking demands. Instead, open the negotiation with a question and then proceed gingerly and gently.

No Flexibility

If, by chance, your hiring manager responds by stating that there is no flexibility in the offer, you may still negotiate. How? First, by emphasizing the concessions you are making. For example, mention that the job change would be just a lateral one for you; or that it requires you to sacrifice vacation, sick leave, or other benefits; or that it causes you to pay moving expenses or significantly raise your living costs.

Then, ask your hiring manager to consider evaluating you in six months' time if you take the job, and agreeing to give you a merit-based step increase or cash award if she or he is happy with your productivity, as you are certain will be the case. (Agencies can grant an employee a cash award based upon a favorable rating totaling up to 10 percent of salary.)

In the unlikely event that your hiring manager does not offer you any concessions, you've lost nothing just by attempting to negotiate. And if nothing else, you have established yourself as an assertive, goal-oriented professional and have set the stage for future promotions.

Yes, We Do Have Flexibility!

Alternatively, the hiring manager may respond to your invitation to negotiate by saying something like, "What did you have in mind?" Here are some possible responses:

1. **Suppose you've received a competing offer.** Present documentation of your competing offer, and say, "I understand that the government usually matches reasonable competing offers. I wonder whether you could match or come closer to my other offer." Alternatively, if your research has revealed that another agency is paying people at your level better than your agency's offer, ask whether your agency could pay comparably.

2. **Suppose you're a current fed.** If you're currently eligible for a grade or step increase and/or have been promised a promotion from your current employer, explain to your hiring manager that accepting a job offer at your current level would require you to sacrifice an impending job offer. Note that when a GS employee is promoted to a higher grade, he or she may receive a pay increase equal to two steps above the individual's current grade and step.

   If you're a current fed who is ineligible for a promotion because you have not yet fulfilled your time-in-grade or step requirements, ask your hiring manager if she or he can commit to giving you a grade increase or a merit-based step when you fulfill whatever time requirements apply to your situation and/or a bonus after six months if she or he is happy with your contributions.

Hot Tip

Pick an Employer Who Can Help You Lose Your Loans. Federal agencies can repay up to $10,000 of an employee's academic debt per year, up to a total of $60,000. In return, the employee must agree to stay with the agency for at least three years.

Some agencies use the student loan repayment program more than others. To find out which agencies use this program, type "Student Loan Repayment Program" into the search window at http://opm.gov/.

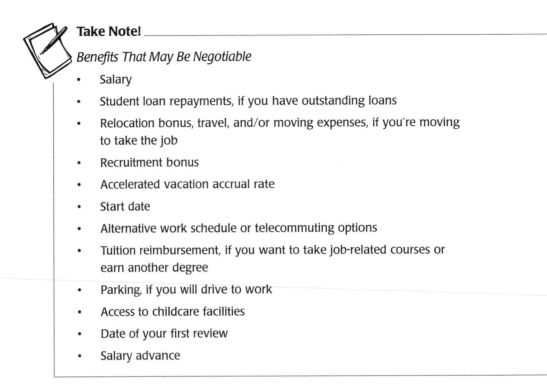

Take Note!

Benefits That May Be Negotiable

- Salary
- Student loan repayments, if you have outstanding loans
- Relocation bonus, travel, and/or moving expenses, if you're moving to take the job
- Recruitment bonus
- Accelerated vacation accrual rate
- Start date
- Alternative work schedule or telecommuting options
- Tuition reimbursement, if you want to take job-related courses or earn another degree
- Parking, if you will drive to work
- Access to childcare facilities
- Date of your first review
- Salary advance

3. **Suppose you're a new grad with outstanding student loans.** Ask your hiring manager for coverage in the Student Loan Repayment Program. (See the Hot Tip box, page 189.) (Also, note that the College Cost Reduction and Access Act of 2007 established a new public service loan forgiveness program, which cancels academic debt remaining after ten years of full-time employment in public service. See http://www.finaid.org/ loans/publicservice.phtml.)

4. **Suppose you're an experienced nonfed or a returning fed.** Request authorization to accrue vacation time at the same rate as feds whose experience levels are similar to yours instead of at the standard accrual rate for new feds—four hours per two-week pay period. Your hiring manager can credit your previous work experience so that you will meet seniority requirements for accelerated leave rates. (Feds with three years of seniority earn six hours of vacation every two weeks, and those with at least 15 years of seniority earn eight hours.)

   If you are very experienced and your hiring manager refuses to immediately start you at a higher than standard vacation accrual rate, request credit toward receiving an accelerated accrual rate. For example, depending on your experience level, you could ask your hiring manager to credit you for two years of work experience, so that you would only have to work one year for the federal government, instead of three years, to qualify for six hours of vacation time per pay period.

   Strengthen any request for increased vacation time by telling your hiring manager how much vacation time you will sacrifice by leaving your current job.

5. **Suppose you've received bonuses, awards, or overtime on previous jobs.** Cite such awards/extra income as evidence of your superior performance and that your previous salary was underestimated by your previous base pay, which provided the basis for the hiring agency's salary offer.

6. **Suppose your qualifications match the ceiling of your opening's grade range.**
    Show your hiring manager the position classification criteria for the higher grade
    and explain how your credentials match the criteria for the higher grade.

7. **Suppose you have truly superior qualifications.** Your hiring agency can set your pay
    at a middle step—instead of at the lowest step—of your grade level. Explain why your
    educational and/or work experience exceeds your opening's basic requirements and
    ask whether you qualify for Superior Qualifications and Special Need Pay-Setting
    Authority. If you have a security clearance, mention it. If you're a recent grad,
    underscore your exceptional academic record and the relevance of your major or
    degree to your target job. For more info, type "superior qualifications and special
    need pay-setting authority" into the search window at http://www.opm.gov/.

8. **Suppose you want to
    continue your education.**
    Request reimbursement for
    your tuition. Agencies can
    pay for job-related degrees
    and nondegrees. For more
    information, type "training
    and development policy"
    into the search window at
    http://www.opm.gov/.

9. **Suppose you're a nonfed
    who has been offered a job
    in a high-demand field.** Ask
    your hiring manager if he or
    she will authorize a recruit-
    ment bonus for you. A
    recruitment bonus may
    range up to 100 percent of
    your annual salary. For more
    info, type "recruitment and
    relocation incentives"
    into the search window
    at http://www.opm.gov.
    (Chapter 2 identifies many
    agencies that offer recruitment bonuses.)

*"I can only discuss salary and benefits. You'll have to
analyze the babe situation yourself."*

10. **Suppose that taking the job would require you to move to a new location.**
    If you're a current fed, ask your hiring manager for a relocation bonus. (The cap for
    a relocation bonus is 100 percent of your annual salary.) Alternatively, if you're
    currently a nonfed, ask whether your hiring agency would cover your transportation
    and moving expenses. For more info, type "recruitment and relocation incentives"
    into the search window at http://www.opm.gov.

11. **Suppose you want scheduling flexibilities.** Request telecommuting or an alternative
    work schedule involving working nine hours per day in exchange for a long weekend
    every other week or working four 10-hour days per week.

12. **Suppose you plan to drive to work.** Request free parking. In some cities, this benefit is worth several thousand dollars per year. In a lesson in creative negotiating, one recruit convinced her new boss to give her the parking privileges of her predecessor and thereby enabled her to avoid joining the agency's waiting list for free parking.

13. **Suppose you're short on cash.** Your hiring agency can advance up to two paychecks to a new fed.

Sealing the Deal

Your hiring agency may pressure you to make a quick decision on an offer. Nevertheless, you are completely within your rights to ask for a day or two to consider any offer. Also, request an offer letter.

CHAPTER

17

Responding to an Agency's Decision

"The world is all gates, all opportunities, strings of tension waiting to be struck."
—RALPH WALDO EMERSON

You Got the Job!

So you've received an offer! You won the jackpot . . . the grand slam . . . the ultimate prize. Give yourself a big, fat slap on the back and collect some kudos from friends and relatives.

You Want the Job

Sometimes, the decision on an offer is a no-brainer. The job would be perfect for you, and you're chomping at the bit for it. But no matter how heavenly an offer may be, consider negotiating your salary, as well as other benefits, as covered in Chapter 16.

Here are some additional tips for what to say when you accept a job offer:

➤ Thank the hiring manager for the offer.

➤ Express excitement about the job and say something like, "I will make sure that you will be pleased that you selected me."

➤ Politely request an offer letter that summaries the terms of your agreement, including your start date, salary, and title.

Uncertainty

Although it is always flattering to be selected for a job, do not reflexively accept a questionable job just because it was offered to you or because it represents a new opportunity. Change merely for the sake of change will not necessarily make you happier or advance your career. You should only accept a job because you really want it, or really need income . . . now!

Yes, bills or the need "to get your foot in the door" might justifiably compel you to accept a questionable job—despite its imperfections. But in such cases, be honest with yourself (but not with your hiring manager) about your needs and continue your job search accordingly.

But don't accept an unappealing job just to escape a current unappealing job. By doing so, you will only jump from the fire into the frying pan. After all, if a potential boss or a job description rubs you the wrong way, your affection for the person on the job is unlikely to grow once you dive into the job's day-to-day drudgery. Moreover, remember that the demands of a new job would probably complicate your continued job search.

If you feel undecided about an opening, more information about it might help you clinch your decision. If this is the case, when you talk to the hiring manager, thank him or her for the offer, express enthusiasm about the job, and then ask for a meeting to clarify a few points. If salary is the sticking issue, see Chapter 16 for negotiating tips. Once you gather more information, ask the hiring manager for a day or two to finalize your decision, if you need it.

Rejecting an Offer

If the offer isn't right for you, let the hiring manager down courteously, quickly, and graciously. Don't burn any bridges unnecessarily; you never know if you might cross paths again with the hiring manager. Here are some tips for turning down an offer:

➤ Thank the hiring manager for taking the time to interview you and for selecting you.

➤ Cite something impressive about the organization.

➤ Say that you gave the offer much thought and that turning it down was a tough decision.

➤ Give a specific reason for turning down the offer, such as the salary, or leave your reasons vague by saying something like, "It isn't the right fit for me right now."

If at First You Don't Succeed

"Success is the ability to go from failure to failure without losing your enthusiasm."
—WINSTON CHURCHILL

Although it is understandable to be disappointed by a rejection, never regard your standing in a job competition as a referendum on your credentials, smarts, or personality. As one recent rejectee sensibly explained, "I don't take it personally. It's not like the hiring manager really knows me or what I can do."

Also, take solace in the fact that almost everyone—even the most fabulously successful people—have, at one time or another, been rejected for a job that they knew they were perfect for. Indeed, many roads to success are rutted with potholes, riddled with speed bumps, blocked by barricades, and traversed by blind alleys.

And even if you're rejected for a job that seemed like it was the best job in the world, another exciting opportunity will almost certainly eventually develop.

Keep On Keeping On

Many job searchers let their fear of failure derail their job search. Instead of rolling with the punches, they allow rejections to confirm their conviction that they are destined to fail, and so they suspend their job search—sometimes indefinitely. They thereby succumb to a self-fulfilling prophecy: By stopping their job search, they guarantee that they will not find a job and thereby further reinforce their poor self-image.

Remember: The quality that distinguishes many successful people from others is neither intelligence, nor talent, nor luck, but sheer persistence. Successful, persistent professionals take setbacks in stride; instead of turning away from obstacles, they step around or over them. They incorporate any lessons that might be gleaned from setbacks into their strategies without losing their resolve, their determination, their self-confidence.

Indeed, many high-profile people achieved their goals only after tenaciously toiling through humiliating defeats. Consider, for example, politicians—many of whom apparently regard a lost election as encouragement to run for an even higher office. And why not? After all, many presidents—including Lincoln, Nixon, Reagan, Clinton, and both Bushes— lost major elections before ultimately winning the White House.

Take Note! _____

The Power of Persistence

If you recently experienced a professional disappointment, you're in good company. In fact, many of the most fabulously successful people have overcome setbacks that would have thwarted less determined people. For example:

• The Beatles were turned down by Capitol Records four times before Capitol signed them.

• *Chicken Soup for the Soul* is one of the best-selling nonfiction books in United States history. But the proposal for the book was rejected by more than 24 publishers before it found a publisher.

• Screenwriter Marc Cherry spent three staffing seasons without so much as an interview, let alone a job. He told the *Washington Post* that his spec script for the blockbuster *Desperate Housewives* was itself "born of desperation" and was initially turned down by all four networks.

• High-jumper Dick Fosbury failed at conventional straddle jumping. So he pioneered the goofy backward "Fosbury Flop," and won the Gold Medal in the 1968 Olympics.

Maximize Your Odds

I have frequently been amazed to hear unemployed job seekers say things like, "I once got rejected from a federal job, so it would be useless for me to apply for another federal job." By contrast, no reasonable person would ever say, "I once got rejected from a private-sector job, so it would be useless to apply for another job in the private sector." Nevertheless, it is just as unreasonable to paint all federal jobs with a broad brush as it is to paint all private-sector jobs with that same broad brush.

Federal agencies are as different from one another as are private-sector organizations. Every federal office is run by different people with different priorities, and every opening is screened by different managers. So any rejection you receive in a federal job competition would not impact your standing in any others.

But the raw reality is that no matter how impressive your application is, there will always be uncontrollable factors that can nix your application. For example:

➤ Another applicant may have pivotal connections or more experience than you.

➤ You may be beaten out for a job by a veteran who has veterans' preference.

➤ A hiring manager may have a wacky bias against some innocent and even admirable aspect of your background. For example, I know of a professor at a top university who automatically rejects all applicants for a professorship who does not cite her articles in their own scholarly publications.

➤ A hiring manager may have poor judgment.

➤ The selection may hinge on unstated criteria. For example, a hiring manager recently told me that he based a selection on his "sense that my pick would thrive in this office's chaos." But an "ability to thrive in chaos" was never identified as a selection criterion.

➤ Your target job may be cancelled because of hiring freezes or changing priorities.

➤ You may be overqualified—a particular liability before insecure hiring managers who fear being outshined by subordinates. (Remember why the first President Bush selected the inexperienced lightweight Dan Quayle as his running mate?)

> ### Take Note!
>
> *Torn Between Two Agencies?*
>
> If you receive an offer from your "second choice" opening before receiving a decision from your "first-choice" opening, here is what to do: Ask your contact at your second-choice opening for time to think over their offer. Then, call your contact at your first-choice opening, explain the situation to him or her, and ask whether a decision about you has already been made.
>
> If your first-choice opening won't give you a decision before you must respond to your second choice, accept your second choice. But back out of it if you are later offered your first choice. Remember: You should accept the best offer you receive at any time, even if doing so would—through no fault of your own—unfortunately inconvenience an employer.
>
> By the same token, if you start a new job that ends up disappointing you, keep looking for other jobs. If, during your continued job search, an interviewer asks you why you want to jump ship so soon after starting a new job, simply explain that your current job is not a good fit for you, and you would rather find a better fit immediately than stay in the wrong job for a prolonged period. Remember: You are not an indentured servant; you are free to leave any job at any time.

To a large extent, hiring decisions are based on chance; they hinge on the vagaries of your hiring manager's judgment, the credentials of your competition, and other fluky and sometimes kooky factors. You can always increase your odds by acing your application and interview. But no matter how impressive you are, success is never guaranteed.

The best way to improve your odds in the job-searching numbers game is to apply to as many jobs that suit you. Moreover, the more logs you keep in the fire, the less disappointed you will be if any one of them is snuffed out.

*"I'm not against public service. I just think I can
do more damage in the private sector."*

Reevaluate Your Approach

If employment pay dirt is eluding you, you would be wise to calmly and objectively evaluate your strategy, and to—if possible—seek a fresh, objective perspective from a trusted source. Here are some ways to do so:

1. Check that you are qualified for your target jobs and are not overreaching.

2. Call a previous interviewer and ask for candid suggestions on how you could improve your performance in future interviews.

3. Ask friends, relatives, and colleagues to give you honest feedback on your résumés and essays, and to practice interviewing with you. Incorporate any reasonable advice that you receive into your job searching strategy.

Take Note!

Has Your Job Hunt Sent You Out Onto the Ledge?

"And this, too, shall pass."
—ANONYMOUS

One of my clients observed, "When you're looking for a job, you feel particularly fragile, insecure, and nervous." Another says that "a job search is about as much fun as unrequited love." As you thanklessly pound the cyber-pavement day after day searching for a break, it can be tough to maintain your morale and fighting spirit. Some tips for staying off the ledge:

- Continually give yourself things to look forward to and celebrate every little victory, like finishing a long application. After receiving good or bad news, splurge on special treats for yourself—even modest ones, such as time off with a great book, a movie, a walk through the park, or a special meal.

- This one is not negotiable: Keep up your exercise program. If you don't have one, start one. (I would have attached a free pair of sneakers to each copy of this book if I could have.)

- Don't bottle up your frustration: Discuss it with friends and relatives and seek pep talks from them. And if you live in an isolated area, occasionally open the window, stick your head out the window, and yell: "I'm mad as hell and I'm not going to take it anymore." (Then close the window and get back to work on your job search.)

- Harden yourself to rejections. Because of the unpredictability and capriciousness of selection processes, there is an excellent chance that you won't hit employment pay dirt on your first try. Many extremely qualified job seekers receive a number of rejections before they ultimately get hired. As one successful EPA attorney recalls, "Before I landed my EPA job, I received enough rejections from EPA to wallpaper my apartment."

- If you are currently unemployed, consider working a temp or contract job during your job search. By doing so, you will add credentials to your résumé, increase your cash flow, and generate contacts that could lead to permanent jobs. (See Chapter 2 for leads.)

- Throughout your job search, keep participating in activities, including professional activities and hobbies, that you enjoy and are good at—whether they be playing musical instruments, painting, gardening, cooking, coaching sports teams, volunteering for an advocacy group, organizing community events, or anything else. The emotional lift and positive feedback you receive through such activities will help you maintain your equilibrium throughout the vicissitudes of your job search.

- Remember that your fortunes can, and probably will, change on a dime. A case in point: A federal IT expert who had submitted fantastic applications consulted me in tears because her job search had generated a 4-inch folder of applications without a single job offer. But one week after her tearful meltdown, my client was invited on three interviews. And two weeks after that, she received an offer for a choice executive job. Several months after she started on her new job, she was featured on the cover of *Federal Computer Week*.

- Never let anyone, particularly strangers, make you feel bad about yourself. As Eleanor Roosevelt said, "No one can make you feel inferior without your consent."

4. Review this book's application and interviewing advice again.

5. Seek advice from a career coach. Yes, such advice may cost you. But if your career is stalled, the real question is, can you afford not to seek it?

Remember: Perseverance is a critical component of success. If you keep improving your application, keep plugging, and keep applying, you will eventually land a career-boosting job.

PART

ACCELERATING YOUR ASCENT

Two new feds who start out on the same rung on the career ladder may soon find themselves on different rungs, with the distance between them only growing with time. Why? Because the speed of a fed's climb up the career ladder—just as the speed of a private sector professional's climb up the career ladder—usually depends not only on each professional's smarts and dedication but also on each professional's savvy use (or lack of use) of go-getter strategies for speeding the career ascent.

Part IV provides a bevy of career-accelerating strategies—available nowhere else—for earning an enviable reputation, generating high-level connections, getting the credit you deserve, amassing key credentials, boosting your salary, and making the right moves at the right time.

This is the kind of practical, potentially pivotal advice that they never taught you in school, your friends don't know, and your boss won't tell you.

CHAPTER

18

The Fed "Get Ahead" Guide

"Luck is what happens when preparation meets opportunity."
—SENECA

"Did you think the ladder of success would be straight up?"

What is success? You're successful at work when you're doing the most interesting and important work possible, getting the recognition you deserve, and making as much money as possible.

This chapter is loaded with tips for achieving work success and accelerating your ascent. Some of them may be more appropriate for you at certain times than at others. So, as you review these tips and strategies, don't pressure yourself to do them all at once, or even to ever do them all.

Instead, cherry-pick the strategies that suit you now, and then periodically review this chapter to remind yourself of strategies that will help you keep improving and advancing.

How Fast Will You Move Up? There are no formulas for how fast feds rise. The speed of your climb will depend on many factors—some that you can control and some that you can't. For example, your agency's budget will probably influence how generously it rewards producers. Nevertheless, by continuously gathering résumé-stuffing experiences and seizing opportunities to grow and excel, you will surely accelerate your ascent.

Why Initiative Beats Inertia

Even if you have the best boss in the world, you are, at most, only your boss's second most important priority. Indeed, no matter how kind and caring your boss is, how much camaraderie you share with your colleagues, and how loving your family is, you're the only person in the world who has true pride of ownership over your career; it is your career.

Sure, managers, colleagues, and your inner circle may provide guidance and support. But whether you're in government or the private sector, you can't expect anyone else to vigilantly look out for your career, make sure you get the recognition you deserve, and devote his- or herself to your advancement.

Also, remember that pivotal opportunities to shine and advance probably won't just drop into your lap. To find and pursue them, you must be enterprising, show initiative, and apply savvy strategies.

First Impressions

When you start your job, your main goal should be making a good first impression with your boss. The single most important factor determining your quality of life on any job is your boss. In fact, your boss is as critical to your happiness at work as your parents were to your happiness at home while you were growing up. Moreover, first impressions make lasting impressions. That's why it's much easier to make a good first impression than to correct a bad first impression. If you get off to a good start with your new boss, you will be paving the way for a smooth long-term relationship with him or her.

Start working on your relationship with your boss even before your first day on the job. For example, ask your future boss what you should read to be able to hit the ground running, and then read what has been suggested. Also, if possible, take off a few days before you start your new job so that you will arrive rested and energetic, and not frazzled from finishing up old commitments. Then, once you start your new job:

> **Hot Tip**
>
> **Getting to Know You.** Position a candy jar near the entrance to your cube or office. Your candy jar will entice your new colleagues to stop by and introduce themselves.

➤ Give your all to your job for at least the first few months. Go above and beyond the call of duty whenever possible, even if you slack off later; be punctual; work extra hours if necessary; double-check and proofread your work; and meet your deadlines.

➤ Ask for "getting started" suggestions. On your first day, ask your boss which people you will be working with most closely and frequently so that you can introduce yourself to them. Follow through on any other "getting started" suggestions your boss offers.

➤ Be enthusiastic and positive. Act like you feel privileged to work there, even if you had to miss a free Hawaiian vacation to take the job. Be friendly and courteous to everyone.

➤ Charge out of the gate. During your first couple of week(s) on the job, bite off a contained, easy-to-accomplish project and finish it quickly and effectively, if possible.

Second Impressions

An axiom of life is that if you make life easier for other people, they will probably like you and seek out your company. If you make life harder for others, they probably won't. Apply this principle to your relationship with your boss; in other words, win your boss over by solving problems—not by creating them. Some ways to do this are:

➤ **Priorities, priorities.** Identify your boss's priorities and, as much as possible, make them your own. By helping to push his agenda, you will make his life easier and thereby make your life easier as well. After all, your efforts will take you further if you swim with the tide rather than against it.

➤ **No cattle prodders.** Finish assignments quickly, enthusiastically, and without prodding, even taxing, dull projects. If you need clarification on assignments, request it. If you have ideas on how to improve projects, suggest them tactfully.

Take Note!

Free Advice on Career Advancement Strategies

My recent "Career Matters" columns in *Federal Times* cover everything from avenues into the senior executive service, to landing overseas jobs, to effective communication skills. To access an archive of my columns, visit the "Career Information" section of http://www.FederalTimes.com. Additional free advice is posted on my Web site at http://www.IGotTheJob.net.

➤ **Volunteer to do more.** If you're underbooked or you would like to do higher-level projects, ask your boss point-blank: "How can I make a bigger contribution here? Is there something else I could take off your plate? Don't worry about giving me tough assignments. I will do what it takes to get them done." As one hiring manager said, "If you want to be promoted, it's usually not enough to just do your job well; you must usually succeed at higher level work in order to move up."

➤ **Do crisis management.** Be the unflappable, indefatigable troubleshooter during crises.

➤ **Don't be a clock watcher.** Work extra hours, if necessary and if you can.

➤ **No disappearing acts.** Your boss shouldn't have to put your photo on milk cartons in order to find you. A case in point: I once had a colleague who arrived on time every morning only to strategically place his jacket over his seatback in order to create the impression that he was in the building. Then, he would run out to who-knows-where for most of the rest of the day. My colleague's gimmick fooled his boss—but only for a while.

➤ **Be a problem-solver.** If you can independently troubleshoot through obstacles and problems without supervision, do so, and then tell your boss about such successes. Generally speaking, your boss will be happier to hear about problems you solved than problems you created or can't solve.

➤ **No surprises.** If you anticipate missing a deadline, don't blindside your boss. Instead, warn her of the problem while there is still time to develop work-around strategies. And even though you should attempt to work as self-reliantly as possible, by the same token, if you need help tackling important technical or administrative obstacles, ask for it. Remember: Part of your boss's job is to make sure that you have everything you need to do your job.

   In addition, if you're involved in snags that your boss will inevitably learn about from others, break the news to her first yourself. Why? For the same reasons that a defense attorney presents the weaknesses of his own case to the jury before the prosecution does: to establish credibility, put bad news in the best possible light, explain mitigating circumstances, and steal the thunder of those who would joyfully harp on their misfortune.

➤ **Schmooze.** Managers are more likely to trust members of their inner circle with important, career-boosting assignments and promote them than hostile outsiders. So try to become one of the gang. When appropriate, engage your boss, other managers, and colleagues in conversation and attend office parties and outings.

➤ **Never say:** "That's not my job" (even if you're thinking it).

Start Spreading the News

As your projects progress, ask yourself whether you think your boss knows what you do. I mean really knows what you do, as in all the troubleshooting, barrier-busting, and going the extra mile-ing that you do.

The Danger of Communication Gaps

Unfortunately, many bosses—overtaxed and untrained in supervising—rarely take the time and trouble to say to their staffers those five little words, "What are you working on?" This principle was underscored by the manager of a large federal accounting office who confessed to me as we strolled through his staff's cubicle farm, "I probably know about 10 percent of what each of these people does daily." The problem with such communication gaps for employees is that they generally don't get credit on their annual evaluations for achievements that their bosses don't know about. In other words, what your boss doesn't know about you *can* hurt you.

But beware: Your annual evaluations are important to you for several reasons. For one thing, pay for performance evaluation systems, which base annual raises on employees' evaluations instead of on automatic increases, are proliferating throughout the government.

In addition, your evaluations will probably impact your prospects for promotions. This is because many federal job applications require submission of recent annual evaluations. And even if your future applications don't require you to submit your evaluations, you may want to cite your record of earning positive evaluations and quote praising comments from your evaluations in your résumé and application essays in the future.

> *"If you done it, it ain't bragging."*
> —WALT WHITMAN

If you feel self-conscious about encouraging positive feedback, remember:

➤ You're as entitled to your hard-won positive feedback, such as positive annual reviews, as to your paycheck—you worked hard for it and you deserve it. So if it doesn't come to you spontaneously, go get it, just like you would if you were denied your paychecks.

➤ Bad news and criticism travel on their own wings, but good news needs a nudge. Yes, when things go wrong for you, news of the problem will fly up and down the gossip wires. But when things go right for you, you may have to telegraph the news yourself.

➤ Your work won't speak for itself because inanimate objects can't talk.

➤ No one is going to advocate for you. So if you don't advocate for yourself, you will be advocate-less. It is up to you to sing your own praises, toot your own horn, and trumpet your own achievements. And if you do so by sticking to the facts without exaggerating, and by using tact, common sense, and moderation, you won't sound egocentric and brassy.

Nine Ways to Close Communication Gaps

Here are some specific ways you can get the word out about what you've achieved:

1. **Introduce yourself.** If your boss is replaced, your new boss probably won't know anything about what you have already done or can do. And so you'll probably have to reestablish your reputation from scratch with your new boss.

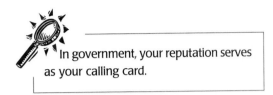

In government, your reputation serves as your calling card.

Don't just settle for a hallway handshake introduction with your new boss. Instead, make an appointment to introduce yourself to her. During your meeting with your new boss, sell yourself and make her excited that you are on her team. How? By quickly reviewing your best credentials—telling her about your biggest projects; showing her some of your relevant work products; identifying your upcoming projects and the approvals you will need on them; suggesting some future projects, if appropriate; and by conveying zest about taking on the future, and working hard to help advance her agenda! One more thing: No griping or complaining in this first meeting!

2. **Cultivate a friendly rapport.** Without being obsequious, complement your boss on his successes and chat with your boss when you both have the chance. By doing so, you will make it easier to deliver your good news as it develops.

3. **Be direct.** Many professionals only hint about their extra efforts. For example, they assume that if they send their boss an e-mail late at night, their boss will notice the time stamp on the e-mail, make a mental note of the long hours, and remember those efforts at review time. But will she? And isn't it risky to rely on the selective and perhaps defective memory of a pressured, distracted boss?

    Alternatively, when you're working like a harnessed beast, take the bull by the horns and tell your boss about your extra effort. Say something like, "I just wanted to let you know we are making good progress on Project X. . . . Sharon and I are working hard on it; we put in 12-hour days on it every day this week."

    In addition, if you put in extra hours, claim it on your time card. You shouldn't anonymously donate your time to your office any more than you would make anonymous financial donations to your office.

4. **Provide updates.** Establish a regular method for updating your boss on your projects. This mechanism may involve regular or occasional meetings; generating some sort of cyber or paper trail—such as regularly e-mailed status reports. Be sure to describe in your updates special obstacles you conquered, such as repeated system crashes or staff shortages. Also mention in your updates how you are going the extra mile. A sample project tracking sheet to help you impress your boss with your ongoing achievements is included on the CD accompanying this book.

    One great way to avoid any misunderstandings about projects with your boss is to e-mail him or her a summary of assignments he or she has given you immediately after you receive them.

5. **Maintain up-to-date records.** Create and maintain a table that lists all of your ongoing projects with their major milestones and deadlines, the positive results or feedback that they have generated, and obstacles you have conquered. Periodically, review your table with your boss to ensure that the two of you agree on your progress, you haven't forgotten about any of your assignments, and your boss gets a bird's-eye view of everything you do. (See Chapter 9 for ideas on how to describe your achievements in impressive terms.)

6. **Participate in meetings.** If you've completed an important phase of a project, tell your colleagues about it in staff meetings. Also, mention any major positive feedback you've received. For example, if your office's top banana just approved your organization's annual report that you wrote, say so.

7. **Show-and-tell.** Show to your boss or leave in your boss's in-box documents that validate your success. These may include, for example, evaluations from trainings

or events you organized; complimentary e-mails from top managers; agendas from conferences at which you gave presentations; articles you published; or printouts from Web pages you created. Also, invite your boss to presentations, trainings, or other events that you organize.

8. **Write about it.** Offer to write articles about your projects for your office's newsletter or Intranet site or for professional publications.

9. **Express gratitude.** When projects that you lead conclude, e-mail each member of your team a thank-you note that cites some of the team successes and c.c. your boss on it.

Get Juicy Projects for Greater Visibility

Some ways to get assigned to interesting, important projects are to:

➤ **Be proactive.** Read everything you can about your office's activities, ask your colleagues about their work, and stay alert at staff meetings. By doing so, you will find ongoing projects that interest you. Volunteer to contribute to them instead of passively waiting to be assigned your next projects.

➤ **Create new projects.** Identify new projects that would fill unrecognized needs, explain to your boss how your office would benefit from these projects, and then offer to do them yourself. I can personally testify to this approach because I have used it to my own advantage many times. For example, some years ago, I worked for the Plain Language Initiative (PLI)—a government-wide campaign to improve federal communications. Because I am interested in science communication, I suggested to my boss that I develop communications trainings for various science-based agencies, and so began my training career. What's more, the experience I gained on that job training scientists in communication skills helped me land my current job as a science writer at the National Science Foundation.

➤ **Be a pinch hitter.** When your colleagues permanently leave their jobs or go on extended leave, offer to cover projects for them. Opportunities for doing so will probably increase as the retirement tsunami washes over the federal workforce. I know, for example, a federal accountant who was itching for a career switch. So she volunteered to help the director of her agency's Alternative Dispute Resolution (ADR) program manage some of her cases. Some months after the accountant started her ADR work, the director went on maternity leave, and so the accountant slid into her job as a temporary substitute. Then, when the director finished her maternity leave, she decided not to return to work, and so the accountant was selected to replace her.

➤ **Track changes.** When you attend staff meetings and read publications targeting feds, stay alert to mentions of reorganizations, the creation of new offices, and government-wide commissions and task forces. Why? Because such organizations may need your temporary or permanent help. This principle was exploited by a U.S. Postal Service (USPS) professional that I know; immediately after hearing about the creation of a new USPS division, he e-mailed the chief of the new division a summary of his credentials and a description of some ways that he could contribute to the new division. Two weeks later, he was on staff in the new division, and six months after that, he was promoted.

> **Get supervisory and project management experience.** Because many senior-level jobs require such experience, experience supervising others in any capacity—even without serving as a direct-line supervisor—is an excellent credential for landing senior-level jobs. So, if your office has interns, entry-level employees, or experienced employees whom you are qualified to supervise, guide, or mentor in any way, volunteer to do so, if appropriate. Also, make yourself available to serve in "acting" positions, when possible.

Likewise, project management experience is a sought-after skill. Therefore, seize all opportunities to manage projects and to obtain formal training in project management, including training that leads to certificates. (See http://www.federalpm.com.) Brandish any resulting supervisory and project management experience in your job applications.

Also, experience in contract management and certification as a Contracting Officer's Technical Representative (COTR) is valued. Potential training sources for such certification include the Federal Acquisition Institute and the Defense Acquisition Institute.

Grow Your Reputation

Do you have fantasies of being plucked from the obscurity of your cube and instantly elevated into the lofty position you deserve, the way Lana Turner was "discovered" at the soda fountain in that old "we're going to make you a star!" Hollywood legend? Sorry to be the bearer of bad news, but your agency's star-making machinery is about as likely to happen upon your cube as someone from the Publishers Clearing House is to ring your doorbell.

Remember: If you want to move up, it's not enough to simply toil in obscurity, hunkered alone in the bunker of your cube—no matter how great your work is, nobody knows you or knows about your stellar contributions. Relationships matter.

But take heart; here are simple things you can do to progressively spread your reputation so that:

> Your boss won't be the only manager who knows what a great job you're doing. This is important because, after all, your boss could leave his job at any time. And if he does leave before you, you don't want your reputation to walk out the door with him.

> You will get the credit you deserve.

> Managers will invite you to work on hot-button projects, provide you with good references, and maybe even recruit you onto their staffs.

Here are some ways to shine:

1. **Follow the power.** Pounce on any and all opportunities to interact with the front offices of your agency and department. Even better, arrange a detail or transfer into a front office, if possible. Why? Because the front offices of your agency and department are loaded with highly-graded positions, big budgets, and senior managers who have the power to promote. It's usually easier to move up in front offices than in backwater offices. Moreover, if you hitch your wagon to one of the front office's rising stars, you may rise with her. Remember: When it comes to success, in many cases, it's not about who you know but who knows what you can do.

2. **Follow the controversy.** If possible, volunteer to work on your organization's high-profile, high-priority projects. Your contributions to such projects will be more appreciated and will provide more exposure to high-level officials than will your contributions to back-burner projects.

3. **Talk to the crowds.** Offer to help work on high-profile events that will draw staffers from various offices. Also, don't wait to be invited to give presentations before large groups, volunteer to do so. If, for example, you know of an upcoming conference in your field, offer to give a presentation at it. To select good topics to cover, consider what specialized knowledge you have that others would find useful. For example, describe a successful case study, provide how-to instruction, or discuss lessons learned from a policy or system implementation. Alternatively, summarize the state of knowledge on a topic, or discuss ways to adapt to changes in your field.

4. **Bust out of your office.** Join interoffice and interagency work groups that will help you generate outside contacts. Tell your boss about your desire to join such groups.

5. **Advertise your availability.** When your office is short staffed, tell your office director that you're available to help. For example, a policy analyst at the Department of Housing and Urban Development did just that on July 3, after most of her colleagues had already left for the holiday. The result was that, by the end of that July, the policy analyst had been hand-picked by the assistant secretary to become her special assistant.

6. **Develop a useful high-demand specialty.** This technique helped a young financial planner catapult into the senior executive service. He explains: "I volunteered to distill complex data and trends into bite-sized descriptions and easy-to-understand graphs for managers. I thereby helped them find good answers to hard problems. Soon I was getting invited to high-level meetings where these conceptual skills were useful. And those meetings provided a good vantage point for me to spot opportunities for advancement."

7. **Be a "friend in need."** Extend yourself to managers and colleagues in need, even if doing so requires you to do menial tasks. That way, they will see for themselves what a trooper you are, and reciprocate when you're in a crunch. (And believe me, you will have at least a few crunches of your own.)

8. **Solicit advice.** Many people who would be happy to help you won't volunteer their help; they'll only give their help if asked for it. So seek career advice from people you admire inside and outside your office.

9. **Stay in touch.** Keep in contact with as many of your current colleagues as possible—even those whom you may not necessarily like (if you can stand it). And whenever you change jobs, send out a global e-mail with your new contact information to your contacts, and announce your job change on social networking sites. This is important because as you move up the career ladder, so will your current colleagues and supervisors. Even if they can't hire you now, they may be able to do so in the future. In addition, some of your current contacts will inevitably move into different organizations. Therefore, if you stay in touch with them, they will serve as your tentacles throughout the government.

10. **Exit gracefully.** Last impressions often leave lasting impressions. So if you leave a job with loose ends hanging, unfinished assignments, and unfulfilled commitments, your last-minute irresponsibility (no matter how much time pressure caused it)

On the CD...

This book's CD includes: (1) a list of professional organizations for feds of various career levels and in various fields; (2) my *Washington Post* articles on the career-boosting advantages of participating in professional organizations and creating a success portfolio; (3) a cheat sheet to help you ace annual reviews; and (4) a sample project tracking sheet to help you impress your boss with your successes on your ongoing projects.

may overshadow the years of diligence and dedication that proceed it. Remember: A disorganized, neglectful rush from a job may ultimately come back to haunt you if you need references from your boss for that job in the future.

So, before you give notice on a job, generate a final to-do list of obligations as well as documents that should be handed over to your successor before you leave. Shortly after you give notice, review our to-do list with your supervisor and inquire about (and build time into your schedule for) your agency's "check out" requirements, which may consume significant chunks of time. If you anticipate not having enough time to complete your to-do list before your last day on the job, prioritize and then devise a plan B accordingly for potentially unfinished business with your supervisor.

Warning: Build into your schedule for your final days' time for attending "going away" celebrations, visiting with well-wishing colleagues who drop by your office (and may overstay their welcome while you are scrambling to finish your work), and cleaning your computer and office—all of which will likely take up more time than you anticipate. On your last day, give a copy of your to-do list of obligations to your supervisor with each item checked off or alternative provisions for it notated.

Join Professional Organizations

You're probably already taxed to the max with work and personal commitments. So why should you try to squeeze time into your jam-packed schedule for professional organizations? Because these organizations provide excellent opportunities to do the following:

> **Meet kindred spirits.** Each professional group brings together professionals who belong to the same demographic group, minority group, or profession, or have another interest in common. By interacting with one another and sharing ideas, these like-minded professionals find camaraderie and achieve strength in numbers.

> **Stuff your résumé.** Because professional groups are smaller and more nimble than federal organizations and because they are run by volunteers, they offer great opportunities to gain top-management experience. This type of experience usually impresses hiring managers as much as paid experience. For example, one of the founders of Young Government Leaders (YGL)—a turbo-charged professional organization of 22- to 40-year-old feds from over 30 agencies—says, "at YGL, I am doing things I want to do on a grand scale." His achievements include building YGL's IT infrastructure, appearing on national radio shows, delivering presentations to executives about federal recruitment at Brookings Institution conferences, and receiving *Federal Computer Week*'s Rising Star Award.

> **Find new jobs.** Professional organizations provide informal and formal mechanisms to inform members of job openings that they would not otherwise learn about. They also provide platforms for members to exhibit their skills to hiring managers.

> **Advocate for important causes.** Professional organizations create opportunities for their members to get published, make media appearances, give presentations, and organize events that are of common concern to their members.

➤ **Get mentored.** Professional organizations provide training to feds of all levels and offer advice on varied issues, such as strategizing career moves, dealing with difficult bosses, fighting discrimination, and motivating staffs.

➤ **Meet colleagues from other agencies.** Professional organizations provide all-too-rare opportunities for employees of different agencies to interact with one another. They thereby enable members to broaden their perspectives and make more informed professional and life choices.

➤ **Socialize.** Professional organizations sponsor happy hours, networking events, lectures, cultural outings, vacation packages, and other recreational activities.

Details, Details

A "detail assignment" is a temporary assignment for a specified period of time in another office or agency. While "detailed," an employee remains an employee of his or her home office and continues to be paid by it, but works for another organization.

You may want to do a detail to get experience working on new and different issues from your current ones, completing different types of assignments, networking, working for a more prestigious organization, or scoping out another organization. Moreover, detail assignments, like rental-with-option-to-buy agreements, frequently lead to permanent jobs.

Details are occasionally posted on USAJOBS; you may find them by doing keyword searches on the word *detail*. However, many details are never advertised. Look for unadvertised details by asking around among your current and previous colleagues and supervisors.

Also, when you read the newspaper and publications that target feds, look out for discussions on temporary government-wide organizations, like task forces and commissions, that may need temporary staff; call the staff directors of those that interest you and volunteer your services. Alternatively, contact the managers of agencies where you would like to work, describe your credentials and your interest in joining their staffs, and then ask if they would be interested in helping you arrange a detail.

Your boss is most likely to approve your request for a detail if he tends to encourage professional advancement; believes that you will return from your detail with new skills that will be helpful to your home office; or is sympathetic with your desire to jump ship. One way to encourage your boss to approve your detail is to arrange for a senior executive from the detail agency to contact your office director and request you for the detail. The more senior your requesting official is, the better.

Training and Education

By pursuing training and education opportunities on your government job, you will:

➤ **Stay current.** Every field, no matter what it is, is continually advancing. So if you just tread water without advancing with your field, and without learning the latest methods and software tools, you will fall behind. Alternatively, if you stay on top of your field, your commitment to staying current will serve as a great selling point to hiring managers.

➤ **Keep evolving.** As you evolve, your interests may change. By getting training in your new areas of interest, you will improve your ability to pursue them further.

➤ **Become management material.** No matter how good your leadership, communication, team-building, and project management skills already are, you can improve them more. And the more you do, the more you will increase your credentials for moving into management.

➤ **Network.** Classes provide great opportunities to interact with feds from other agencies.

Where to Get Training

More and more agencies are creating varied types of training programs for their employees. Ask your boss and your agency's training department if your agency has one. If it doesn't, seek out mentors on your own. In addition, these sources provide training to feds:

➤ The U.S. Office of Personnel Management's Federal Executive Institute and Management Training Centers in Virginia, West Virginia, and Colorado. See http://www.leadership.opm.gov/.

➤ Fed LDP: the Catalogue of Federal Leadership Development Programs at http://www.opm.gov/fedldp/index.aspx. The Department of Transportation lists federal training programs at http://www.dotcr.ost.dot.gov/asp/trainingprog.asp.

➤ The Graduate School offers day and evening classes and certificate programs especially for feds. See http://graduateschool.edu.

➤ Various degree programs and classes for feds listed on the training tab at http://www.govleaders.org. Find a additional training programs by typing *training for federal emploees* into the search window at http://www.usa.gov.

"*It's the old story. I was in the middle of a successful acting career when I was bitten by the accounting bug.*"

➤ The Center for Excellence in Public Leadership at George Washington University offers leadership and management programs for managers in the public sector. See http://www.gwu.edu/~cepl/about/about.html.

➤ The Center for Federal Management Leadership at George Mason University. See http://publicservicecenters.gmu.edu/federal.

➤ Web Manager University provides training to anyone who works on a government Web site (http://www.howto.gov/training).

➤ Fellowships for current feds are covered in Chapter 3 and this book's CD.

➤ Federal Executive Boards, which are located throughout the United States, provide leadership training programs and classes. See http://www.feb.gov. The Greater Los Angeles Federal Executive Board sponsors a Leadership Associates program for feds at the GS-9 through GS-12 level. For more information, Google the program name.

➤ The Congressional Black Caucus Foundation's Leadership Institute for Public Service prepares the next generation to take its place in community service and policy development arenas. The Leadership Institute's primary goal is to increase the pool of black leaders in community-based programs and public service careers. The institute offers numerous educational and leadership development programs for individuals ranging from junior high school students through young adults (generally ages 40 and under). Participants are provided with opportunities to learn the inner workings of Congress, explore public service and public policy careers, discuss current events and policy initiatives, and see close up leadership at its very best by working with and learning from Congressional Black Caucus members. For information, see http://cbcfincorg/internshipsandfellowships.html.

➤ Various federal organizations provide training in specific disciplines. For example, the Federal Acquisition Institute (http://www.fai.gov) and the Defense Acquisition Institute (http://www.dau.mil) provide training to federal contract managers. In addition, since 9/11, many defense and intelligence agencies have created new training programs for their employees.

Getting Trained on the Government's Time and Dime

Many agencies allocate a certain amount of money to each employee's training and/or attendance at conferences per year and associated travel expenses. They also allow employees to use work time to attend such events. If your boss hasn't already explained your agency's training policy, ask her or your agency's training department to do so.

Note that if you pursue a college or advanced degree related to your job, you may be able to cover some or all of your tuition through your annual training allocation or through your agency's student loan repayment program. I know, for example, a GS-14 Public Affairs Specialist at the Environmental Protection Agency whose department covered her entire tuition for a master's degree in public administration that she earned at night; this degree helped her qualify for a GS-15 position.

In addition, find out if your agency has an employee scholarship program. Also, the University of Maryland's Robert H. Smith School of Business in College Park, Maryland, offers partial-tuition scholarships to federal managers.

Finding a Mentor

Remember that reassuring line "I'm on your side," from the Simon & Garfunkel song, "Bridge Over Troubled Water"? Wouldn't it be nice to have someone on your side at work—someone who would be willing and eager to offer you professional advice? That's a mentor.

Some potential sources of mentors include:

> **Professional organizations devoted to a particular field.** Once you find relevant organizations, search their Web sites for potential mentors and training opportunities. And if possible, participate in these organizations' events. Even better, contribute to events in order to showcase your skills and cultivate contacts whom you may turn to as mentors.

> **Professional organizations devoted to a particular demographic.** For example, the organizations Blacks in Government and Federally Employed Women both run training and mentoring programs. Also, the Senior Executives Association offers a "flash" mentoring program that arranges for retired SEA members or SEA volunteers to offer advice on personal growth and career development to newly appointed members and GS-14/15 members. Each mentor-mentee pairing lasts for a one-hour, one-on-one meeting. And Young Government Leaders sponsors occasional mentoring events.

> **Federal development programs.** The Senior Executive Candidate Development Program, the Executive Leadership Program, the Presidential Management Fellows Program, and the USDA Graduate School Executive Leadership Program mentor program participants.

> **Programs for feds at nonprofit organizations.** For example, the Voyagers Program of the American Council for Technology-Industry Advisory Council offers mentoring. The Partnership for Public Service's Strategic Advisors to Government Executives provides mentoring to senior leaders in government from their predecessors and private-sector counterparts. This mentoring is usually designed to help mentees implement discipline-specific strategies.

> **Agency mentoring programs.** Among agencies that have programs are the State and Energy departments, Nuclear Regulatory Commission, Environmental Protection Agency, NASA, the Justice Department Bureau of Alcohol, Tobacco, Firearms and Explosives, and the Corporation for National and Community Service. Ask your boss or your training department if your agency offers such programs.

> **SCORE, a program of Counselors to America's Small Business.** Through this national organization, retired business experts offer free online and in-person advice and classes to professionals who are starting or expanding their own businesses.

> **The International Mentoring Networking Organization** offers mentoring from leading authorities to everyone, anytime, anywhere at its Web site, www.imno.org.

Still stuck? Contact successful individuals in your field and tactfully ask for advice. You may find such individuals from these and other resources:

> *Federal Times*, the *Fed Page* of the *Washington Post*, other publications devoted to federal audiences, and other books, periodicals, and Web sites. If you read about someone whose achievements you would like to emulate, contact that person, tell him why you admire him, and ask specific questions that would help you achieve your goals.

➤ GovLoop.com, a social networking site devoted to government employees. By starting and contributing to discussions on this site, you may meet potential mentors.

➤ **Managers at your job.** Engage potential mentors in conversations about common ground you share, your interests, and their favorite topic: their own rise to the top.

Once you've identified potential professional confidantes, build relationships with them by:

1. **Offering them assistance.** By volunteering to help role models, you will generate opportunities to work shoulder-to-shoulder with them.

2. **Engaging leaders.** If you reach out to conference presenters, authors, columnists, federal managers, or other prominent professionals, try to bring something to the table before you request their advice by, for example, referring them to a relevant article or event.

3. **Expressing gratitude whenever someone goes out of his or her way for you.** Send a card, gift, or at least a thank-you e-mail, and report back to your mentor how the assistance helped you.

Are you a manager who wants to learn more about the benefits of mentoring programs? If so, search for the Office of Personnel Management's online publication "Best Practices: Mentoring" at www.opm.gov.

Your Success Portfolio

No matter how preoccupied with your current projects and proud of your achievements you are now, I guarantee you that your memory of them will soon fade as you move onto new projects. Moreover, the evidence of your success will vanish as Web sites are revised, key documents get lost, and supervisors who witnessed your achievements leave your organization.

Nevertheless, by maintaining a complete inventory of your achievements and resulting positive feedback, you will generate important supporting grist for your future requests for promotions and future job applications. So continually track your achievements and preserve the evidence of your success. For guidance on how to do so, see the discussion "Validating Your Success" in Chapter 9, "The Portfolio Treatment" in Chapter 15, and my *Washington Post* article, "Make Every Interview a Show and Tell," which is included on this book's CD.

Getting Great Evaluations

Make it easy for your boss to give you a great review by:

➤ **Answering the question, "What have you done for me lately?"** If your boss was replaced midyear, he probably doesn't know much about what you did before he arrived. And even if you have had the same boss all year, he probably doesn't remember all of your important accomplishments for the year.

So instead of relying on your boss's selective or defective memory, submit to your boss a concise, bulleted list of this year's achievements before review time. That way, he will have sufficient time to incorporate it into your review.

Your achievements list should succinctly review your success portfolio's recent additions, describe how your achievements added value, and review the positive feedback you received. Also, describe how you went above and beyond the call of duty, completed projects that exceeded your grade level, and stayed current in your field. And, if possible, describe any of your "Superman"/save-the-day achievements, decisions, and strategies that saved your organization's hide, prevented disasters, and/or contributed to particularly quick disaster recoveries. (For guidance on how to describe your achievements in compelling terms, see Chapter 9 and the "Cheat Sheet for Annual Review Prep," which is included on this book's CD.) Also, attach any relevant documents to your list.

If your boss ignores your list, during your review meeting, request that he attach it to your review. That way, it will become a formal part of your record. So, even if you receive a commentless review, you will still get credit for your achievements and the positive feedback they drew.

➤ **Making detail assignments count.** If you're detailed to another office for any extended time period, ask your detail boss for a written evaluation when your assignment ends, and then give it to your permanent boss.

➤ **Requesting what you need.** Your review is a great time to request training, discuss the types of projects you would like to take on, and ask for any additional administrative or equipment supports you need.

➤ **Proactively defusing criticism.** If you had any significant setbacks this year, acknowledge them and affirm your commitment to doing better in the future. Even if you had a great year, solicit suggestions from your boss on potential improvements.

➤ **Doing better next time.** If you get a poor review, develop with your boss an action plan for improvement and follow through on it. Ask for another review in six months.

➤ **Asking for what you deserve.** If you had a good year but your boss doesn't schedule a review meeting, schedule a meeting for a review with your boss. Then, during the meeting, explain to your boss what you accomplished during the year and show him/her evidence of your success.

Alternatively, if your permanent or temporary boss is too busy to write your evaluation, politely volunteer to write it yourself for her signature. By using this technique myself when I completed a detail at the White House Conference on Aging, I earned a positive evaluation that I deserved but otherwise wouldn't have received. Then, I submitted my detail evaluation to my permanent boss in the Treasury Department, and thereby bolstered my reputation on my permanent job. Finally, by incorporating comments from my detail evaluation into job applications (as explained in Chapter 10), I helped generate many interviews when I was job hunting.

➤ **Push back if you feel you've been wrongly evaluated.** If, by chance, you receive an annual evaluation that does not do justice to you, consult your union on potential ways to request a reconsideration of your evaluation and/or submit a more formal objection—and then consider your options carefully.

Harness the Power of an Effective "Thank You"

Are you expressing gratitude frequently and forcefully enough to people who help you? If not, you are probably sacrificing important opportunities to:

➤ Strengthen ties with friends, colleagues, and other associates.

➤ Encourage people who have helped you to help you again.

➤ Show that you have good manners—a rare trait that can help you stand out from the pack.

➤ Reward and lift the spirits of deserving people.

Who should you thank? Each of your personal or professional contacts who extends him- or herself for you or provides you with particularly helpful advice, connections, or information. Such people may include:

➤ Professional associates—such as bosses, colleagues, and mentors—who create career-boosting opportunities for you; direct you to promising job openings; organize special events that are particularly instructive; advise you on professional, financial, or personal decisions; provide you with pivotal contacts or leads; or help you do your job better or give you glowing references.

➤ Outstanding members of your staff.

➤ Professionals, such as doctors and accountants, who devote special attention to your case, conduct extensive research for you, or make themselves available to you during off-duty hours.

➤ Experts who present effective lectures, seminars, or training sessions that you attend.

➤ Your former teachers or professors whose instruction influenced you in important ways.

➤ Clerks in stores or employees in restaurants or on telephone help lines who go the extra mile for you. (That way, you will practically be guaranteed good service next time you return to that venue.)

How should you thank people who help you? First and foremost, say "thank you" to them early and often. And when you do so, specify why their contributions were so special and helpful to you.

Remember that even the most accomplished and successful people are not too accomplished or successful to get a charge from your positive feedback and to benefit from learning how their expertise helped you. So by, for example, telling a speaker how his presentation rocked your world, you will almost certainly rock his world.

But when a mere verbal "thank you" does not do sufficient justice to good deeds, also consider the following:

➤ Sending a thank-you card or letter to an expert, such as a lecturer, conference presenter, or author whom you admire. (This is a great way to initiate networking contacts with such experts.) And a written thank-you is always much more forceful and memorable than merely a spoken one.

> ➤ Passing on praise to the supervisors of people who go the extra mile for you. You may do so in-person, by phone, by mail, or by e-mail (with a cc to the recipient of your praise). If, for example, you work closely with other feds or contractors who put in stellar performances, tell their supervisors about their productivity.

> ➤ Similarly, if a clerk in a store or someone on a "help" line extends him- or herself for you, reward that person by telling, e-mailing, or leaving a note for his supervisor about your positive interaction.

> ➤ When someone helps you in a big way, honor your associate's contributions with a gift; such a gift need not be hulking and expensive—only thoughtful; nothing expresses heartfelt appreciation as effectively as a considerate memento.

Some caveats. Don't make preliminary comments to mentors, such as, "if X happens from all of this, I'm going to take you out to dinner," or to only thank mentors when their assistance is fruitful. Rather, if your mentor's efforts are worthy of a thank-you dinner, they are worthy of that dinner even if her efforts, for whatever reason, fail to bear fruit. And by all means, if you ever promise to take someone out for thank-you drinks, dinner, or anything else, be sure to fulfill your promise.

Warning: Be careful not to give gifts that violate ethics regulations. (Consult your agency's ethics officer, if necessary.)

Keep people who advise you on your professional, business, or academic choices informed of your progress. For example, report back to mentors how their advice helped you. If your mentor's advice does not work out exactly as planned, tell your mentor what you learned from the experience anyway.

Also, consider turning help from your mentor into a gift that keeps on giving. How? By mentoring another professional who would benefit from your advice. Tell your mentor(s) about the mentoring altruism he helped inspire in you, and how you are passing on his approach/knowledge to other worthy professionals.

Last but not least, remember that it is never too late to thank a mentor. Even if a teacher, professor, supervisor, colleague, manager, or someone else provided you with important guidance years ago—perhaps, it was guidance or inspiration that served you well during a pivotal time or throughout your career—and you didn't give him the thanks she deserved at the time, or her advice has continued to help you long after she initially gave it to you, contact her now. Fear not: there is no expiration date on a thank-you. Even if your mentor doesn't even remember you, or your thank you is belated, your expression of appreciation will give your mentor a well-deserved thrill.

Asking for a Promotion

Do you think that your boss will automatically give you a promotion when you deserve it, or that promotions only come to those who don't ask for them?

Well, think again. Remember that your boss's primary concern is probably not your well-being, but his own well-being. And to be brutally honest, he probably remembers his fifth-grade report card better than what you did five months ago. So if you have done a stellar job on a demanding project, put in a banner year, or are handling increased responsibility, your boss may need a tactful reminder that you are due for some financial positive feedback.

How Big Will Your Promotion Be?

Under the General Schedule (GS) pay plan, a supervisor usually can:

➤ Give you a cash award worth up to 20 percent of annual salary.

➤ Give you a Quality Step Increase (QSI), which will move you up one step within your grade before the required waiting period has passed. (In some agencies, employees who receive the highest rating in tiered annual evaluations must receive either a QSI or a cash award.) If you have a choice between a cash award and a QSI, you should usually opt for the QSI because its long-term value will probably exceed that of a cash bonus; unlike a one-time bonus, a QSI is a gift that keeps on giving.

➤ Give you a grade increase, if your job has promotion potential. In most cases, you would become eligible for a grade increase after spending one year at your current grade. This means that you would probably become eligible for a grade increase on the first anniversary of your first day in the government.

Contrary to popular belief, if you receive a grade increase, you won't automatically be promoted to Step 1 of the grade immediately above your current grade. Instead, your promotion would probably follow the two-step rule. (See http://www.opm.gov/oca/pay/HTML/promotion.asp.)

To find your salary under a two-step promotion, go to the salary table that covers your current job. (Find current salary tables by entering the phrase "salary tables" into the search box at http://www.opm.gov.) Next, find your current step and grade on your table. Then find the step that is two steps above your current step at your current grade. Next, go to the grade that is immediately above your current grade, find the salary that is equal to, or immediately above, your two-step salary, and that step will be your promotion destination.

But if your position doesn't currently have promotion potential, your boss might be able to give you a grade increase by upgrading your job because of additional duties and responsibilities under an "accretion of duties." To do so, your boss would have to submit a justification to your agency's human resources office that explains how your duties increased and so now warrant classification at a higher grade level. Alternatively, your boss may be able to give you a grade increase by advertising a job with a higher grade level than you now have and putting it out to competition. Under this alternative, you would have to apply for the job and win the competition to land the higher graded job.

Strategize Your Promotion Request

Whenever you request a promotion, QSI, or cash award, give your request extra *oomph* by submitting a clear justification of why you deserve it—including a concise explanation of how your responsibilities have increased, a bulleted list of your achievements, and how they benefited your organization and a description of the positive feedback they generated.

A particularly strategic time to remind your supervisor of your recent glories is before your annual review and in time for your supervisor to incorporate your list of successes into your review. If you're confident that your boss values you but is resistant to rewarding you, you may want to put the squeeze on him. How? By getting a better, competing offer from another organization, and then asking your boss to match it.

One more thing: If your boss announces her impending departure from your agency, be sure to ask her to finalize any promotions she has promised you before departing.

This is important because your boss's replacement will be about as likely to honor your current boss's promises as the next U.S. president will be to honor the current president's promises.

Earn Professional Awards

A professional award may boost your career long after your awards ceremony. An award's long-term benefits may, for example, include:

> ➤ Establishing you as an expert and validating your approaches.

> ➤ Generating exposure for you when you are publicly honored in the sponsoring organization's events or publications or in media outlets. Such exposure may yield new professional opportunities for you.

> ➤ Providing you with a monetary reward.

> ➤ Enable you to—like an Oscar winner—raise your asking price on your next job.

To maximize the benefits of any awards:

1. Position discussions of awards prominently in your cover letters and résumés. Also, include flattering write-ups that accompany your awards in your success portfolio.

2. Mention your awards and why you received them during interviews.

3. Create a networking business card that states that you are a "Recipient of the XYZ Award."

Types of Awards You May Receive

There is a wide variety of awards that you might be able to win. Consider the following:

> ➤ Bonuses, which are usually doled out during annual reviews.

> ➤ Federal incentives awards. During or between annual reviews, your boss may reward you with a cash award or a time-off award. You may also receive a Quality Step Increase, which would advance you one step within your grade before the required waiting period has passed. And successful teams may be awarded "team awards." Tip: If you are asked in an interview about your ability to work with others, cite any team award(s) you may have received as tangible evidence of your team-friendly approaches.

> ➤ Agency or departmental awards, such as a "Director's Award" from your agency ahead.

> ➤ Presidential Rank Awards, which honor members of the Senior Executive Service.

> ➤ Agency or departmental awards.

> ➤ Awards from organizations addressing federal management, such as the Council for Excellence in Government, the Partnership for Public Service, the National Academy of Public Administration, and American Society for Public Administration.

> ➤ Awards from professional organizations or associations that address your field.

Helping Yourself Win Awards

Rather than passively waiting to be recognized with an award, use strategies that will increase your odds of receiving awards. For example:

➤ Identify and lead high-profile and high-impact projects that would increase your eligibility for awards.

➤ Ask for what you deserve. If you think your achievements qualify you for an incentive award, ask your boss if he would consider giving you one. If he turns you down, ask him what else you would have to do in order to qualify for an award in the future.

➤ Ask your boss or office director to enroll your office in competitions for awards in your field. For example, if you work in a federal public affairs office, ask your agency's public affairs director to submit your office's best work products, including your best work products, to competitions sponsored by the Association of Government Communicators.

➤ Arrange to be nominated. Instead of expecting a manager to spontaneously notice your work and nominate you for an award, ask a colleague or manager who appreciates your work to nominate you. If you do so, volunteer to complete the associated paperwork yourself. I know, for example, an environmental educator who recruited a former colleague to nominate her for a prestigious lifetime achievement award from an ecological association while taking two years off to take care of her baby. The result: The environmental educator won the award, which—in addition to serving as a huge feather in her professional cap—provided her with grist for her résumé covering her maternity leave.

➤ Convey compliments. If another manager besides your boss or a client, stakeholder, colleague, or any other noteworthy figure compliments your work orally, say to him: "I'm sure my boss would like to know that my contributions were helpful to you. Would you mind e-mailing her a short note telling her what you just said to me, and cc-ing me on that as well?"

➤ Write your acceptance speech. Imagining your victory may help motivate you to achieve it.

Moving On to Move Up

Here are some ways to boost your salary besides, as discussed above, earning a promotion:

1. **Get a retention bonus.** You may be eligible for a retention bonus if you're a prized employee and are considered likely to leave the federal government for any reason, including retirement. (You can help prove that you may be likely to leave the government by providing letters for other job offers.) For more info, type "retention bonus" into the search window at http://www.opm.gov/.

2. **Get a better job.** To keep moving up in government, you may have to keep moving on to different jobs, different offices, and different agencies—just as many private-sector employees must do. Why? Because even if your job was perfect for you when you were hired, perfection is usually a temporary state with only a limited life span. Any number of circumstances can damage the magic of a great job. For example,

opportunities on your job might not evolve as quickly as you do. Your relationship with your boss may deteriorate. Your agency may have thorny organizational problems. Or you may deserve a promotion that you're not getting.

Deciding to Make a Move

How do you know when it's time to go? Someone once suggested to me that as soon as you land a new job, you should start looking for your next job. While instant job searching may be a bit premature, it's a good idea to:

1. Continually scope out opportunities in your field even if you like your current job. By doing so, you may get ideas on how to slant your career or unexpectedly stumble across a job that you like even better than your current job

2. Cultivate and maintain a broad array of professional relationships throughout your career, not just when you're in crisis-management mode or when you're job hopping. Once you're in a crisis or ready to bolt, it's too late to stock your Rolodex with contacts who can provide advice, feedback, and job leads.

As a general rule of thumb, it's time to start looking to jump ship when you realize that your current job doesn't offer advancement, interesting projects, and/or a respectful, dignified work environment—and probably won't do so in the future. However, I have known many intelligent, energetic, and accomplished feds who—almost resembling the victims of Stockholm Syndrome—stayed in jobs long after they had, for one reason or another, become hopelessly unrewarding and unpleasant. Why? Usually because these stagnating feds were afraid of change.

But to be successful, and keep advancing, your fear of not achieving your potential must exceed your fear of change. If your fear of change—or anything else—is blocking your ascent, it's a good idea to address your fears by discussing them with friends, reading self-help books, joining self-help groups, or getting professional help. After all, if you don't wrestle your fears to the ground, they will wrestle you to the ground.

And if you expect things to get better by themselves even when management is not addressing the situation, ask yourself whether your expectations are reasonable. In my experience, problems rarely fix themselves.

Here's another way to look at it: Conventional wisdom says that about 50 percent of all marriages end in divorce, even though most marriages were formed out of love. Most employee/employer relationships were formed out of a lot less than love, and so are destined to ultimately end in divorce.

Landing Your Next Job

As a current fed, you may find openings in your current agency and other agencies by any of the following:

1. Regularly checking USAJOBS and the other sources of openings listed in Chapter 2. If you apply to openings that are advertised through multiple announcements, be sure to apply to the announcement that is only open to current and

"Actually, it was more of a lateral move than a promotion."

former feds. For more info on this, see "Steps for Reading a Vacancy Announcement" in Chapter 6.

2. Finding hiring managers who will either create a position for you or hire you into an existing opening. You may find such networking contacts among your existing contacts or through networking activities discussed in Chapter 2 or in this chapter.

Here are a few tips on moving around in government:

➤ If you're willing to accept a position at your current step and grade without a promotion, in many cases, you can be lateraled into any equivalent position within your current agency or another agency without competition. That is, a hiring manager can select you without considering any other applicants. Unfortunately, this option is not well publicized, and so even many managers don't know about it. So if you are willing to accept a lateral transfer and you suspect that a particular federal manager might be interested in hiring you, consider tactfully reminding him/her of the option of moving you onto his or her staff via a lateral transfer.

➤ If a federal position is created for you, ask your hiring manager to build promotion potential into it; otherwise, you will probably eventually have to land another job or have the position redesigned in order to move up.

➤ Because excepted service agencies generally pay better and have more flexibility in setting pay than competitive service agencies, if you switch from the competitive service to the excepted service, you will have an excellent chance of getting a big salary boost.

➤ No matter where you land your next job, see Chapter 16 to prepare for salary negotiation.

Becoming Executive Material

Thinking about aiming for a job in the senior executive service (SES)? If so, the first thing you should do is learn as much as possible about the SES and confirm that you do, in fact, want to be an SESer.

What the SES Is

The SES is the federal government's corps of executive leaders; about 6,000 career SESers manage about 1.8 million civilian feds. The ratio of about one SESer to about every 300 feds underscores the selectivity of the SES as well as the responsibility and authority wielded by its members.

SESers devote the majority of their time to leadership, as in setting goals for their organizations and marching their organizations toward them. (READ: respect, power, and influence.) To succeed as leaders, SESers must form alliances with other executives, regularly communicate with staffers, and motivate and evaluate them. They must also make high-impact decisions about the structure and strategic plans of their organizations and the allocation of large budgets, contracts, and other resources.

The rewards of SES jobs include the satisfaction of improving government programs that can impact the health, education, security, and standard-of-living of people all over the world, as well as the uses of worldwide natural resources. As one SESer says," Everyone in government can make a difference. But in the SES, you have a chance to make a big difference."

The Pressures of the SES

SESers usually pursue management and leadership career tracks rather than purely technical tracks. Therefore, if you want to devote your time and effort to advancing in your technical field rather than in management, the SES might not be for you. Moreover, SESers must regularly interact with staffers throughout the hierarchy and implement tough decisions, sometimes unpopular ones. So if you are not people-centric, or are conflict-averse or meeting-averse, you might not be a good fit for the SES.

Mapping Your Path into the SES

In addition, SESers must regularly commit to achieving specific quantifiable goals that may, for example, involve streamlining or automating processes, reducing costs, or improving customer services. The pressure resulting from such rigid accountability energizes some personality types but overwhelms others.

Last but not least, SES jobs demand great quantities of time, devotion, and toil. So, if you aim for the SES, be certain that, at this stage of your career, you are willing to spend more time at the office and are not aiming to wind down your career. (See Table 18-1 for more about the advantages and disadvantages of joining the SES.)

If you want to land an SES job, strategize your ascent. This is important because entry into the SES requires specific, extensive experience—the type of experience that you would be able to gain only with targeted, long-term efforts, rather than by happenstance or by slapping together necessary prerequisites in a last-minute all-nighter.

Take Note!

Discounts and Freebies for Feds

- **Rental Cars.** Fed up (no pun intended) with renting wrecks? Avis, Alamo, and Budget discount their rates for off-duty feds; Hertz, Dollar, and E-Z Rent-A-Car offer government rates to off-duty feds; and Thrifty gives off-duty feds a free class upgrade. Some price breaks also cover federal contractors. Request price breaks when you reserve cars.

- **Computers.** Feds get hardware discounts ranging from 6 to 10 percent, and software discounts up to 18 percent at most Apple Stores (bring your federal ID) and online at http://www.apple.com/r /store/government/. Many PC vendors also give discounts to feds. For example, see http://www.mil- itary4life.com/discounts/computers.shtml and http://www.dell.com/content/segmenter.aspx?c=us&l =en&cs=6099. Also, members of the American Federation of Government Employees receive dis- counts on computers.

- **Hotels.** Many domestic and overseas hotels give their government rate to feds even when they're on personal time. (But don't try to get an unwarranted discount by claiming that you're on federal busi- ness when you're not.) See the Federal Discount Lodging Directory at http://www.hotels.idt.net/.

- **Insurance and Other Services.** GEICO offers discounts to feds. Also, the National Active and Retired Federal Employees Association offers various types of insurance and discounts on moving expenses to its members.

- **Scholarships and Loans.** The Federal Employee Education & Assistance Programs provides scholar- ships and emergency financial assistance to feds and their families. Some professional organizations for feds also offer scholarships.

- **Agency-Sponsored Services.** Many federal agencies sponsor employee assistance programs (EAPs) that offer free confidential support, including emotional counseling, legal services, and financial advice. So check whether your agency has such a program.

  What types of problems do EAPs address? An EAP may be helpful to anyone who is battling his or her own or a family member's substance-abuse problem; is searching for affordable day care or elder care; wants legal help after a car accident; is engaged in a dispute with his or her landlord; is trying to decide whether to pay off a mortgage early; has tax questions; needs advice on how to craft a standard will or living will; needs advice on how to pay for a child's college tuition; or is experienc- ing depression—to name just a few examples. In addition, some EAPs provide around-the-clock crisis counseling by phone. To find out whether your agency has an EAP, consult your agency's human resources office or Intranet.

  If, by chance, you are dissatisfied with a referral you receive from an EAP, inform an EAP manag- er of the problem. I learned this lesson after seeking legal advice from an EAP years ago. Unfortunately, I was initially referred to an attorney who was obviously only interested in recruiting me for more consults than were covered by the EAP. After I informed my EAP contact of the situation, she paired me with a different attorney who provided all the advice I needed in one free consult.

- **Cell Phones.** Some major cell phone companies give discounts to feds on their monthly bills. For example, Sprint gives a 15 percent discount on monthly cell phone bills to employees of some feder- al agencies. Ask for the discount when you buy your plan. But beware: My research indicates that many sales reps at cell phone companies don't know about discounts offered by their own compa- nies. So, if necessary, ratchet up your inquiries about discounts to managers at your target compa- nies, and keep saying that you seek the Federal Telecommunications Act of 1996 discount to feder- al employees past and present.

TABLE 18-1	Advantages and Disadvantages of Being an SESer	
Job Characteristic	**Advantage**	**Disadvantage**
You're a member of an elite corps.	It's an honor to be admitted into a highly selective, respected, elite organization composed of high-achieving leaders. Each SESer has great opportunities to make big changes in the federal government.	To your colleagues, you may go from being "one of us" to being "one of them."
You're perched in a lofty position at the top levels of government.	Finally, you're in a position to translate your visionary ideas into reality. You're a leader. You have arrived!	Translating your visionary ideas into reality may be harder than it looks. To do so, you must lead people, with all of their foibles and resentments. Yes, you have arrived, but you have arrived at an organization that, like all other organizations, has flaws.
Influence and visibility	You advance the president's agenda, you can improve government on a big scale. When things go well, you get credit—whether or not you deserve it. Because you're working on a public stage, everyone sees you succeed.	You must advance the president's agenda, whether you agree with it or not. When things go poorly, you get the blame, whether or not you deserve it. And because you're working on a public stage, everyone knows it when you fail.
High stress, long hours, and interruptions at home	If you thrive under pressure, enjoy the limelight, and are prepared to be accountable for organizational results, you're in your element.	Obvious disadvantages.
Your pay	Your salary and bonuses may be significantly higher than those of your previous GS-14 or GS-15 job. Plus, you're eligible for prestigious and lucrative Presidential Rank Awards (see http://www.opm.gov/ses/performance/presrankawards.asp).	You probably earn less than you would as a private-sector executive.
You belong to a community of high-achievers	You receive a great deal of training and collaborate with other high-achievers whom you may learn from and enjoy.	Possibility of death by meeting.

A regularly updated hyperlinked directory of dozens of types of discounts for feds on everything from hotels to child care to auto repair to computers and more is posted by *Governement Executive* at http://www/govexec.com/federal-news/2012/02/gimme-my-discounts/29165.

Note that if you decide to pursue the SES, be aware that some SES jobs are open to GS-14s (or equivalents) and some are restricted to GS-15s. Some more tips:

> **Assess.** Start considering your potential SES prospects by reviewing the SES Web site at http://www.opm.gov/ses, particularly the section on the five Executive Core Qualifications (ECQs). These ECQs are: (1) Leading Change; (2) Leading People; (3) Results Driven; (4) Business Acumen; and (5) Building Coalitions. Remember that your application for the SES must include essays addressing each of these five ECQs. This means that you must gain significant experience in all five ECQ areas to qualify for the SES.

"I say, if at first you don't succeed, redefine success."

So identify gaps between the ECQs and your credentials and the types of experience you would need to fill those gaps. When doing so, solicit advice from your supervisor, current SESers, your agency's SES training coordinator, and managers inside and outside your chain of command. Why? Because, says a Department of Energy (DOE) SESer, while managers inside your chain of command are uniquely positioned to evaluate your productivity, managers outside the chain of command are particularly likely to provide you with the "brutally honest feedback" that you need about your deficiencies.

You will receive different and complementary advice from the various managers whom you consult, assures the DOE SESer. To chart his own climb to the top, the DOE SESer says he "sat down with my boss, various mentors, and two human resources directors who gave me candid assessments of my skills. They told me where I should be to get into the SES." In addition, he also recommends analyzing the winning ways of federal leaders whom you admire, and identifying how you could acquire their expertise.

> **Get Training.** Take SES prep courses offered by the Federal Executive Institute (https://www.leadership.opm.gov), the Graduate School (http://www.graduateschool.edu), Harvard's Kennedy School (http://ksgecprogram.harvard.edu/Programs/sef/overview.aspx), Brookings (http://www. brookings edu/execed/pr grams/catalog/sesbootcamp_s.aspx), the Partnership for Public Service (http://ourpublicservice.org/OPS/pr grams/cgl/index.shtm), and by other training centers discussed in the "Where to Get Training" section of this chapter. Also, consider participating in fellowships for current feds that provide leadership experience. (See the list of fellowships provided on this book's CD.)

 **Caution**

Feds may only accept discounts that are offered to feds from all or multiple agencies, not just to those of particular offices or to particular employee(s). (This is an anti-bribery restriction.) If you're unsure whether to accept a particular discount or gift, ask your agency's ethics attorney.

> **Lead on Your Current Job.** Request new assignments that would help you round out your experience and add to your leadership experience. Seek and seize opportunities to lead projects, task forces, committees, and change management programs, whenever possible. Such opportunities may be particularly abundant during reorganizations and after other professionals in your organizations quit or retire.

Also, identify unrecognized needs in your agency and volunteer to lead projects addressing them. For example, I know a writer at NOAA who volunteered to offer a one-time seminar to agency scientists on how to communicate scientific information to the public. She received so many requests for more seminars that providing such training became a regular part of her job.

Another case in point: I know a mid-level fed who was assigned to be her agency's representative to the charity effort known as the Combined Federal Campaign (CFC). At first, she resented the assignment because it took time away from her assignments that she enjoyed more. But once she discovered that the assignment helped her generate high-level contacts throughout her own and other agencies (which ultimately helped her ascend the career ladder), she came to delight in it.

> **Lead Outside of Your Job.** Volunteer for leadership positions outside of your current job. Yes, your nonwork leadership experience will help you get into the SES. For example, you could gain required budget experience by serving as the treasurer of your condo board or by running charity fundraisers; or you could gain communications experience by managing public relations projects for a professional organization.

> **Transfer Jobs, If Necessary.** Apply for new jobs, even lateral jobs, if your current job does not offer opportunities for you to fill your ECQ gaps.

> **Schmooze with SESers.** If you are currently a GS-14 or GS-15, join the Senior Executive Association (http://www.seniorexecs.org). Also, seek training and mentoring from professional organizations in your field and from professional organizations for federal executives and managers. (See the list of professional organizations provided on this book's CD.) Also, seek situations in which you can contribute to these organizations because they provide ideal opportunities to impress potential hiring managers. Many of these groups invite feds at the GS-13 through GS-15 levels to join.

> **Cultivate High-Level References.** Your references for SES jobs should do more than just testify to your reliability and effectiveness; they should also attest to your leadership and management abilities. And it's all the better if your references are from SESers themselves. So as you advance, cultivate high-level contacts, keep them informed of your activities, be as helpful as possible to them, and stay in touch with them.

> **Soak up Knowledge.** Throughout your career, seize formal and informal opportunities to master the nuts and bolts of running federal offices by learning about budget management, human resources, information security, communications, procurement, and other management issues, whether they interest you or not. As one SESer observes, "If you're going to run a large department, you need to know it all." If you aspire to the SES, it is particularly important to learn about federal budget processes because so much about the management of every agency and department hinges on its budget, and because understanding budget fundamentals will increase your marketability in every agency.

It is particularly helpful to learn about the budget both from the perspective of Congress, which sets the budget, and from federal agencies that must adhere to them. You may learn about federal budget processes by landing detail assignments in federal offices that liaison with Congress, training courses discussed in this chapter, and fellowships in Congress covered on the CD accompanying this book.

Also, review the discussion of entry into the SES provided in Chapter 6 of this book.

APPENDIXES

APPENDIX

1

Tip Sheet for Veterans
and Their Families

The federal government is a very veteran-friendly employer.

> More than 500,000 veterans currently work for the federal government.

> Veterans currently account for almost 30 percent of the federal workforce, which is more than triple the percentage in the private sector. What's more, more than 40 percent of upper-level hires are currently veterans.

> The representation of veterans at all levels of the federal workforce is steadily rising.

The federal government is currently becoming even more veteran friendly. This trend is being encouraged by the new Veterans Employment Program, which is designed to help former members of the military land federal jobs. The program's Web site provides many resources to veterans and their families, including a directory of program managers throughout the federal government who are helping to run the Veteran Employment Program. (See FedsHireVets.gov.)

These program managers offer varied services, including providing one-on-one feedback to veterans for preparing their résumés and other application materials, notifying veterans of appropriate openings including unadvertised openings, answering logistical and substantive questions about openings and hiring agencies, and advocating for veterans to hiring managers. The Veterans Employment Program, which began in 2010, is already credited with significantly boosting the hiring of veterans by federal agencies and for helping vets land particularly high-paying jobs.

Described below are various other widely used programs that give veterans important advantages over nonveterans in landing federal jobs.

Get Hired Through a Competition

Several programs give veterans an edge in landing federal jobs that are filled through open competitions involving the rating and ranking of applicants and interviews.

Bookmark These Sites. For more information on federal programs for job-seeking veterans, visit http://www.dol.gov/vets/ and http://www.vetsuccess.gov.

Veterans' Preference

Veterans' preference gives points to qualified veterans in competitions for federal jobs, and requires federal agencies to hire a qualified veteran over an applicant who scores similarly in a job competition. Veterans' preference has make-or-break power; it often serves as the deciding factor in selections.

There are two types of veterans' preference:

1. **Five-Point Veterans' Preference:** Typically given to veterans who served on active duty for at least two years during a period of war or in a campaign or expedition for which a campaign badge was authorized.

2. **Ten-Point Veterans' Preference:** Typically given to a disabled veteran, a Purple Heart recipient, the mother of a veteran who is disabled or who died in active duty, and the spouse of certain disabled or deceased veterans.

To determine whether you have veterans' preference and to count your points, go to http://www.jobsearch.usajobs.gov/veteranscenter. Additional information about veterans' preference, including a videotaped Webcast, is posted at http://www.opm.gov/veterans. To learn about your rights if you believe your veterans' preference has not been honored, go to the Labor Department's Veterans' Preference advisor at http://www.dol.gov.

Note that veterans' preference counts in competitions for most jobs that are: (1) in the competitive service or excepted service; and (2) open to the public. But because veterans' preference does not count in competitions for jobs that are only open to current feds (feds with status), veterans usually can't use it to land promotions. Another restriction: applicants for senior executive service jobs cannot count veterans' preference.

Other Competitive Programs

These programs allow nonfeds who are vets to compete for federal jobs that are otherwise open only to all current feds (feds with status):

 Hot Tip

In some cases, late applications from veterans are accepted by federal agencies. For more information, type "filing late applications" together with "veterans" into the search window at http://www.opm.gov.

> **The Veterans Employment Opportunities Act of 1998 (VEOA).** Note that veterans using VEOA cannot count veterans' preference and so VEOA does not give veterans an advantage in job competitions; it only allows them to compete in competitions that would otherwise be off limits to them.

> **Reinstatement eligibility.** The right of former feds with veterans' preference and former career feds to apply for jobs that are only open to current feds (feds with status). For veterans with veterans' preference and former career feds, reinstatement eligibility never expires; for many other types of former feds, it lasts for three years after their federal job ends.

Get Hired Without Competition

The following programs enable veterans to be selected for jobs without competing against other applications.

> **Veterans' Employment Recruitment Act (VRA):** Enables veterans to be noncompetitively hired into two-year temporary jobs at or below the GS-11 level or equivalent. (A GS-11 job is a mid-level position.)

> **Thirty Percent or More Disabled Program:** Enables veterans who have a service-connected disability of 30 percent or more to be noncompetitively hired into temporary jobs that may be converted at any time into permanent positions. There is no grade-level limitation to this program. Note that more positions are available under this program than under VRA.

> **Reinstatement Eligibility:** In addition to the rights described above, reinstatement eligibility allows former feds with veterans' preference to be noncompetitively hired into positions at grades that are equal or lower than those previously held.

> **Take Note!**
>
> *Operation Warfighter Placement Program*
>
> DOD's Operation Warfighter Program matches veterans who are receiving treatment at Washington, DC, area facilities with temporary federal jobs that match their skills and interests. Many of these temporary jobs lead to permanent jobs. To access this program's Web site, Google the program name.

Some openings that can be noncompetitively filled by veterans through the above programs are not advertised. You may find them by contacting your target agencies' Selective Placement Coordinators; these coordinators stay current on noncompetitive hiring and match applicants with openings. To obtain a list of Selective Placement Coordinators, go to http://www.fedshirevets.gov.

Programs for Family Members of Vets

Some military spouses may be quickly hired for federal jobs without competing against other applicants. This hiring mechanism covers spouses of active service members who must move when their military spouses change duty stations, including spouses of Guardsmen or reservists who are called up for more than 180 days of active service excluding time for training. (Note that to be eligible for this hiring mechanism, a spouse must move to another duty station accompanied by his or her service member spouse.) Agencies may use this mechanism to hire spouses for two years after their moves.

This hiring mechanism also covers former service members who are listed as 100 percent disabled and separated or retired, as well as widows or widowers of service members who have died on active duty and who have not remarried. Agencies are not bound by any time limit to use this hiring mechanism.

A few notes: To be hired via this hiring mechanism, eligibles must meet the qualification criteria of their target jobs. And hiring agencies are not obligated to use this hiring mechanism; they use it at their own discretion.

For more job-hunting advice for members of military families, see the above discussion of 10-point veterans' preference and http://www.fedshirevets.gov.

How to Find Job Opportunities

Plan your transition early. Before you leave the military, take courses that will boost your marketability, and participate in your base's Transition Assistance Program. Use online transitioning resources posted at http://www.turbotap.org/register.tpp. And stay in touch with colleagues who leave the military before you do. Once you join them on the outside, they may provide you with pivotal contacts and job-hunting advice. In addition:

1. You may find some openings that accept VEOA, VRA, or the 30 Percent or More Disabled Program by doing keyword searches of vacancy announcements using the names of these programs at http://www.usajobs.gov.

2. Some federal agencies recruit veterans from lists of job seekers provided by the VA. For more info, contact your state VA office, which you can find on http://www.va.gov.

3. Defense Department agencies currently employ far more veterans than other agencies. For example, almost 50 percent of Air Force employees are veterans. In addition, veterans account for about 25 percent of the workforce of the Department of Homeland Security (DHS). Other organizations with particularly good track records in hiring veterans include the VA, the intelligence community, and the Departments of Justice, Treasury, Labor, Transportation, Energy, and Agriculture.

4. Consider openings with federal security organizations, including police organizations in the Treasury Department, the U.S. Capitol Policy, the U.S. Supreme Court Police, and Customs and Border Protection.

Here are some key federal Web sites for job-hunting veterans:

➤ DoD's Web site is http://www.dodvets.com/index.asp. This site connects veterans with job openings as well as dynamic Professional Development Programs (entry-level internships) for recent college graduates that provide formal classroom and on-the-job training, and lead to permanent positions within DoD.

➤ The career Web sites of the Veterans Administration are http://www.vacareers.va.gov and http://www.vetsuccess.gov. The Web site of the VA's Vocational Rehabilitation and Employment Program is http://www.vba.va.gov/bln/vre. The Web site of the Veterans Job Bank, which provides a central resource that allows veterans to access jobs available specifically for them, is https://www.nationalresourcedirectory.gov /jobSearch/index.

➤ The career Web site of the intelligence community is http://www.intelligence.gov. The CIA's career Web site (https://www.cia.gov) and DHS's career Web site (http://www.dhs.gov) have special pages for military transitioners. Note that agencies in the intelligence community, DHS, DoD, the FBI, and the State Department frequently hold job fairs throughout the nation that are announced on their respective Web sites, USAJOBS, and http://www.FedsHireVets.gov. In addition, DoD's Hiring Heroes program sponsors job fairs (frequently located near military hospitals) that match veterans with government organizations. (See Chapter 2 for tips on faring well at career fairs.)

➤ The Defense Logistic Agency's Web site for military transitioners is http://www.hr.dla.mil/prospective/military.

➤ The Labor Department's site for transitioners and job-hunting veterans is http://www.dol.gov/vets.

➤ The Web site of the Army Materiel Command, which helps disabled veterans find jobs, is http://www.amc.army.mil/AlwaysASoldier.

In addition, the Office of Personnel Management runs the Veterans Outreach Offices at the Brooke Army Medical Center in San Antonio, Texas; Walter Reed Army Medical Center in Washington, DC; Brooke Army Medical Center in San Antonio, Texas; and at Fort Carson, Colorado. These offices provide various services, including help finding federal openings and preparing applications.

Note: See Appendix 2 if you are a disabled veteran. See the internship and recruitment programs that are covered in Chapter 3 and on this book's CD, and discussions of contract and temp jobs requiring security clearances that are covered in Chapters 2 and 7. See Chapter 2 for more ideas on finding permanent and temporary openings.

Conduct Google searches on terms like *military transition*. In recent years, many new Web sites connecting veterans with employers have appeared. Moreover, since 9/11, defense contractors—particularly DC-based ones—have grown like gangbusters.

Also, network via professional organizations in your field and via military-oriented associations, such as the Military Officers Association of America, Veterans of Foreign Wars, and Disabled American Veterans.

The Small Business Administration's nationwide offices help veterans start and run their own businesses by providing them with grants as well as free training, help winning federal contracts, mentoring, and other resources. For more information, type *veterans* into the search window at http://www.sba.gov. Other related Web sites are hyperlinked to http://www.dol.gov/vets/programs/empserv/main.htm.

Hot Tip

If You Have Security Clearance. . . . Identify your current or previous security clearances prominently on your cover letter, résumé, and other application materials, and mention them in your interviews. Such clearances may increase the number of jobs that you qualify for and significantly boost your salary offers for federal and contracting jobs.

Caution

Submit All Required Documents. Many veterans inadvertently sabotage their applications by neglecting to submit or failing to label documents proving their military service and/or disability or by neglecting to bring such documents to career fairs. To visit a site that can help you request documents that provide proof of your service, Google the terms *national archives* and *veterans service records*.

On Your Application

The federal government's special programs for veterans never guarantee jobs to applicants. To be offered a job, you must, at the very least, prove that you meet the job's minimum requirement. Also, be sure to clearly and prominently identify on your applications all of the relevant veterans' hiring programs that you're using.

To translate your military experience into civilian terms:

➤ Identify your final rank, promotions, medals, honors, the number of people under your command, and the training you received.

➤ Clearly identify the challenges you faced in the military and the generic skills they taught you. For example, describe how your experience as a combat infantry leader sharpened your ability to lead and supervise, as well as to quickly make high-stakes decisions, allocate assignments to team members based on their skills, develop quick responses to threats, adapt to changing circumstances, quickly communicate with people of diverse backgrounds, and conduct post-action reviews. Other important selling points frequently offered by military experience include high-tech proficiency, loyalty, self-diligence, experience managing confidential information, troubleshooting skills, attention to detail, international experience and knowledge of particular regions, language skills, team-friendly approaches, strategic planning skills, grace under pressure, and ability to excel in high-pressure environments.

Take Note! _____

Salary Savvy

Your hiring agency will probably base its salary offer on your military salary. Therefore, when discussing your current salary with federal employers, explain how your military salary underestimates your true income by, for example, excluding bonuses, overtime pay, or valuable benefits, such as housing allowances and child care. And if accepting the job offer would require you to move to a city that would increase your cost of living, say so.

By using these techniques, one of my clients, who transitioned from a military weapons specialist to a weapons analyst at a federal agency, increased his salary offer by more than $25,000. (No, that was not a typo.) Also, in addition to requesting a higher salary offer, request reimbursement for moving expenses, tuition costs, and support for continuing education, if appropriate.

Remember that a hiring manager won't be impressed by your application if he doesn't understand it. So avoid or define technical terms and acronyms that are commonly used in the military but will stump civilians, and explain the importance of your contributions. Here's an excerpt of a federal job application from a veteran who unfortunately violated these principles:

> *I wrote Mission Need Statements (MNS) and Capstone Requirements Documents (CRDs) that were mandated when Joint Strike Fighters or IMDs are introduced. The audience of these documents was the Flag-level officers in the J1, J2, and J3 Directorates.*

You can find help in translating military occupations to civilian terminology at http://usajons.gov/ei/tutorials.asp.

One more thing. Are you a current or former fed with veterans' preference applying for a federal job that is open to the public? If so, you can apply under Competitive Procedures or Merit Promotion Procedures. Look up these terms in the Glossary (Appendix 4) to evaluate the relative pros and cons of applying under each of these procedures.

APPENDIX

2

Tip Sheet for Applicants
with Disabilities

The federal government is the largest employer of people with disabilities, and is currently working hard to increase its hiring of people with disabilities. The federal government currently employs about 125,000 people with disabilities and almost 20,000 people with severe disabilities. About 7 percent of feds have a disability.

Job applicants with disabilities may be hired for federal jobs through the same competitive procedures as nondisabled applicants. But disabled applicants may also be hired through special procedures that allow them to bypass job competitions. These procedures are called "noncompetitive Schedule A Appointments."

Under a noncompetitive Schedule A Appointment, a federal agency can simply hire an applicant with a disability into an opening without considering other qualified applicants—as long as the disabled applicant meets at least the opening's basic requirements. This means that an applicant with a disability does not necessarily have to be the best qualified applicant to get the job; she or he only has to be qualified.

Using Schedule A Appointments minimizes red tape for federal agencies and applicants, and helps agencies fulfill their obligation to increase their hiring of people with disabilities. For more information about Schedule A Appointments, see http://www.opm.gov/disability.

Get Certified

To be considered for a noncompetitive Schedule A Appointment, you must have a severe physical disability, psychiatric disability, and/or be mentally retarded. You must also have proof of your disability and a certification of your job readiness that describes your ability to perform the essential duties of your target positions. You can obtain these documents from any of these sources:

> A licensed medical professional (e.g., a physician or other medical professional certified by a state, the District of Columbia, or a U.S. territory to practice medicine)

> A licensed state or private vocational rehabilitation specialist

> Any federal agency, such as the Department of Veterans Affairs, state agency, or agency of the District of Columbia or a U.S. territory that issues or provides disability benefits

If you have proof of disability but don't have a job readiness certification, you may be hired into a temporary federal job. Once you obtain the job readiness certification or your on-the-job productivity convinces your agency that you are able to fulfill the duties of the job, you may be hired into a permanent job or into another temporary job.

Find Openings

Some federal agencies do not advertise some openings that they want to fill with disabled applicants. Instead, they may recruit for these openings via methods that target disabled applicants. Once you get certified, find these openings by contacting the Selective Placement Coordinators, the Special Emphasis Managers (SEP) for Employment of Adults with Disabilities, or equivalents, who help agencies recruit, hire, and accommodate people with disabilities. These coordinators stay current on job openings for disabled job seekers, including unadvertised openings, and match applicants to them. To find these coordinators, type "Selective Placement Coordinators" into the search window at http://www.opm.gov. Also Google "Selective Placement Coordinators" along with the names of your target agencies.

If you're a veteran, see Appendix 1. If you're a student or recent grad, review the internships and recruitment programs discussed in Chapter 3 and listed on this book's CD, particularly the Workforce Recruitment Program and other programs that are flagged for favoring people with disabilities.

Consider the following:

1. Some federal agencies recruit applicants with disabilities from state vocational rehabilitation agencies. Therefore, you may find some unadvertised federal openings by contacting your state agency. To access a list of state vocational rehabilitation agencies, Google them.

2. Some agencies recruit people with disabilities through organizations such as the American Association for People with Disabilities, Easter Seals, and The Arc and by advertising in *Careers & The Disabled* magazine.

3. The Computer/Electronic Accommodations Program (CAP) provides assistive technology and services (at no charge) to employees of dozens of federal agencies. See http://www.tricare.mil/cap. The CAP Web site also posts updates on federal disability hiring and links to other sites addressing federal opportunities for people with disabilities.

4. Bender Consulting Services, Inc., places professionals in varied fields in federal jobs throughout the United States. See http://benderconsult.com/index2.html.

5. USAJOBS works with screen reading software like JAWS (Job Access with Speech). You can increase the font size of USAJOBS screens on Internet Explorer.

Reasonable Accommodation

The federal government is required by law to make reasonable accommodations for a worker's disabilities. Examples of reasonable accommodation include providing interpreters, readers, or other personal assistance, modifying job duties, restructuring work sites, and providing alternative work schedules and/or work-at-home options.

Hiring agencies also provide special accommodations to help disabled applicants take tests or be interviewed for openings if they are asked to do so. For more information on reasonable accommodation, go to http://www.eeoc.gov, then type "reasonable accommodation" into the search window.

On Your Application

If you want to be considered for a job opening under a noncompetitive Schedule A Appointment, say so in your cover letters, the short-answer questions addressing Schedule A Appointments in online applications, your job interviews, and any other potential opportunities. Although you are not required to do so, you may provide assurance in your application of your ability to get the job done with reasonable accommodation.

You will probably want to begin your cover letter just like any other applicant for a competitive appointment would begin the cover letter. (See Chapter 13 for more instruction on writing cover letters.) But after you identify your target job and review your credentials, you could say something like this:

> Please consider me for the [name of the position goes here] opening under a noncompetitive Schedule A Appointment because I am deaf. I assure you that I am a top-notch producer, and I could perform the job effectively; my certification letter is attached.
>
> I can communicate articulately as long as I have an interpreter for meetings and telephone calls. I offer a solid record as a team player. My contributions to group projects are reflected in my successful completion of [cite specific types of projects you completed and objective validation of your success, as discussed in Chapter 9].
>
> I would be happy to show you my portfolio of work and discuss my communication abilities in person. My references can verify my skills, positive attitude, and reputation as a team player, as well.

In job interviews, employers are technically restricted by law to asking if the applicant could do the job and, in some cases, to asking the applicant for an illustration of how he/she would do so. This means that interviewers are prohibited from asking you questions about your disability that are irrelevant to your functioning on the job and you are not required to discuss your disability during interviews. Nevertheless, you are certainly permitted to answer the unspoken questions that may loom large in the interviewer's mind. For an excellent article on how to address disabilities in interviews, see http://www.quintcareers.com/disabled_job_strategies.html.

You may ask your references to specifically discuss your disability with potential employers and provide additional validation of your effectiveness.

More Resources

> ➤ For the federal government's fact sheets on federal disability hiring, type "Federal Employment of People with Disabilities" into the search window at http://www.opm.gov.

> ➤ Professional organizations for disabled feds include Deaf and Hard of Hearing in Government at http://www.dhhig.org and the Association of Persons with Disabilities in Agriculture at http://www.apda.usda.gov.

> ➤ For the U.S. Labor Department's one-stop Web site for government disability information, go to http://www.dol.gov, and then select "disability resources" in the A-to-Z site index.

> ➤ See *Job Hunting for the So-Called Handicapped or People Who Have Disabilities* by Richard Nelson Bolles and Dale Susan Brown. This book explains rights guaranteed by the Americans with Disabilities Act and provides insightful job-hunting tips. (Bolles also wrote the job-hunting blockbuster *What Color Is Your Parachute?*)

> ➤ *Careers & the Disabled* magazine provides insightful job-searching articles. See http://www.eop.com/cd.html.

> **Hot Tip**
>
> **Agencies with Good Track Records.** Many agencies, including the Department of State, the IRS, the U.S. Postal Service, and the Defense Department (DoD), have won awards from *Careers & the Disabled* magazine for their records in disability hiring.
>
> The Department of Homeland Security is working particularly hard to recruit people with disabilities. For a list of Homeland Security's Selective Placement Coordinators, type that phrase into the search window at http://www.dhs.gov.
>
> The Social Security Administration is eager to hire people with disabilities. See http://www.ssa.gov/work/scheduleA/hiring.htm.
>
> In addition, agencies with particularly good track records in disability hiring include the VA and the Departments of Treasury, Energy, Housing and Urban Development, Agriculture, Commerce, and Labor.

Formatting Tips

The most important formatting principle is: What stands out on the page is what will stand out in the reader's mind.

In order to format your résumés and cover letters so that your most important credentials leap off the page and into the reader's mind, you must use effective formatting techniques. This appendix provides tips for attractively formatting your documents in Microsoft Word and in automated applications systems. Note that all of the formatting features incorporated into the résumés included on the CD accompanying this book are explained here.

To Add Special Characters

The diamonds in the résumé header below are an example of a special character.

JOE SIXPACK
Certified IT Specialist

1234 Yellow Brick Road ♦ City, State Zip Code
Work: (123) 123-567 ♦ Home: (123) 123-4567 ♦ E-Mail: JSixpack@E-mail.com

---

Steps to Add Special Characters

1. Position your cursor where you would like to position a special character.

2. In the toolbar, click on the "Insert" option at the top of the menu.

3. Select "Symbol" in the "Symbols" option.

4. Click on the symbol you want to select.

5. Click "Insert."

To Create Bulleted and Numbered Lists

Capitalize the first letter of the first word in each bullet of a bulleted list. If each item in a list consists of a word or just a few words, don't punctuate listed items with periods. If each listed item is a sentence, end each item with a period. Use numbers when rank or sequence is important. Use bullets when rank or sequence is not important.

Steps to Format and Position Bullets

1. Select text to be bulleted.

2. In the toolbar, click the "Home" button.

3. In the "Paragraph" options, click on the downward pointed arrow immediately next to the button showing bullets.

4. Select the desired symbol for bullets from menu box options.

5. Hit "Enter" at the end of your last bullet to create the next bullet in your text.

6. To add or decrease the distance of bullets from left and right margins, click on the tiny box on the lower right corner of the "Paragraph" options and adjust numbers in "Left and Right" under "Indentation.

7. To add or decrease the space between bullets, click on the tiny box on the lower right corner of the "Paragraphs" options, and adjust numbers in "Before and After" under "Spacing."

8. Select "OK."

Alternatively, create a bulleted list by typing each item of the list on a separate line, selecting the entire list, and then hitting the icon representing bullets located in the "Paragraph" section of the toolbar.

Steps to Create a Bulleted List Inside of Another Bulleted List

1. Complete steps 1–4.

2. Select a different symbol for subbullets than for bullets.

3. Specify higher numbers for "Bullet Position" and "Text Position" for subbullets than selected for bullets, such as .3 and .6, respectively.

4. Select "OK."

Steps to Format Numbered Lists

Follow the steps provided above in "Steps to Format and Position Bullets," except that, at Step 3, click on the downward pointed arrow next to the button showing numbers under the "Paragraph" options instead of the downward pointed arrow next to the button showing bullets.

To Create and Manipulate Tables

You may want to include a "Your Needs/My Skills" table in your cover letter as demonstrated in Chapter 13.

Steps to Create a Table

1. On the toolbar, click the "Insert" button.

2. Click the "Table" button.

3. Click "Insert Table."

4. Enter the number of columns and rows needed for your table.

5. Adjust the sizes of the table's columns and rows by clicking on the gridlines and moving them.

6. Bullet items in the table's cells, if you so desire.

7. Bold the table's headings.

Steps to Delete a Table and Its Contents

1.   Select the entire table.
2.   Click the "Del" key on your keyboard.

Steps to Delete a Row or Column of a Table

1.   Select the column or row you would like to delete.
2.   Right-click your mouse.
3.   Select the "Delete Rows" or "Delete Cells" from the pull-down menu, as appropriate.

Steps to Insert a Row or Column of a Table

1.   Select the column or row you would like to delete.
2.   Right-click your mouse.
3.   Select the appropriate "Insert" option from the pull-down menu.

To Adjust a Document's Margins

Steps to Adjust a Document's Margins

1.   On the toolbar, select "Page Layout."
2.   Click "Margins."
3.   To create ample white space with your margins, set all margins to 1 inch.
4.   To shrink margins so that will be able to fit more text on your page, click one of the options displayed or click "customs margin" to size margins to your specifications.
5.   At the bottom of the menu box, click "OK."

To Create Horizontal Lines Across the Page

You can sandwich text, such as a heading in a résumé, between various types of lines, some of which are showcased below:

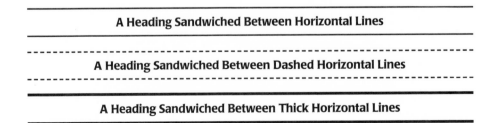

Steps to Sandwich Text Between Lines

1. Select the text that you want lined. If you want the sandwich lines to extend across the entire page, extend the selected area beyond the last letter in the text that you want lined. Alternatively, if you want the lines to end where the text ends, end the selected area where the text ends.

2. In your toolbar, click "Home."

3. In the lower right side of the "Paragraph" section, click the "Borders and Shading" button, which looks like a square inside a square.

4. On the bottom of the pull-down menu, click the "Borders and Shading" option at the bottom of the list.

5. Under "Setting" on the left side of the menu box, select "Custom."

6. Under "Style" in the center of the menu box, specify a style.

7. Under "Preview" on the right side of the menu box, select the icon representing a line positioned above your selected text, and the icon representing a line positioned below your selected text.

8. At the bottom of the menu box, click "OK."

9. Justify or center the text between the lines by selecting the text and then clicking the appropriate justification button in the "Paragraph" section of the toolbar at the top of the page.

Steps to Create a Single Horizontal Line Under Text

1. Complete Steps 1–4 from "Steps to Sandwich Text Between Lines" as explained above.

2. Under "Preview," on the right side of the menu box, select the icon representing a line positioned under your selected text.

3. At the bottom of your menu box, click "OK."

4. Justify or center the text.

Steps to Create a Single Horizontal Line Without Text

1. Hit the "Shift" key.

2. While holding down the "Shift" key, hit the dash key (the key next to the zero key) at least three times.

3. Release the "Shift" key.

4. Hit "Enter."

To Shade a Heading

You can emphasize text, such as a heading in a résumé, by shading it.

Steps to Shade a Heading

1. Select the text to be shaded. If you want the shading to extend across the entire line, extend the selected area beyond the last letter of the text. Alternatively, if you want the shading to end where the text ends, end the selected area where the text ends.

2. In your toolbar, click "Home."

3. In the lower right side of the "Paragraph" section, click the "Borders and Shading" button, which looks like a square inside a square.

4. Click the "Borders and Shading" button on the bottom of the list.

5. To erase lines, click on the "Borders" tab. Then, on the right side of the menu box under "Preview," click the icon representing the line(s) you would like to erase.

6. At the top part of the menu box, select "Shading."

To Shade and Sandwich a Heading Between Lines

To shade and sandwich a heading between horizontal lines, combine the instructions provided above for shading a heading and sandwiching a heading between horizontal lines.

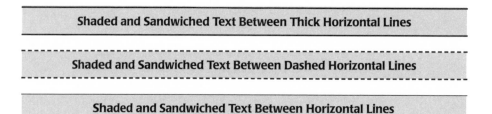

To Erase Lines and Shading

Use the steps below to erase lines and/or shading that you have just created.

1. Follow Steps 1–4 from above.

2. To erase lines, click the "Borders" tab. Then, on the right side of the menu box under "Preview," click the line icon(s) representing the line(s) you would like to erase. Then, click "OK" at the bottom of the menu box.

3. To erase shading, click the "Shading" tab. Then select "Clear" as the "Style" option, and select "No Color" as the "Fill" option. Then click "OK" at the bottom of the menu box.

Alternatively, you may erase lines and/or shading around text by selecting the shaded or lined text, then access the "Borders and Shading" menu and select the "No Fill" option for shading and the "None" option for borders.

To Expand the Spacing Between Letters in a Heading

You can emphasize a heading by expanding the spaces between its letters. Here are the steps for doing so:

1. Select the text that you would like to expand.

2. From your toolbar, click the "Home" option.

3. Click the small box located in the lower right box of the "Font" section of the toolbar.

4. Click "Character Spacing."

5. Adjust the "Scale and "Spacing" options, as desired.

6. Click "OK."

To Create Borders Around Each Page

Steps to Create Borders Around Each Page

1. From your toolbar, select the "Home" button.

2. In the lower right side of the "Paragraph" section, click the downward pointing arrow immediately next to the "Borders and Shading" box, which looks like a box within a box.

3. Click the "Borders and Shading" button at the bottom of the list.

4. Click the "Page Border" tab.

5. Click the page border option that you desire under "Setting."

6. If you would like to delete a border line(s), click on the lines in the picture in the preview box that represent the line(s) you would like to delete.

7. Click "OK."

Steps to Erase Borders Around Each Page

1. Follow Steps 1–5 from above.

2. On the top of the menu box, click the "Page Border" tab.

3. In the "Setting" box, select "None."

4. At the bottom of your menu box, click "OK."

To Save Space on the Page

You can save space by shrinking the size of the empty lines between items in bulleted or numbered lists (without shrinking the font of listed items) and/or by shrinking the size of empty lines before or after headings (without shrinking the font of the heading) to an 8-point font.

Steps to Shrink the Size of Empty Lines

1. Select the empty line that you would like to shrink.

2. Access the "Format" pull-down menu from the toolbar.

3. Click on "Font."

4. Change the font size to "8."

5. Click "OK."

To Make Long Lists More Readable

By breaking up lists of achievements, training courses, or other credentials with headings, you will make them easier to skim and remember. This principle is demonstrated by the two lists of training courses provided below, which contain the same course titles. But isn't List 2, which has headings, easier to skim and remember than List 1, which is long and unbroken?

List 1: Long, Unbroken List

Training Courses

- PowerPoint—January 2007

- Using Spreadsheets—November 2006

- Direct Marketing Math & Finance Seminar—November 2005

- High Impact Business Writing—October 2004

- Public Speaking—September 2007

- Mediation and Conflict Management Skills—January 2001

- Project Management Principles—March 2005

- Crash Course in Direct Marketing—September 2000

- Diversity Training—August 2007

- Dispute Resolution—October 2007

- Fundamentals of Writing—February 2006

List 2: List Broken Up with Subheadings

Training Courses

Management
- Diversity Training—August 2007
- Project Management Principles—March 2005

Marketing
- Direct Marketing Math & Finance Seminar—November 2005
- Crash Course in Direct Marketing—September 2004

Conflict Resolution
- Dispute Resolution—October 2007
- Mediation and Conflict Management Skills—January 2001

Communication
- Public Speaking—September 2007
- Fundamentals of Writing—February 2006
- High Impact Business Writing—October 2004

Software
- PowerPoint—January 2007
- Using Spreadsheets—November 2006

Essential Features for Hard-Copy Applications

Pay particular attention to all of the following when submitting a paper application:

1. Type your name and the title of your target job at the top of each page.

2. Number your pages.

3. If your application includes essay questions, answer your essays in the same order in which they appear on the application.

4. Repeat the question with each essay.

5. Use margins that are between 1 and 1.5 inches wide. Instructions for manipulating margins are provided in this Appendix.

6. Try to limit each essay to one or two pages.

7. Use a font size of at least 9 or 10 points.

8. Use plain fonts, such as Calibri, Arial, Helvetica, or Trebuchet.

9. Print your applications as a single-sided document, so that they can be photocopied without losing content.

10. Do not print your application on odd-sized paper.

11. Print your application on white or off-white paper. Do not print your application on colored paper or include any other formatting gimmicks.

APPENDIX

4

Glossary

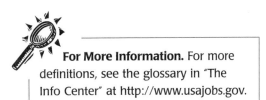

For More Information. For more definitions, see the glossary in "The Info Center" at http://www.usajobs.gov.

30 Percent or More Disabled Program: Program that makes some disabled veterans eligible to be directly hired into some federal jobs without competing against other applicants.

Appointment: A federal job. Each federal job is filled either through a competitive appointment or noncompetitive appointment.

Basic Qualifications/Minimum Qualifications: The criteria that applicants must meet to be seriously considered for the job. Applications that don't meet these qualifications are rejected.

Best-Qualified Applicant: An applicant who was among one of the top scorers in a job competition. (In government lingo, the applicant has "made the cert.") The applications of best-qualified applicants are forwarded to the selecting official for further consideration; other applications are rejected.

BRAC: The Defense Department's (DoD) Base Realignment and Closure program. This program is shutting down some DoD facilities and expanding others.

Career Appointment: Type of position held by feds after completing career-conditional appointments in the competitive service. It usually takes three years to progress from career-conditional appointments to career appointments with career status (or tenure). If you have career status, you have two main advantages: (1) it would be harder to lay you off than career-conditional feds; and (2) if your resign your federal job, you can be rehired by the federal government at any time in the future without competing with the general public. Also see Status.

Career-Conditional Appointment: Type of position held by most new feds in the competitive service. The first year of service in a career-conditional appointment is usually a probationary period. Usually after serving three continuous years in a career-conditional appointment, an employee automatically receives a career appointment. If you have conditional status and: (1) if your agency is involved in a layoff (RIF in government lingo), then you are more vulnerable to being RIFed than feds who have career status; (2) if you resign from federal service, then your ability to be later reemployed without having to compete for a job with the general public is limited to the three-year period after resignation. Also see Status.

Career Transition Assistance and Special Selection Priority (CTAP): Program that gives selection priority to displaced federal employees for some job openings in their own agencies before their federal employment ends.

Certification List: The list of most qualified or best-qualified applicants developed either by a peer-review panel or an online hiring system during a competitive examination for a federal job. The certification is given to the selecting official who makes a final selection. In government lingo, applicants listed on the certification "made the cert."

Civil Service: Includes the competitive service, excepted service, and senior executive service.

Civil Service Laws: Laws designed to ensure that hiring is strictly merit based. Civil service laws apply to all jobs in the competitive service. The Office of Personnel Management establishes regulations for implementing civil service laws. Jobs in the excepted service are specifically exempted from civil service laws.

Closing Date: The deadline for applications for federal openings. Late applications are almost always rejected. On rare occasions, a closing date is extended to encourage more applications or because of other reasons.

Competitive Appointment: A federal job that is filled through a merit-based competition.

Competitive Examination: A merit-based competition that is used to screen applications for federal jobs that are open for competition. In a competitive examination, applications are rated and ranked with a numerical score based upon merit and veterans' preference; an applicant who ranks as most qualified for the position is selected. (Only relatively few competitive examinations involve tests or exams.) Most jobs posted on http://www.usajobs.gov are screened through competitive examinations.

Competitive Procedures: Procedures used to rate outside applicants to vacancy announcements that are open to the public. Under competitive procedures, applicants may use their veterans' preference. But applicants hired under competitive procedures must undergo a one-year probationary period that is not required under Merit Promotion procedures. (See Merit Promotion Procedures.)

Competitive Service: Includes all jobs covered by federal civil service law. (Civil service laws are designed to keep hiring procedures strictly merit-based.) Competitive service jobs are filled through open job competitions (competitive examining procedures). Most federal jobs are in the competitive service. All federal jobs that are not in the competitive service are exempt from civil service laws and are in the excepted service. Personnel regulations for competitive service jobs are set by the Office of Personnel Management.

Competitive Status: See Status.

Contact Person: Agency employee identified on a vacancy announcement who answers questions about the job opening.

Detail Assignment: A temporary assignment of a federal employee to a different position for a specified period, with the employee returning to his or her regular duties at the end of the detail.

Direct Hire Authority: Special streamlined procedures used to quickly fill openings when there is a severe shortage of candidates or when there is a critical mission need.

Excepted Service: Excepted service jobs are outside of the Competitive Service and can be filled via more flexible procedures than competitive service jobs. That is, an agency can decide to select an applicant for an excepted service job without a competition designed to identify the best-qualified applicant. Agencies set their own qualification requirements and salary rules for excepted service jobs (though some excepted service agencies do follow some Office of Personnel Management regulations). Excepted service jobs include:

- All political positions in the federal government.
- All federal jobs filled through special appointments instead of through competitive procedures.
- Some categories of jobs in all federal agencies such as attorneys, chaplains, doctors, dentists, and nurses.
- All jobs in some federal agencies. The primary common denominator of many of excepted service agencies and positions is that they address national security, international, and/or intelligence functions, such as the Central Intelligence Agency, the Department of State, the National Security Agency, or the Federal Bureau of Investigation, or address financial, banking, or trade issues. To access a list of excepted service agencies, look up excepted service on Wikipedia.
- Jobs in the foreign service.
- Some jobs in the Department of Veterans Affairs and Department of Defense.
- Most jobs on congressional staffs and in the Judiciary.

Note that excepted service employees generally have fewer appeal rights (compared to positions in the competitive service) in the event of disciplinary actions or job termination. In other words, jobs in the excepted service are not quite as secure as jobs in the competitive service. However, jobs in the excepted service generally pay better than comparable jobs in the competitive service.

The classification of some federal jobs can change. For example, when a competitive service job is filled through a noncompetitive appointment under a special hiring authority, it becomes an excepted service job. If this excepted service job is then filled again through a competitive appointment, it converts back into the competitive service.

Executive Core Qualifications (ECQs): Qualifications required for obtaining a senior executive service (SES) job. Essays addressing ECQs are required in applications for SES jobs. Note that ECQs are very similar to KSAs.

Federal Wage System: The personnel and salary scale for blue-collar federal employees.

Federal Résumé: Type of résumé required for applying for jobs in federal agencies. Federal résumés are required to contain more information than standard résumés.

Foreign Service: The federal government's diplomatic corps that helps design and support U.S. foreign policy from Washington, DC, at over 250 international posts and runs all U.S. embassies, consulates, and other diplomatic missions. The foreign service comprises branches from the Departments of State, Agriculture, and Commerce and U.S. Agency for International Development. The foreign service is part of the excepted service.

General Schedule (GS) Pay: The pay scale for most federal white-collar positions. GS positions range from GS-1 to GS-15.

Interagency Career Transition Assistance Plan (ICTAP): Program that gives selection priority for some federal openings to displaced federal employees after their jobs have ended.

Knowledge, Skills, and Abilities (KSAs): Criteria used by federal employers to screen applications for federal jobs. Most federal applications used to require applicants to write lengthy essays addressing each KSA in each application. However, in 2011, federal employers were directed to drop requirements for KSA essays from applications used in initial screens.

Therefore, almost all federal employers now primarily evaluate applicants' abilities to fulfill KSAs through their answers to short-answer questions on job applications and their résumés and interviews. However, applicants may occasionally be required to write KSA essays on follow-up screens. In addition, applications for jobs in the Senior Executive Service still require applicants to answer essay questions.

Lateral Transfer: Current federal employees may be transferred to other federal jobs at their current grade without competition. Former feds who have reinstatement eligibility may be noncompetitively hired.

Locality Pay: Special pay increases that apply to federal workers in cities with high costs of living, such as New York City, San Francisco, and Washington, DC.

Merit Promotion Procedures: Procedures used to rate and rank applications for vacancy announcements that are only open to current and former feds. (Specifically, merit promotion procedures may apply to applicants who have status or reinstatement eligibility.) Applicants hired under Merit Promotion Procedures cannot count their veterans' preference; but if hired, they do not have to fulfill a probationary period. By contrast, applications for vacancy announcements that are open to the public are rated and ranked according to competitive procedures. Table A4-1 explains the differences between merit promotion and competitive procedures.

TABLE A4-1	Merit Promotion vs. Competitive Procedures	
	Merit Promotion Procedures	**Competitive Procedures**
Coverage	• Applicants with status. • Applicants with reinstatement eligibility.	• All applicants without federal experience. • All applicants who have status or reinstatement eligibility and opt to be covered under competitive procedures.
Veterans' Preference	Veterans' preference does not count. Applicants who are rated and ranked under merit promotion procedures do not gain points for veterans' preference.	Veterans' preference counts. Applicants who are rated and ranked under competitive promotion procedures may gain points for veterans' preference.
Probation Period, If Hired	No probation if applicant is hired.	One-year probation period if applicant is hired.

Noncompetitive Appointment: A federal job that is not filled by the hiring agency through a merit-based competition involving the rating and ranking of applicants; noncompetitive appointments are filled by agencies by using special hiring programs for veterans, returned Peace Corps volunteers, students, former feds, or others who can bypass competitions under some circumstances or by transferring, reassigning, or promoting current feds. Each vacancy announcement for a noncompetitive appointment specifies what types of noncompetitive appointments can be used to fill the position.

Noncompetitive Schedule A Appointment: A federal job that can be made available to disabled applicants without competition. See Appendix 2.

Office of Personnel Management (OPM): Sets hiring procedures for all federal agencies in the competitive service. Some excepted service agencies also follow some OPM procedures, but the degree to which they do so varies from agency to agency.

Optional Application for Federal Employment (OF-612): Form that may be submitted with a federal job application instead of a résumé. However, hiring managers universally prefer résumés over this form, which has a bureaucratic, hard-to-read format and is essentially an anachronism.

Personal Service Contract: A contract between a federal organization and a professional for providing specific services during a specified period of time.

Probation: The first year of service of an employee who has a career or career-conditional appointment in the competitive service. After an employee completes probation, it becomes much harder to fire him/her. In practical terms, the overwhelming majority of employees complete the probationary period without any problems. See also Trial Period.

Promotion Potential: The promotion potential assigned to each job defines the highest level that can be reached by a person holding that job without competing against other applicants. To climb higher than his/her current job's promotion potential, a fed must either land another job or convince their boss to extend their current job's promotion potential.

Quality Step Increase (QSI): A faster than normal step increase that is used to reward employees at all General Schedule grade levels who show high-quality performance. To be eligible for a QSI, an employee must be below Step 10 of his grade level; have received the highest rating available under his performance management program; have demonstrated sustained performance of high quality; and have not received a QSI within the preceding 52 consecutive calendar weeks. See http://www.opm.gov/perform/articles/1999/apr99-7.asp.

Reduction-in-Force (RIF): The federal government's version of a lay-off. RIFed feds receive priority for other federal openings.

Reinstatement Eligibility: Right of former feds who held career appointments and former feds with veterans' preference to: (1) be noncompetitively rehired into federal jobs at grades equal or lower than those previously held; and/or (2) apply for jobs that are open only to applicants with status. For former career feds and former feds with veterans' preference, reinstatement eligibility never expires. For other former feds, it usually expires 3 years after end of federal employment.

Security Clearance: Authorization awarded by the federal government to a fed or contractor to access classified materials needed to do a job. In many cases, security clearances signficantly increase salary offers. You can only get a security clearance if you: (1) work for a federal agency or a federal contractor who requests a security clearance for you because you must access classified materials to do your job— you cannot get a security clearance by applying for it yourself; and (2) pass a security investigation. Your security investigation, which may last months, may involve reviews of where you've lived, worked, and gone to school; checks of credit and police records; interviews; and a polygraph. The main types of clearances from lowest to highest level of security are: (1) confidential, (2) secret, (3) top secret, and (4) sensitive compartmented information. Some job offers are contingent upon receipt of a security clearance. In recent years, the processing of security clearances has been significantly speeded.

Selecting Official: Person who makes a hiring selection from best-qualified candidates in a job competition (competitive examination). The selecting official usually interviews at least some of the best qualified candidates to help them make the decision, but does not always do so. The selecting official is usually the supervisor of the new employee.

Senior Executive Service: The federal government's corps of executive managers.

Special Hiring Authorities: Authorities that enable federal agencies to hire applicants who meet specified criteria without an open competition. Special hiring authorities are commonly used to noncompetitively hire veterans, people with disabilities, RIFed feds, returned Peace Corps volunteers, applicants for internships and student jobs, and former feds. Note that applicants in these categories are not guaranteed jobs. To be hired for a job, an applicant must meet or beat its minimum qualifications.

Status: Possessed by career employees and career-conditional employees who have served at least 90 days. (Includes employees hired under noncompetitive appointments working in the competitive service; excludes employees of agencies in the excepted service.) It is advantageous to have status (also known as "competitive status") because some federal jobs are only open to those who have it. In addition, a status employee may be promoted, transferred, or reinstated without an open competition. Take care not to confuse "competitive status" with "career status" possessed by feds with career appointments.

Step Increase: Each General Schedule (GS) grade has 10 steps. Step increases or within-grade increases (WGIs) are periodic increases in a GS employee's rate of basic pay from one step of the grade of his or her position to the next higher step of that grade. See http://www.opm.gov/oca/pay/html/wgifact.asp.

Temporary Appointment: Temporary job that lasts one year or less; usually benefits are not provided.

Term Appointment: Temporary job that usually lasts one to four years. Benefits are usually provided.

The Two-Step Rule: The formula that determines which grade/step a fed on the General Schedule (GS) would be eligible to be promoted into upon reciept of a salary grade increase. See Chapter 18 and http://www.opm.gov/oca/pay/html/promotion.asp.

Trial Period: The excepted service's version of the probationary period. This period may last up to two years.

USAJOBS: The federal government's official jobs Web site. See http://www.usajobs.gov.

Vacancy Announcement: The announcement of a job description(s) and application requirements for one or more federal job openings.

Veterans Employment Opportunities Act of 1990 (VEOA): Program that allows veterans to apply for some federal jobs that would otherwise be off-limits to them.

Veterans' Preference: Preferential treatment given to the applications of some veterans, and some spouses and mothers of veterans for federal jobs. See Appendix 1.

Veterans Recruitment Appointment (VRA): Program that enables veterans to be hired into temporary positions that may lead to permanent positions.

INDEX

ABOUT THE AUTHOR

A Leading Authority on Federal Cases

Lily Madeleine Whiteman is:

> **Federal Career Coach:**
> Lily has helped hundreds
> of professionals of all levels—
> from recent grads to execu-
> tives—land jobs and earn
> promotions.

> *Washington Post* **Contributor
> and** *Federal Times*
> **Columnist:** Lily has written
> for the "Jobs" section of
> *The Washington Post* and
> WashingtonPost.com and
> her "Career Matters" column
> appears twice a month in
> *Federal Times*. Her career
> advice has also been featured
> by CBS, *The Wall Journal*,
> National Public Radio, and
> many other media outlets.

> **Savvy, Seasoned Fed Who Knows the Federal System Inside Out:** Currently is sen-
> ior science writer at the U.S. National Science Foundation, Lily has climbed the
> career ladder at six agencies, including the White House Conference on Aging and
> the Vice President's National Partnership for Reinventing Government. As an expe-
> rienced job seeker herself, Lily relates to other job seekers with empathy and humor.

> **Hiring Manager:** Lily knows how to instantly impress federal hiring managers
> because she has served as a hiring manager herself and has interviewed hundreds of
> others about their hiring decisions.

> **Award-Winning Communicator:** Lily received three "Awards of Excellence" from
> the National Association of Government Communications.

Communications Consultant

Known for her informative, entertaining approaches, Lily has led seminars for many organizations including Harvard's Kennedy School of Government, The Council for Excellence in Government, The Department of Interior University, and the American Association for the Advancement of Science. Dozens of her articles have appeared in national publications including *Audubon*, *The Magazine of the Discovery Channel*, and in-flight magazines.

Education

Lily has a Master's degree in Public Health and a Master's degree in Environmental Management from Yale University. She received her BA in Earth Science from Wesleyan University in Connecticut.

Websites

http://www.IGotTheJob.net

http://www.CrystalClearCommunications.com